WEB-BASED SERVICES:
A Transforming Revolution in Modern Libraries

WEB-BASED SERVICES: A Transforming Revolution in Modern Libraries

DR. SANGEETA DHAMDHERE
Librarian
Modern College of Arts, Science and Commerce,
Ganeshkhind, Pune, India

DR. RAMDAS LIHITKAR
Librarian
Government Institute of Science, Nagpur

Ess Ess Publications
New Delhi

WEB-BASED SERVICES:
A Transforming Revolution in Modern Libraries

ISBN : 978-93-87698-32-1

Price: Rs.1000/-

First Published 2021

Published by:
Ess Ess Publications
4831/24, Ansari Road,
Darya Ganj,
New Delhi-110 002.
INDIA
Phones: 23260807, 41563444
Fax: 41563334
E-mail: info@essessreference.com
www.essessreference.com

Cover Design by *Patch Creative Unit*

Printed and bound in India

Dedicated to
My Father
Late Mr. NAMDEV MARUTI DHAMDHERE

Contents

Acknowledgements

I would like to express my deep gratitude to my Ph.D guides Dr. Ramdas Lihitkar, Librarian, Government Institute of Science, Nagpur and Prof. Dr. Egbert De Smet, Head of the Department, Antwerp University, Belgium for their constant guidance and suggestions throughout this research work. I would like to thank Prof. Dr. Ramesh Babu a Senior Library Professional for encouraging me to publish this work in book form. I wish to express my gratitude to Dr. Mangala Hirwade, Head of the Department, Library and Information Science, Nagpur University for her support. I would like to extend my grateful thanks to RTM Nagpur University for awarding my doctoral degree. My special thanks to the Principal Dr. Sanjay Kharat, Modern College of Arts, Science and Commerce, Ganeshkhind, Pune for his motivation and support. I wish to acknowledge the help of library staff, professional colleagues and friends. Without support, help and blessings of my loving parents and family members, I would not have completed this book. Lastly, I would like to thank Mr. Sumit Sethi, Ess Ess Publications for publishing this book.

Dr. Sangeeta Dhamdhere

Librarian, Modern College of Arts, Science and Commmerce, Ganeshkhind, Pune – 411016

Preface

Modern libraries are changing so fast and adopting new ways of services, technologies and best practices both online and physical. Developed country libraries are much ahead than developing countries in terms of their remote access/online services. Under developed and developing countries libraries are still proving traditional services to their readers. Many libraries have discovered the advantages of having a presence on the internet and have successfully addressed their objectives by integrating their website as part of their daily functioning. It is a challenge in front of all libraries to accept new technologies and offer new services due to many constraints like funds, trained staff, technologies, space, etc.

The idea of carrying out the study and publishing book on modern web-based services offered by top world university libraries came in my mind couple of years back and therefore registered this topic for my doctoral program at the RTM Nagpur University. To carry out this study I spent more than four years. This book is the outcome of my research work carried out during my research, I had browsed hundreds of university libraries website, blog and searched these library services on various social platforms, and Google, collected data from the librarians and used translation services for few libraries to translate their website contents. Total fifty nine different web-based services are shortlisted and mentioned in this book with few examples of how libraries are offering these services. The book is not only focusing on web-based library services, but also most important area in the success of quality enhancement i.e. web-based best practices. This will be a unique work where the top libraries from all parts of the world are studied and findings are not restricted to a specific country, region or area. In this book the Webometric Ranking is used very first time for selecting university libraries in library and information science field.

The main objective of this book is to give the current status of online library services of universities in the World, to give overview of analysis of the web based library services, best practices and technology used by these libraries, to promote web presence and web-based services in university libraries, to correlate the rankings of world university with their library rankings which has not done earlier, to identify the areas to improve on in developing countries libraries and to suggest the best practices to be followed by University libraries from developing countries to change their profiles into more modern information centres with higher education potential.

This book can be used as a guide to web-based services and best practices top world university libraries are offering. These web-based services are classified in four clusters depending on their scope and type as follows 1. Web-based Bibliographical Services, 2. Web-based Patron Education Services, 3. Web-based Patron Communication Services and 4. Web-based Publishing Platform for patrons. The details of library web-based best practices offered by top world universities are also covered.

Chapter 1 is an introductory chapter in this the overview of the whole book is given. Why web-based services are studied and why they are important now a days. How the libraries from the World are selected and a list of all web-based services clusters and best practices covered in this book are mentioned.

Chapter 2 "Libraries on Web" emphasis on earlier studies carried out so far and clears concept of audiences about what the web is, web 1.0-4.0, uses of the web in the libraries over the years, library web-based services and how the shortlisted web-based services are different than the services covered in earlier studies.

Chapter 3 is dedicated to the overview of web-based bibliographical services which mentions how traditional bibliographical services are now offering using web and internet. Total 12 web-based bibliographical services along with different examples and screenshots are explained.

Chapter 4 discusses the web-based patron education tools/services. Educating the patron is a big challenge libraries are facing. At University thousands are students are studying and giving them education physically in the class is quite difficult task. This chapter explains how using web technology library professionals can teach or educate their patrons about services and how to access the resources online. Total 27 different tools and techniques libraries spread across the world are using to educate their patrons effectively. All information along with a couple of examples are given in this chapter.

Chapter 5 emphasizes on web-based patron

communication tools/ services. Top University libraries are using which platforms, tools to communicate or reach their patrons are explained here. Total 14 web-2.0 platforms, including social media are elaborated in this chapter. What precautions one should take while using social media to communicate and update is also mentioned in this chapter.

Chapter 6 presents the publishing platforms university libraries using to publishing facility or services. Total six web-based publishing services provided by the top world university libraries like open access initiatives, publishing platforms for journals and authors, university records management, anti-plagiarism software access and help, citation tools and help and course work are covered in this chapter along with how they are offered by different libraries.

Chapter 7 is dedicated for innovative best practices offered by top world university libraries through their website or blog. More than 14 best practices are covered in this chapter, which will help other libraries to improve their best practices and adopt a few of them.

Chapter 8 in this chapter authors have given the revolutionary changes going on across the world in terms of web-based services and best practices are mentioned. Important suggestions and precaution library professionals need to take care while starting new services and best practices via the web are given.

Library web-based services and best practices are explained in this book with a good number of examples and screenshots which will help the library professionals to understand and implement these services in their libraries very easily and effectively. The authors have also given the instructions and tips to use online tools and platforms and precautions library professionals' needs to take while offering web-based services professionally.

This book is useful to library professionals all over the world, LIS students and administrators of an educational institutes. The web-based services mentioned in this book will help the university libraries to improve their rankings at global level.

Dr. Sangeeta Dhamdhere

Librarian, Modern College of Arts, Science and Commerce,
Ganeshkind, Pune
librarian@moderncollegegk.org
(M) +917972092077

Abbreviations and Acronyms

API	Application Programming Interface
ARL	Association of Research Libraries
AUB	American University of Beirut
CAS	Current Awareness Service
CGPA	Cumulative Grade Point Average
CWUR	Centre for World University Ranking
FAQs	Frequently Asked Questions
HSL	Health Science Libraries
HTML	Hyper Text Markup Language
HTTP	Hypertext Transfer Protocol
ICT	Information & Communication Technology
ILL	Inter Library Loan
IR	Institutional Repository
ISBN	International Standard Book Number
ISMN	International Standard Music Number
ISSN	International Standard Serial Number
JUIT	Jaypee University of Information Technology
KU	Kesetsart University

LMS	Learning Management System
LRC	Learning Information Center
NAAC	National Assessment and Accreditation Council
OA	Open Access
OPAC	Online Public Access Catalogue
RSS	Rich Site Service
SDI	Selective Dissemination of Information
SMS	Short Message Service
TISS	Tata Institute of Social Sciences
UKZN	University of KwaZulu-Natal
UPR	Universidad de Puerto
URL	Uniform Resource Locator
WWW	World Wide Web

1

Introduction of Web-Based Services Offered by University Libraries at the Global Level

INTRODUCTION

The success of any library is in its innovative services and best practices. Total Quality Management (TQM) stresses upon continuous improvement in services as core values (T, S.D, 2009)[6]. To cope with the timely challenges, every library has to identify and develop its own tailor-made best practices to enhance the collection development process, services dissemination and use of the library as a whole. Several factors are forcing academic libraries to change. The drivers of change include social and economic factors along with technological innovations which affect higher education in general and libraries in particular. The main factors behind the change are changes in literate habits, changes in students and the curriculum, and changes in the technological infrastructure and expectations. Open Access, E-publishing, automation, digitization and Internet have made impact on users and slowly the number of library users visiting libraries is decreasing. In many countries, patrons as well as library staff work from home or on the web with their flexible timetable, and more and more virtual communities are emerging in library field.Therefore, it is a challenge in front of all libraries and forces them to make appropriate planning, thinking ahead, detailed analysis of their user base, the objectives of the institution and its future strategies towards accepting new technologies in libraries.

Many library stakeholders grumble that any best practice means involvement of a lot of resources, especially in terms of money and equipment. In fact, it requires active participation, willingness, creativity and problem solving attitude from all library stakeholders. Developing best practices, analyzing and revising them at a regular interval will lead to continuous improvement in overall performance of the library and the whole institution. Almost all the services and outputs of a library are associated with these two aspects. These can be strengthened further with the help of additional best practices. A best practice may be innovative and be a philosophy, policy, strategy, program, process or practice that solves a problem or create new opportunities and positively impact the whole organization (NAAC, 2006)[1]. Best practices are nothing but developing tailor-made services, reaching beyond with available resources and delighting the customers (Tikam, M)[4].

The WWW offers libraries the potential for more revolutionary change as well. The library website can become the main point of access to all library services; it can integrate services across libraries, and can become a catalyst for new services. Web Services are self-contained, modular applications that can be described, published, located, and invoked over a network, generally, on the Web. Web-based library services mean that library users can obtain services whenever they need them and scholarly databases are accessible twenty-four hours per day (except for scheduled maintained and occasional system failures) from anywhere on or off campus.User can check books and journals, holidays or library hours, even when the phones are busy or the library is closed. Library staff members can be reached via e e-mail links when they are not available in the library. Using various educational and web 2.0 technologies it has become very easy for university library staff to prepare instructional videos, blogs, tutorials, demos, subject guides and reach the students via various social networks and educate them, update them. Many top university libraries providing many of their services via the web using such technologies.

Many libraries in India are following the practices followed by British Libraries and American Centre libraries operating in India (Vyas, 2009)[6]. NAAC is also recommending those practices and services. Libraries in developed countries are much ahead in providing various innovative services to their users. But slowly the same trend is not very far away in India. While working in digital, web and electronic environment all librarians are curious to know what new they can do to attract readers and give prompt service to the users. Here in this book we are mentioning the web-based services, best practices and technology used in modern libraries from all over the world.

WHY CHANGE REQUIRED?

With the new trends in technology, publishing and users' expectations, libraries need to change a lot. The new trends in libraries are present and visible already in developed countries like UK, USA and top universities or institutes of these countries. They are moving ahead in this. They are already providing better services personally as well as online. Because of the web and new library technologies it has become very easy to reach patrons and provide them resources at their finger tip where ever they are.As per law of librarianship library is for all and access to library material should be easy to save the time of the reader. To fulfill this purpose Open public access catalogue, information discovery tools are there. Many developed country's libraries provide access to their catalogue and electronic resources online forall and on the other hand still many libraries in developing countries keep the access to catalogue limited to their users and password protected.With emerging online educational technology, libraries are using different tools and application to educate their patrons online by using social networking sites, by preparing blogs, subject guides, video tutorials, audio tutorials, PDF instructions, PPTs, etc. Many innovative ways are accepted in many libraries to attract readers and inculcate reading habits and support research activity. If we compare these library web-based services, practices and technology, Indian libraries are lagging behind in offering such web-based services because of various reasons like lack of trained staff to manage these kinds of services, websites are outsourced and lack technologies and tools used behind such service but Indian university libraries can see the way ahead.

The web is the main tool for scholarly communicationnow a day. The web is accessible from all over the world and reaches every country. It can reflect all missions of university libraries to make a vibrant learning unit of the university. It provides easy access to relevant indicators.The global ranking of universities is also depending on how this university is representedon the web. According to Webometric Ranking of Universities[2], the university or institutional websites should accurately represent their resources; activities and global performance, providing visitors with a clear vision of the university or institution. They intend to motivate both institutions and scholars to have a web presence that reflect accurately their activities. They suggested that if the web performance of an institution is below the expected position according to their academic excellence, university authorities should reconsider their web policy, promoting substantial increases of the volume and quality of their electronic publications. Here university libraries can play a major role to improve university ranking[3].

It has been observed that in QS world university ranking or Times Higher Education World University ranking, top Indian universities failed to make a mark. There are many reasons for that as Indian universities do not document their systems, processes and outputs and so unable to produce this data when asked by ranking agency. Another reason is universities do not have the number of research papers produced and the number of citations those papers received to the international faculty and international student ratio. The Times Higher Education places emphasis on citations per faculty member for their research work. So to improve this situationbeing the heart of universities, university libraries in India should take lead role in promoting web-based services, open access, online bibliographical services, research support and training along with online education and communication. Along with library services on the web, there is need to transform library users into precious researchers. Many university libraries give access to OPAC, institutional repository and electronic resources online, but still the use of all these resources in universities is low. The main reason behind this is that the student number strength is very high in universities. In many universities there is no fixed schedule to give information literacy programs and orientation for all staff and students. Every year all universities organize such sessions, but only interested and present staff and students attend such classes. Remaining students and staff then remain unaware about library services and facilities. The common lecture and orientation model of teaching does not lead to achieve the desired outcome. Patron-centric strategy like flipped the classroom using e-learning method is an extremely useful alternate learning model in this digital environment and therefore study is beingcarried out to study web-based patron education and communication tools and research promotion tools by top university libraries and give suggestions to Indian university libraries to maximize use of these tools and services.

It has been observed that on library websites and web based services earlier many researchers emphasized on application of web 2.0 tools in university libraries. Hardly 15 web 2.0 tools were studied and other studies were on the usability of library websites. Therefore, inthis book authorstried to search and shortlist the web based services offered by top world university libraries and Indian university libraries,including web-based bibliographical services, web-based patron education tools to educate patron, web-based patron communication tools,web-basedresearch support and publishing support and best practices offered by selecting 70 libraries in the world and 39 NAAC[5] "A" Grade traditional university libraries in India. Inventory of university library web based services and best practices are prepared and divided into following three parts web-based library services, web-based best practices and single web page university libraries. The first part, i.e. total 59 web-based library services are divided into fourclusters,namely 12 bibliographical services, 27 patron education services, 14 patron communication web tools, 6 web-based publishing platform for patrons. Total 64 web based services and practices are shortlisted. From thisbooklibraries in India, developing countries and underdeveloped countries will get more ideas to improve and give the best services to future digital generation users and improve their university ranking at global level.

WEB-BASED SERVICES AND BEST PRACTICES

In this bookthe web-based services and best practices offered by the top selected world university libraries and Indian university libraries are divided into three parts as below

PART A: Cluster of Web-based Services

In this partthe web-based services offered by selecting university libraries are categorized into four different clusters namely

1. Bibliographical services:
2. Patron education tools:
3. Patron Communication Tools:
4. Web-based publishing platform for patrons

Below is the inventory of library web based services offered by all selected university libraries.

1. Bibliographical Services

- Datasets
- Access to Databases
- FederatedSearch/E-Information Discovery Tools
- Web OPAC
- Find a Library
- Archieves /Digital Collection/IR
- Visual Database
- Off campus access
- New arrivals
- ILL
- e-document Delivery
- Book Recommendations

2. Patron Education Tools

- News
- Upcoming Events
- Weblog
- WordPress
- Instant Chat/messaging
- Ask Us
- Research/Subject guides
- Video Tutorials
- FAQs
- YouTube
- Service Directory
- PPTs/PDFs
- Research Tutorials
- Tips for access and use
- Newsletter
- Help/User guides
- RSS Feeds
- Mobile App
- Live/Online Sessions
- Prezi(PPT tool)/slideshare
- Audio Tutorials
- Maps Directions
- Feedback
- Live/online Videos Library
- Library Calender
- Photo Gallary
- Text Instruction

3. Patron Communication Tools

- Facebook

- Twitter
- Email
- Tumblr
- Stumbleupon
- Linked in
- Flickr
- Pinterest
- iTunes
- Instagram
- Delicious
- Google+
- Foursquare
- Whatsapp

4. Web-based Publishing Platform for Patrons

- Open Access Initiatives
- Platform to authors and journals
- University Records Management
- AntiplagarismSoftware access/Plagarism help
- Citation Tools
- Coursework

PART B: Best practices Web-based Best Practices

- Online Exhibitions
- Virtual Tour
- Wikis
- Interactive games, puzzles and movie/short films

Each services are explained in this book along with examples in third to sixth chapters.

REFERENCES

1. NAAC (2016).Best practices in library and information services. Available at: http://webcache.googleusercontent.com/search?q=cache:u9kkKNKW0VYJ:www.naac.gov.in/docs/Best%2520Practices%2520in%2520%2520Library%2520and%2520Information%2520Services%2520A%2520Case%2520Presentation.doc+&cd=3&hl=en&ct=clnk&gl=in
2. Ranking web of universities. Available at http://www.webometrics.info/
3. Ranking web of universities: about us. Available at http://www.webometrics.info/en/About_Us
4. Tikam, M. Best practices in academic libraries. Available at: http://knol.google.com/k/madhuri-tikam/best-practices-in-academic-libraries/35muq6i9t1aro/3#
5. Universities – Accreditation Status (as on 21/02/2014). Available at http://www.naac.gov.in/docs/Status%20-%20Universities%20-5%203%2014.pdf
6. Vyas, S.D. (2009). Best practices in academic libraries in India. *ICAL 2009 – Management models and framework.* Available at http://www.libsys.co.in/download/best%20practices_in_india_libraries.pdf

2

Libraries on Web

WEB

Web is synonymous term of World Wide Web or Internet or Online. But as per Vangie Beal the term WWW and internet are not synonymous[71]. They are separate but related things. Internet is massive network of networks and it connects millions of computers together globally by forming a network in which any two computers can communicate with each other as long as they are part of that network. According to Wikipedia "it is a hypertext and hyperlink system that operates over the Internet." Web, is a way of accessing information over the medium of the Internet. It is an information-sharing model that is built on top of the Internet[77]. The World Wide Web was invented in the year 1989 by a British computer scientist Sir Timothy John "Tim" Berners-Lee who was working at CERN (The European Organization for Nuclear Research) in Geneva, Switzerland. He wrote the world's first web client and server. As of now he is playing active role in maintaining standards for the web and to refine its design as a director of the World Wide Web Consortium (W3C)[1]. In recent years he has advocated his vision of a semantic web. The WWW is more and more used for application to application communication (Naik & Shivalingaiah, 2008)[52] and publishing arm of internet. It is basically a system of Internet servers that support formatted documents.[2]

The Web uses the Hypertext Transfer Protocol (HTTP) protocol, which is only one of the languages spoken over the Internet to transmit data. The programmatic interfaces made available are referred as web services. A web service is a software system designed to support computer-to-computer interaction over the Internet and taking form of an Application Programming Interface (API) (Naik & Shivalingaiah, 2008)[52]. Web services, which use HTTP to allow applications to communicate in order to exchange business logic, use the Web to share information. The Web also utilizes browsers like Internet Explorer or Firefox or Mozilla to access Web documents called Web pages that are linked to each other via hyperlinks. The documents are formatted in a markup language called HTML that supports links to other documents as well as pictures, audios and video files. One can jump from one document to another simply by clicking on the link (hot spots). Not all internet servers are part of World Wide Web (Vangie Beal, Webopedia)[70]. The web is an increasingly important resource in many aspects of life: education, employment, government, commerce, health care, recreation, and more.

Web 1.0 is the first generation of internet technology since 1996. A small number of writers created web pages for a large number of readers. People could get information by going directly to the source (Getting, Brian, 2008)[22]. Using this we can call up pages of text and pictures with incredible speed and facility. Web 1.0 was somewhat mono-directional, static and read only web which allowed us to search information and read it (Aghael, Nematbakhsh & Farsani, 2012)[3]. There was very less possibility of user interaction and content contribution. There is no difference from strolling through a library quickly. We can look at pages on the screen just as we look at the pages in a book. The main goal of the website was to publish the information for anyone at any time and establish an online presence. The websites were not interactive and indeed were as brochure-ware. Core protocols of web 1.0 were HTTP, HTML and URL.

Web 2.0 is the second generation of internet technology which allows for user generated content. The term web 2.0 has been since about October 2004 by Dale Daugherty. In 2004 Tim O'Reilly defined "Web 2.0 is the business revolution in the computer industry caused by the move to the internet as a platform, and an attempt to understand the rules for success on that new platform.[56]" It is known as wisdom web, people-centric web, participative web and read-write web. Along with looking at pages we can alter them. We can write our own blog, comment on someone else's article in comment boxes, can edit an entry on Wikipedia, and can share our thoughts on social networking sites. It is a web where users have more interaction and less control. Through this flexible web design, creative reuse, updates, collaborative content creation and modification were facilitated. It supports collaboration and to help gather collective intelligence rather web 1.0 (Aghael, Nematbakhsh & Farsani, 2012)[3]. If Web 1.0 is like a digital library, Web 2.0 is like a digital 'Letter to the Editor', a digital conference call, a digital group discussion. Web 2.0 is a term applied to a perceived ongoing transition of the World Wide Web from a collection of websites to a full-fledged computing platform serving web applications to end users. Some of the web 2.0 services and technologies are blogging, calendars, chats, collaboration, communication, community, CRM, e-commerce, e-learning, e-mail, file sharing, forums, games, images, knowledge base, lists, mapping, mashups, multi-media, portals, RSS, wiki, shared pictures (flickr), videos (You Tube), news/podcasts (digg, iTunes), knowledge, bookmarks (delicious), projects (Google Docs), you (facebook, myspace), library (Library Thing) and virtual library (Second Life) etc (Wikipedia)[78].

Web 3.0 is where the web is now going 2016 onwards. In Web 3.0 the new media become an essential part of the world in which we are living which help to create the world and we live within them. Web 3.0 is partly about Web 2.0 becoming all pervasive and continuous, so that your connections with the web and your social network is an essential part of every experience – it doesn't get switched off. It is the evolution of web usage and interaction that includes transforming the web into a database. Web 3.0 is defined as the creation of high-quality content and services produced by gifted individuals using web 2.0 technologies as an enabling platform. The Web 3.0 would be something akin to a "read-write-execute" web. It is where the concept of the website or evolution of web usage and interaction along with transforming the web into a database, making content accessible by multiple non-browser applications, the leveraging of artificial intelligence technologies (Jeffrey, 2008)[27]. Web 3.0 is built on semantic web technologies, which will allow data to be shared and reused across application, enterprise and community boundaries. The main components that constitute Web 3.0 are the 3D web, the semantic web, web ontology and the real world web (Warrier, Shivarama&Angadi, 2015)[76].

According to Singh, Bebi & Gulati (2011)[65] web 1.0 was about connecting information and getting on the net. Web 2.0 is about connecting people putting the "I" in user interface, and the "we" into a web of social participation. The next stage, web 3.0, is about representing meanings, connecting knowledge, and putting them to work in ways that make our experience of internet more relevant, useful, and enjoyable.

"Some people say Web 4.0 is the Semantic Web when various programmes, machines, and the web itself becomes 'intelligent', and starts to create new meanings that were not programmed into it, and interact with us in ways that were not predicted or predictable beforehand. It doesn't actually require anystrict definition of 'artificial intelligence' or 'consciousness' for the computers; it just means that they start doing new things themselves – whatever the philosophers judge is or is not going on in their 'minds'. This is when the virtual world becomes physically/biologically part of us, or when we become physically/biologically part of the virtual world. When, in other words, the data is not communicated by phones or earpieces or glasses, but is implanted in us, so that the virtual data is part of our consciousness directly, and not just part of our visual or aural experience and/or, when we control the real and virtual world with some kind of brain or neural interface, so that – in both cases – there really is a seamless integration of the real and the virtual, the personal/biological and the digital." (Fr Stephen Wang, 2012)[74]

USE OF WEB IN LIBRARIES

Information and communication technology (ICT), internetand web technology have dramatically impacted the publishing, research and library world in the last few years and this trend continues going well into the future. Information exchange and information distribution have transformed in disparate formats and by dynamic channels.Many libraries have discovered the advantages of having a presence on the internet and have successfully addressed their objectives by integrating their web site as part of their daily functioning. Mehta & Trivedi (2015)[48] in library field the development of a library website initiated from 1990. When the world's first web browser Mosaic was released in 1993 health science libraries took initiative to develop library websites. The 21st century libraries, demand of library automation, networking and developing digital collections. Patrons need access to digital collections like online databases, e-books, e-journals, multimedia collections from their home. In web

2.0 environment web pages are evolved as blogs, encyclopedias into Wikipedia, and text tutorials into streaming media applications, email to instant chat or messaging and so on (Rath, M & Rath, P)[61].

On Virginia Tech University Libraries website the comparison between library Vs web are given in below table.

Table 1. Library Vs Web (Virginia Tech University Librarieswebsite[73])

Components	Starting with the Libraries	Starting with the Web
Review of Resources	Library resources go through a review process and therefore the library resources are reliable, historically relevant, and valuable.	Most information on the web does not go through a review process as everyone has the freedom to publish on the web without passing the content through an editor. Pages might be written by an expert on the topic, a journalist, and a disgruntled consumer or a sixth grader.
Access to resources	Library resources are free for patron's use	Some information on the web is not free
Organization of Resources	Library resources are classified and organized in the libraries and patrons can locate the item with call no.	Information on the web is searchable and not comprehensive but not organized. Information can be found by using a search engine such as Google or Bing. Most information on the web is not comprehensive
Nature of Resources	Library resources are meant to be kept permanently. Current and historical information can be found in the library	Most information on the web is not permanent. Some well-maintained sites are updated with very current information, but other sites may become quickly outdated or disappear altogether without much notice.

Assistance in locating resources	Library resources come with personal assistance. Library staff is trained to assist you in searching and locating information resources.	The information you find on the web is as varied as the people who put it there. On the web Libraries, universities, government agencies, companies, organizations and people from all over the world publish information and Internet preliminary assist you to search information through web crawlers.
Quality and Quantity	The key idea when using the library is that you are getting QUALITY over QUANTITY.	The key idea when using the web is that you get QUANTITY over QUALITY. The web is a good tool for finding information, but it is usually not the best place to begin academic research.

Though we are making distinctions between library and web but these two are not different things. It's important to understand that there is a middle-ground—the idea of the library on the Web. That is to explain, many libraries have web sites which organize information and provide access to collections of quality resources and library services. Libraries on the web are evaluating, organizing Information available online and sometimes digitizing their collections for the use of patrons around the world to use. Norozi, Alireza(2004)[54]stated five laws of web on the basis of Ranganathan's five laws as web resources are for use, every user his or her web resource, every web resource its user, save the time of the user, the web is a growing organism. Academic Libraries are driven by most of the young generation users,they are frequently visiting net and they are grown up with the internet. Due to the impact ofsocial networking software (SNS) most of them have profiles in Internet in different social networking sites and therefore the need to introduce such tools in libraries rose to provide library services (Dora &Maharana, 2008)[18].

Library Web sites often have information about library hours, policies, and contact information if you need assistance. If you are a student at a university, you can use the library online 24 hours a day, seven days a week from any Internet-connected computer. (http://www.lib.vt.edu/help/research/library-web.html)[69]. Website helps to establish a presence and become an active member of this new and growing cyber-culture, to develop lines of communication with patrons and libraries, to provide information about the library and its services to patrons, to provide remote access to library resources with download facility.

Library 1.0 : The library reform of the early 20th century was based on a set of values, where the patron should have the best possible access to and the best possible benefit of library resources, all built on democratic values. Curran, Murray & Christian (2007)[17] defines Library 1.0 the way resources are kept on shelves or ona computer behind a login. These resources can be taken from a shelf, checked out to the librarian, taken home for a certain length of time and absorbed, and then taken back to the library for someone else to use. Library 1.0 is a one directional service that takes people to the information that they require.

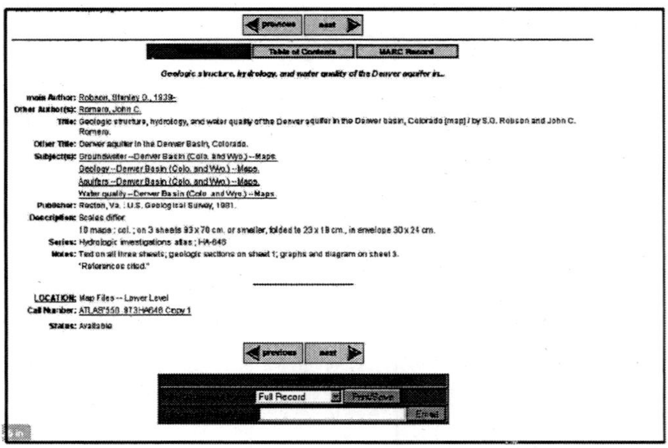

Fig. 1. Library 1.0

Library 2.0 : The term Library 2.0 was first coined by Michael Casey in his blog Library Crunch in September 2005. Chad and Millar (2005)[11] Web 2.0 transferred into the library world as Library 2.0. It is a read-write library that gives library users' power to decide the service that they get. The basic idea of Library 2.0 is to transform library service by making them more personalize, more interactive, collaborative, more web-based, driven by community needs. It replaced traditional one directional library services to more interactive, collaborative and with application of web 2.0 technologies as a Library 2.0. According to Wikipedia[41], "Library 2.0 is a loosely defined model of library services that reflects atransition within the library world in the way that services are delivered to users". Maness (2006)[45] defines Library 2.0 as "The application of interactive, collaborative and multimedia web based technologies to web based library services and collection. Library 2.0 aims to take the information to the users by bringing library services to the internet and getting the users more involved to improve the services by encouraging them to participate in giving feedback. The essential elementsof Library 2.0 are its user-centered participation in content creation and services. It provides multimedia experience and contains audio and video components as well. It's a "social reach"rather communication between library staff and users. It provides community service oriented where not just the librarian has participates butthe entire user community change the library services. The library 2.0 services include synchronous messaging, stream media, blogs, wikis, social networks, tagging, RSS feeds, podcasting, mashups, etc (Rath, M & Rath, P)[61]

Library 2.0 servicesproviding new means of information delivery, distribution and manipulation. For example, library OPAC can link tothe website, and in social networking space (e.g. Myspace or Facebook) with creating an account and providing a search box on that social

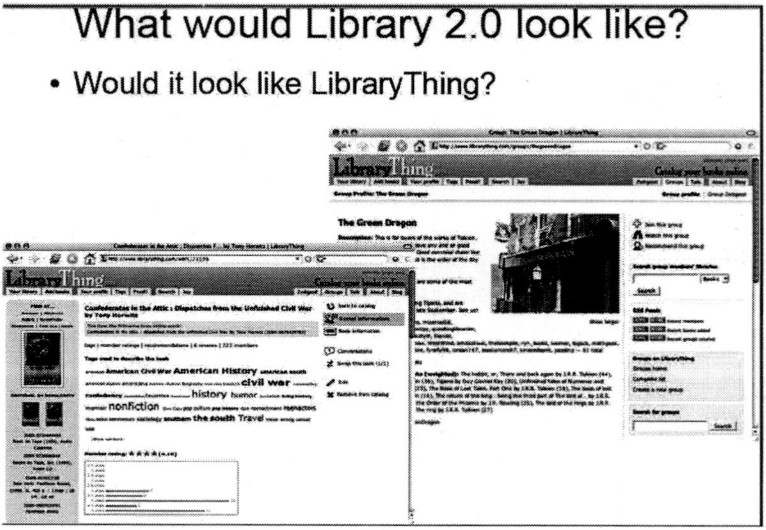

Fig. 2. Library 2.0

space, so that it will be available everywhere, and the user will be happy to search the OPAC from his favorite social software like Myspace, Facebook and Orkut. In other side Library also benefited taking advantage of these services, putting the library in the users' space. Library OPAC is only one example of pushing out the services from conventional library zone to the user comfort zone. There is a lot of the innovative services, library can provide only library has to bend towards its old services, examine holistically, these fundamental services and try to renovate it into 2.0 formats. (Dora &Maharana, 2008)[18]

The difference between Library 1.0 and 2.0: Library 1.0 is in the Library only where as Library 2.0 is every where in the world with internet. In library 1.0, information is controlled by the library and in library 2.0; information is controlled by user/stakeholder. In library 1.0 library website is static where as in library 2.0 library website is dynamic and interactive. Library 1.0 is Publishing platform where as Library 2.0 is Participating platform. Library 1.0 is available locally and library 2.0 available worldwide.

Library 1.0 is one way and library 2.0 is two ways. Library 1.0 is a service and library 2.0 is an experience. (Source: *http://eprints.rclis.org/archive/00012108/*)[85]

Library 3.0 : Lib 3.0 is a product of Web 3.0.Web 3.0 has brought about a revolutionary change in the way we understand the web. Warrier, Shivarama & Angadi (2015)[76] The web 3.0 technologies like semantic web, web ontology and the real world web have a significantrole to play in providing library and information services. The maximization of these services will depend upon how well the services are being executed and how much they are being accepted by the users. In the context of Web 3.0, Crawford and Gorman have re-interpreted Ranganathan's Laws of Library Science[60]. The role of the information professional in the present scenario goes hand in hand with the third law which states that "Use technology intelligently to enhance the service"and forth law "protects free access to knowledge". Accordingly, by using various web 3.0 technologies the library professional will be able to necessarily provide the information as per the requirements of the target users. Library 3.0 projects librarians as prominent apomediaries guiding library users on how best to locate, access and use credible information in myriad formats from diverse sources, at the point of need. The Library 3.0 model has revived hope amongst those who were uncomfortable with the crowd intelligence architecture on which the Library 2.0 model was founded. It provides the tools and framework to organize the info sphere that the Library 2.0 threw into disarray. The authors see the 3.0 library as a personalizable, intelligent, sensitive and a living institution created and sustained by a seamless engagement of library users, librarians and subject experts on a federated network of information pathways (Kwanya, Stilwell & Underwood, 2007)[38].

Library 4.0 : Younghee Noh (2015)[83] now a day's discussions on Web 4.0 and Library 4.0 have begun but very less written on this. Web 4.0 features commonly suggested by previous researchers are: reading, writing, and executing simultaneously, intelligence-based agents, connected web, ubiquitous web, intelligence connections, massive data, augmented reality, context aware, cutting-edge displays, and infinite creative space and the intelligence-based web.

The web has become commonplace throughout the world, a natural complement to traditional library services and develops an innovative ways to meet the information needs of users. Traditional online services have transformed into web based services using web technologies.

LIBRARY WEBSITE

A very large number of studies have been carried out on library websites and web based services offered by various libraries all over the world since 1998. A few examples are cited below:

The library website study has started in 20th century itself by the library professionals as libraries are actively involved in creating the library webpage since then. University websites began as a piecemeal project with varying degrees of complexity in early 1990s. Web site standards have developed since 1990s. Initially they started as informational sites and then became a vital part of postsecondary institutions and one of their most visible faces. On the university website library web pages are most visited one. This to design a well designed library page can be a crucial role for university (Kate Peterson, 2006)[31].

A library website is a virtual public face, the quasi equivalent of the front door, signage, pathfinders, surrogates to the collection, services and it is used as a window to theWorld Wide Web (Diaz, 1998)[18]. Riddle (1998)[62]conducted a comparison of university main pages, not specific libraries. Riddle found that in a survey of twenty-two major university pages, search forms were included only on seven sites and site maps in eight.

A paper by Cohen and Still (1999)[14] offered a fairly detailed analysis of Websites of research university libraries and 2-year college libraries. The authors analyzed 100 websites for specific kinds of resources and information and noted some links from the home page, although they did not analyze other forms of navigation. Categories of surveyed resources included general library information, reference, research, instruction, and functionalities such as search or Web-based forms. Their conclusions listed a series of elements that they considered core to any academic Website. Many of these elements were linked to specific resources, including the library's online public access catalog (OPAC), Internet subject guides, search engines, subscription databases, and electronic journal services. As per his study, he found that patrons turn to the library website for information, reference, research and instruction.

Xue-Ming Bao (2000)[3]surveyed the website home pages of 143 academic institutions and found that only 57% of the institutes' home pages offered links to their libraries' home pages and told the location of a library home page link on its parent institution's home page will determine the visibility of a library and will affect the effective use of the library's online, Web-based resources.

McGillis, L. & Toms, E. G. (2001)[47]described that library web site is its virtual public face—the quasi equivalent of the front door, signage, pathfinders, collections or surrogates to the collections, services, and, to an extent, its people. Because library Web sites compete with a host of other Internet services and organizations for clientele, they must capture and motivate the user; provide useful, innovative, and interactive services and products; give the library some form of identity; and encourage repeat visitation while holding the interest of users and simplifying their tasks. They also must do so while supporting the mission of the library, which for an academic library typically is "to foster the search for knowledge and understanding in the University and the wider community."

According to Jones, an excellent and effective library web site needs two ingredients. First, it has to have the content a user wants and second it needs to allow the user to browse, search and interact with the information in rich and flexible ways (Jones, 2002)[28].

Lesley Moyo (2002)[49] observed that subject areas constitute the main approach to seeking information. Organizing by library function or library organizational structure, although logical to librarians, may not be very useful to library users, particularly remote users.

Stewart M. Brower (2004)[10] found following results from his study of 41 university websites. The most common link of all was to a parent organization. In the case of academic Health Science Libraries (HSL), this link was often to the college or university main page. Thirty-eight home pages, accounting for 93% of the sites, linked to the parent organization.Parent library links were also tracked, with 46% of the academic HSL home pages linking out to a general library home page and 17% of those home pages also linking to the parent library from PNTs.The most prevalent home page links to library-specific information included links to library news or "What's New" features (80%), library education services including tutorials or class schedules (80%), library hours (68%), descriptions of library services (68%), directions or maps to the library (48%), and staff directories (43%).These services, however, were frequently not linked from the navigation tool. Twenty-nine percent of sites (12) linked to descriptions of services from PNTs, and 27% (11) linked to library education services, but no other library general information link ranked higher than 20%.

Broader-scoped comparisons, such as King's analysis year of home pages for member libraries of the Association of Research Libraries (ARL) followed. King found that the average number of links on an ARL library home page was 21.6, and that 37% of the libraries he surveyed had between 10 and 19 links on their home pages. But the specifics of what pages and resources were being linked were not discussed in the article(Brower, Stewart, 2004)[10].

Jasek, Chris (2004)[26] described how to design a library website to maximize usability. Elsevier's User Centered Design Group has conducted usability reviews of several academic library web sitess including the University of Manchester's library web site and Hawaii Medical Library's web site and suggested a few tips for making a library website more usable and effective. Study says to increase use of library website it is necessary to provide hyperlinks for help on every web page, across all web pages fonts and colors should use consistently for a uniform and professional appearance, library website should be directly linked to home page of university website, use one navigation bar to orient users, use different color to differentiate the links, use library page real estate wisely, use only three to four colors for website designing to give professional look, organize information in efficient and flexible way, make website search clear, use meaningful terminology than librarians terminology, make library website accessible and test your website for usability frequently. He suggested that a library Web site should be organized and designed considering the users' point of view.He also pointed out the biggest mistake library web sites were making was not giving enough space to the task 85% of people come to the library web site for finding research materials like journal articles.

In China studies were carried out on the specific library website evaluation since 2004. In 2004 Wu Xiaoxing[80] analyzed the evaluative indicators of library website and suggested some factors in website construction. Wang Zunxin (2005)[75] discussed and pointed out the standard of evaluation indicators related to system for a college library website. Zhao Yuxiang[84] investigated 16 public library websites and developed an evaluative system suitable for a public library website and evaluated the usability of IA of the Shanghai Public Library website. Xiang Liling,Dong Xiaoyan& Qu Baoqiang[81] studied 30 colleges and university library websites and suggested some points for the development of colleges and university library website developments.

The Online Public Access Catalogue is an online bibliography of library collection that is available to the public. (Omoike & Oke, 2014)[55] defined OPAC as computerized databases of library's holding. The new generation of Web OPACs allows users to access resources of libraries, publishers, and online vendors (Guha & Saraf, 2005)[23]

Peterson, Kate (2006)[31] gave the opinion that librarians should work with library and university administrators to create a well designed usable library website. To improve library website library administrators should allocate sufficient resources and staff. The library website template should be selected in such a way that students should keep coming back to access the library website. Library websites are crucial to delivering data, research tools and instructions to patrons and the community. Libraries use their website as marketing, public relations and fundraising tool.

According to Poll (2007)[58] website quality of the library depends on the following criteria: adequate language to the population, clear structure, options given for different user groups, up-to-date information and short and concise information. As per him, the library website should always be the main starting-point for searches and the one virtual "entrance" to the library. He highlighted an important issue that library homepage should guide by the shortest possible way to the most-used information.

As described by Liu (2008)[43] the academic library

websites are libraries' virtual presentation to the world. Academic library websites provide access to online catalogs, electronic databases, subject resources, library instruction/tutorials, digital collections and are gateways to information that supports faculty and students' research and educational needs.

Laouar, Hacken & Miles (2009)[40] outlined a conceptual model of library web portal with ontological classifications and relationships for scholarly resources at the University of Tebessa in Algeria with which they hoped that scholarly work stations that combine local and remote holdings, tools and documents will be created and which will ultimately benefit from inclusion in a nationwide network. Their findings are first the contribution of web-services to the seamless utility of a scholarly portal is indispensable: interoperable features, formats and protocols can be carefully customized. Second, the conceptual model assists not only in visualization, but in implementation phases of the process ofassessment of user needs and behaviors through interface creation and ongoing maintenance. And third, a method for recycling existing applications in constructing new libraryservices is a key component.

According to Jacob Nielson (2010) a better library website is one that helps patrons quickly accomplish their goal. "A user-centered library website can help patrons feel welcomed and valued in the library setting. It can also help them efficiently locate quality information, thus leaving more time for study and reflection "Stephenson, Kimberley (2011)[33]. Kely; Jones & Farrington (2011)[39] suggested that Library website content must be viewed in much the same way as a physical collection. By applying Dr. S. R. Ranganathan's Fifth Law[56], Library website is a growing organism and must be treated as such, especially with the complexity of web content.

In 2011 Kim, Yong-Mi[82]explored the factors affecting users' intentions to use university library website resources and then investigated factors affecting the university library website design and assessed the success of this website from a designer as well as a user's point of view. He suggested that when university plans for the website then web designer should consider university guidelines, he has to review other websites and consult the library experts who are working in that library. With this the website will be successful. He also gave suggestions on enhancing the usage of this website by the users.

Sangeeta Dhamdhere (2012)[19] mentioned that Library website is a part of public image the mirror of library in a community and therefore can be considered as a mirror of the library which shows its services, collection, facilities, communication media and other information.

Becker, Danielle A & Yannotta, Lauren[6] in 2013 wrote in his article that in 2008 Hunter College Libraries launched a two-year website redesign process, keeping goals to update the design to position the library as a technology leader on campus, streamline the architecture and navigation, simplify the language used to describe resources, tools, and services and develop a mechanism to quickly incorporate new and emerging tools and technologies. The library committee considered the principles endorsed solid information architecture, clear navigation systems, strong visual appeal, understandable terminology and user-centered design for the new library website. And accordingly the process led to the development of a strong, user-centered site that can be easily changed or adapted to accommodate new resources and technologies. They also presented a model for creating a strong, user-centric web presence by pairing usability testing and the design process. Four rounds of usability testing were conducted throughout the process of building a new academic library web site. Participants were asked to perform tasks which are based on the guiding principles of web usability that served as a framework for a new site usinga talk-aloud protocol.

Testing the usability of a website is an ongoing search for perfection and not something that is done once. The focus on testing is to find out what does not work and where users run into trouble. Once that is found by testing, the redesigned websites will work better for users than the old ones. The final aim of any testing and redesigning should be to take into considerations user's advice and views on what they need on the website. (Shubhada Nagarkar & Durga Murari)[51]

In 2013 Ellyssa Kroski[36] advised to create person as before designing library website. Person as are fictional depictions of website's target audiences. To develop a persona, one has to learn about users by interviewing (guided, open ended conversation) them and find the distinguishing characteristics about library patrons. Analysis of interview transcripts or notes, though time-consuming, is an invaluable opportunity to get to the heart of your users' behaviors, needs, goals, and motivations. The output is a thematically grouped list of behaviors, which is the raw material for your persona and which represents the cornerstone of your website planning process and have an ongoing role as the site evolves. Personas help to ensure that everyone is on the same page about your main demographic.

The survey of about 210 staff and students (2012-13) who wasusing electronic resources of Nigerian university libraries was conducted to evaluate the quality of online services in academic libraries in Nigeria using questionnaire method. Modified WebQual four performance indicators were designed and used to measure: library equipment, library website, online public access catalogue (OPAC) and e-user education in the university libraries. It was suggested that through adequate funding and prudent management of library funds, online services in Nigerian university libraries could meet the international standards in terms of library web based services (Asogwa, Ugwu, & Ugwuanyi, 2015)[5].

Mehta & Trivedi (2015)[48] carried out study of website contents of 45 central university libraries from 25 states and two territories of India by carefully scanning the websites. In their findings, they observed percentages of libraries, giving following information on their website introduction, about library, history of the library, contact information, copyright information, mission, location information, sitemap of web pages, Library rules, library hours, announcement, membership information, library tour, FAQ, Staff directory, library policies and procedures, library governance, annual reports, library brochure, library collection, e-resources, different sections, library services and technical services along with value added information and services offered by library on their website. They did not studyonly contents and design of university library websites and focused on information provided not web based applications or tools used by those libraries. They concluded that many central university libraries are yet to develop tofull potential and make the web based services more interactive and recommended to add use of social networking sites, web 2.0 tools such as blogs, wikis, RSS feed, you tube, android applications etc for universal identification.

LIBRARY WEB BASED SERVICES

A web service is a software system designed to support computer-to-computer interaction overthe Internet. In today's competition world the web is an increasingly important resource in many aspects of life like education, employment, government, commerce, healthcare, and almost everywhere. The Web services are typically application programming interfaces (API) or Web APIs that are accessed via Hypertext Transfer Protocol (HTTP) and executed on a remote system hosting the requested services. The W3C defines a "Web service" as "a software system designed to support interoperable machine-to-machine interaction over a network. It has an interface described in a machine-process-able format (specifically Web Services Description Language WSDL) (Singh, Bebi & Gulati, 2011)[65].

Historically, library services are typically meant reference and information desk services, reader education programs, interlibrary loan and bibliographic search services. Over last two decades, technology has been used to introduce many new services, either by delivering existing services via electronic media or by developing and implementing entirely new services for a search, delivery and use of information (Poll, 2005)[57]. When focus is given on services provided via library website "Web-based services" is the preferred terminology.

In 1999 Borasky, D[9] in his master's thesis examined the web based library services offered by 15 academic libraries in North Carolina at Chapel Hill (UNC) system via their websites. He used a combination of content analysis and questionnaires. The results of this study demonstrate a broad range of web-based services offered by academic libraries. Most libraries offer a minimum of basic, text-based services, such as descriptive information about the library, policies, and ready reference links. Most libraries also offer web-based access to the mainstay of library services, the online public access catalog (OPAC). Fewer libraries offer more advanced services, such as online request forms, and bibliographies. Fewer still offer innovative services such as digital collections and cross departmental services. This study identified specific ways in which the web, allows libraries to improve and develop services. Some of the key improvements and developments are: a) hyperlinks between resources, such as OPAC records that link directly to web sites or other web-based services; b) cross-departmental services, such as the integration of ILL services with the OPAC; c) simple user interfaces to multiple services, such as the ability to search many electronic databases at one time; and d) remote access to library services, such as digital collections.

Madhusudan (2001) in his survey of 12 selected university libraries in India, he again revealed that Indian libraries are lagging behind in providing web forms to users in different web-based library services which are effective tools for library-user interaction and communication. His findings showed that many of the surveyed university libraries have been yet to exploit the full potential of the web and continually develop an effective web-based information literacy programs to provide a high degree of interactivity and flexibility to enhance the use of web-based library services they offer to the users. His work was earliest work which shaded light on the current level of adoption and use of web based library services in university libraries in India. As per him there was scope to study the university libraries those offers full range of web based services and find the problems faced by users while using them and give direction to other libraries gain a broader perspective on the effective use of web-based library services

Syed Ahmed (2002) surveyed Arabian Gulf university libraries via email to know what type of web based services these universities offer to their users. He found that almost all the libraries are offering web-based services like OPAC, search engines, forms, etc, in one or other way. He also discussed how these libraries can improve and reinforce such services in an effective way and create awareness among the patrons in order to create positive environment about this change. His findings also helped other Arabian Gulf libraries to improve and offer quality web based services.According to him there was an imperative need for libraries to exercise proper awareness, orientation and training to the patrons in order to make them aware about these services and to realize positive change in the environment. To meet these challenges the librarians need to play a leadership role in providing better web-based library service facilities to their current techno savvy users. The librarians should be expert to hold the hands of the users who are moving towards a new communication paradigm a shift from face to face human contact to human machine interaction, from paper to electronic delivery, from text centered mode to multimedia and from physical presence to virtual presence[67].

Contreras, Paula; Probst, Laura K. & Klimczyk, Linda (2004)[15] in their case study of expansionof web-based library services in Penn State University libraries observed that users prefer to use library resources from their home and office to study independently and expect full text web access to all resources and their feedback to the library is depend on the libraries' ability to provide web based services. To support users Penn State University libraries decided to build a comprehensive web-based reference system across their 24 campuses and approximately 50 service points and engage their users in designing new services based on analysis of users needs.

According to Anjana Bhatnagar (2005)[8] mentioned in her paper few emerging web based services in libraries like Virtual library tours, Ask-A-Librarian, Real time services, Bulletin boards, Web based user education and web forms which libraries can adopt. According to her, in the Indian scenario library Web services will continue to spread out, will offer more full-text electronic journals and indexes, Bibliographic access to full-text periodicals. There will be more Web forms for user feedback, and perhaps a virtual librarian who interacts in real time chat or video conferencing. More Document delivery services to distance education or users and Savings on Interlibrary Loan and user convenience are incentives. Information resources through creative consortia purchasing will be popular. A well-developed user education modules or tutorials, especially to support independent exploration of library and Web resources. Somebody will have to figure out how to keep Word users from saving print documents as XML, without thinking in terms of Web, not print, space. XML will be embraced as a way to control page appearance and behavior, but it will take a while for people tofigure out how to use it well and there will be trends we haven't thought of yet. She also concluded that web-based library services will become more widespread and sophisticated as the web becomes common place throughout the world, and to be successful players in the E-world.

LiLi, Li (2006)[42] discussed key issues involved with challenges and opportunities library professionals facing while spreading awareness and instructing patron at the time of delivering dynamic web based resources and services. He mentioned that it is very imperative for libraries and librarians to design, develop, enhance, implement, and deliver high quality user-centered information services, resources, and instruction at the fingertips of library users. He also discussed next-generation web-based client/server library information architecture and services in the foreseeable future. According to Judith Wusteman (2006)[29] until the web services are standardized the advantages of web services will not be realized by the library community.

Kraemer, Elizabeth W. ; Lombardo Shawn V. & Lepkowski, Frank J. (2007)[35] suggested that In comprehensive information literacy program online instruction should be one component and should also include librarian-student interaction. This hybrid instructional model will help librarians to address multiple learning styles, to engage students with the latest technology, to respond to external pressures to move into an online teaching environment, and to maintain the physical contact that is vital to student learning. The students enrolled in Rhetoric 160: Composition II (RHT 160) at Oakland University for the 2005 winter semester was the target population for this study. For this study, they selected twelve sections of RHT 160 during the winter 2005 term to compare three instructional methods: online instruction only, live instruction, and the current "hybrid" combination of live instruction and online tutorials.The sections were assigned to one of the instructional methods and, to assess student learning, all students (n=224) completed identifying pre- and post-tests. The results of the study, including differences in student performance in relation to pedagogy were discussed.

Farkas (2007)[21] gave an excellent example of Georgia State University libraries how academic libraries can leverage their services with Web 2.0. These libraries took blogging to another level of outreach and public service through their subject specialist, liaison efforts by creating subject blogs. The university library uses blogs in conjunction with their reference services where each blog contains a variety of content, including new subject-specific databases, calls for participation and requests for proposals, subject-related world news and studies, book reviews, conference announcements, and relevant library news. He also suggested that academic libraries should try to create more value with social networking profiles by offering a space for patron to give feedback, by providing news and information, or by providing a portal to library services.

Libraries are facing demands from increasingly techno savvy patrons to expand online library services in new and sometimes usual ways using web tools. Web based library services means the services provided using the internet as a medium and though the website as a gateway with the help of integrated library management system (Madhusadan & Nagabhushanam, 2012)[40]. White (2001)[79] defined library web based services as an information access service in which users ask questions via electronic means e.g. email or web form. According to Arora, J (2001)[4] technical infrastructure required for generating web-based library services are divided into three categories Collection infrastructure, Access infrastructure and Hardware & Software Infrastructure.

Web based services require accuracy, promptness, courtesy and understanding of the information need (Sangale, 2015)[63]. The web services are only useful and effective if potential users know that they exist, how they can access and what they offer. Information is available to varying degree and in a variety of formats, depending on the service in question (Judith Wusteman, 2006)[29]

Kataria, Sanjay & Anbu K, John (2009)[30] mentioned in his paper how library committee and the librarian of JIIT University planned to start a new interactive library website and on the basis of user feedback proposed a model for learning information centre in which they planned to add new web 2.0 tools like LRC Forum, LRC Wiki, LRC RSS, LRC YouTube videos, LRC Social Networking, Content Tagging and Media tagging to bring users closer to learning information centre.

Korah & Cassidy (2009)[34] carried out study at Sam Houston State University to assess student use of and satisfaction with the Web Feat federated search tool implemented by their library. Students voluntarily responded to an electronic survey conducted to collect feedback on how often they conducted class research using the federated search tool, individual databases, and online search engines and how well each search tool satisfied their class research needs. In the result, it was found that a high rate of federated search use, but only moderate satisfaction; for most students, federated search did not replace individual databases and online search engines, which also saw frequent use for class assignments. Federated search use was highest among lower-level undergraduates, and both use and satisfaction declined as student classification rose.

Su, Chen,Ouyang, F & Chu, H[12] in 2009 visited 81 academic library websites in the New York State and he found that 42% libraries adopted one or more web 2.0 tools such as blogs while the implementation of these tools in individual libraries varies greatly.

Hatua, Sudip (2010)[25] mentioned about 20 web based services we can apply on our library and information science field, but most of these services we cannot use as library services. They are as following List Serve, Subject database, community information, Government resources, library catalogue, shopping and other commercial transactions, document delivery, commercial resources, bulletin board, email facilities, surfing facilities, access to the database, bibliographical and cataloguing service, bulletin board service, push based services, ICAS, profit based alert service, E-SDI: Link to remote information, list of acquisition, hosting on web, email delivery, FAQ, ILL and document delivery services, newsletter services, OPAC, Webopac, patent information services, reference services, usenet, uncover, webcasting, whiteboard and virtual library. But as he mentioned now libraries are taking full advantages of the internet and web facilities and remarkably changing their mode of provision of services. Western countries have gone far miles than developing and underdeveloped countries. These new modes of service arehighly effective in special libraries than academic libraries. About why Indian libraries are far backward in offering web based services, he mentioned, national policy of India has no intention of implementing. No infrastructure for implementing web based library services, Government policy of restricted employment opportunity compelled not to take professional manpower as muchas required. The various networking system in India issimply failed due to lack of good will, effort and ego problem in big libraries. But if libraries will invest initial installation cost they will enable to provide web based services and make them popular, but only when library and information centre should become professional about their services in future. This scenario has changed now Indian University libraries are getting sufficient infrastructure to provide web based services to the patrons and also internet facility to patrons in library premises.

In 2010 Chua, Alton & Goh, Dion[16] addressed the issues related to application of web 2.0 in libraries. He studied to what extent Web 2.0 applications are prevalent in libraries, in what ways Web 2.0 applications have been used in librariesand Does the presence of Web 2.0 applications enhance the quality of library websites? He studies total 120 library websites, both public and academic from North America, Europe and Asia. He found that libraries are implementing web 2.0 applications like Blogs, RSS, Instant messaging and applications like social tagging to increase the level of user engagement. The presence of Web 2.0 applications was found to be associated with the overall quality, and in particular, the service quality of library websites.

N.S. Harinarayana & N. Vasantha Raju[24] in 2010 studied the web 2.0 features in university library websites in 2010. They selected 57 Universities from the top 100 universities from the Times Higher Education Ranking web site in 2007 out of 200 Universities listed on the basis of whether the site was in English had at least one Web 2.0 feature. Theycollected and analyzed the data visiting their website for web 2.0 features like Blogs, RSS, Instant Messaging, wikis, etc. In his study,theyrevealed that 37 university libraries out of 57 university libraries uses RSS feeds and Instant Messaging feature for dissemination of Library news, events, announcements and reference service. 15 universitylibraries provide blog space for users and only one university uses wiki whereas only three university libraries used Podcast and six libraries were using Vidcast. In their paperthey provided concrete evidence of the application of Web 2.0 in University libraries where most of the earlier studies were on how Web 2.0 tools used in a library context.

Nithya, S; Srinivasaraghavan, S; Surulinathi, M & Gopinath[53], A in their pilot study discussed different ways to reinforce and improve the provision of web based services including effective ways to create awareness and delivering orientation to create a positive environment among the students about this change. According to them Bharatisadan University Library offers following general and common web based services subject gateways, Bibliographic databases and full text databases, Information alert service, web OPAC, Institutional repository service, live chat in the form of a FAQ, and Virtual Library tour.

In 2011 the survey of ARL Library websites was carried out by Khalid Mahmood & John Richardson[32] for adoption of web 2.0 in US academic libraries. They found that all libraries were widely using blogs, micro blogs, RSS, instant chat, social networking sites, podcasts, mashups, vodcasts while wikis, photos and presentation sharing, and vertical search engines were used less. They were using these web tools for marketing their services, providing information literacy instructions and making the users aware about library resources and to collect feedback.

Shubhada Nagarkar[50] (2011) described in her paper how personalized reference services for Bioinformatics scientists of Savitribai Phule Pune University are being developed using a portal. She used various tools and resources starting with Google Sites as the platform and then integrating RSS feeds, Google gadgets, Google News for current awareness services and PubMed and Google for selected dissemination services.

Shri Ram, Anbu K, John & Kataria, Sanjay (2011)[14] carried out a survey to understand the basic awareness of web 2.0 tools and to create information literacy amongst users by knowing their expectations and usage of web 2.0 tools and applications at the Learning Resource Centre (LRC), Jaypee University of Information Technology (JUIT), Solan, Himachal Pradesh, India. It was observed that users of the JUIT library were lacking awareness about various Web 2.0 applications necessary for teaching and learning. Therefore, their study provided an insight into implementation of digital libraries, video on demand, reference services, and database services along with some innovative web 2.0 applications at JUIT library to create information literacy.

Web information services are not widespread and have yet to take off widely in academic Libraries in India; the diffusion rate of Web 2.0 information services is relatively low (Preedip & Kumar, 2011)[59]. Tyagi, Sunil (2012)[69] has observed that a large number of respondents had knowledge about Web 2.0 tools and were more inclined to adopt the Web 2.0 technologies in their personal lives. However, libraries are lagging behind in using the social networking technologies.[47]

According to B.V. Kumar & S.V. Subrahmanya (2012)[37] the web and Internet offered a unique medium for businesses to reach beyond geographical boundaries. Web services are characterized by their ability to work in the interoperability among communicating applications by using XML based data. The applications that offer web services are therefore designed to be loosely coupled withnature and services they are offering could synchronous or asynchronous web services. Web services heralded another significant milestone in the history of information technology. Earlier, Internet catered mostly to the business-to-consumer (B2C) category of the users on the web. As against this, web services enable B2B interactions as well since the interaction/transaction is being carried out on the internet, HTTP, SMTP and such transport protocols are used in communication.The key issues involved with opportunities, challenges, and future development trends of delivering dynamic and distributed web-based library information resources, services, and instructions for library users in the digital age (Madhusudan & Nagabhushanam, 2012)[40].

Madhusudhan & Nagabhushanam (2012)[44] conducted a survey of 20 University libraries in India in 2012 in which he presented current status and use of web by those libraries. They examined how some of the university libraries in India provide web access to their collections and user support for that access and the problems faced by users in accessing Web-based library services. They found that many surveyed university libraries were not exploited full potential of the web forms and are lagging behind in effective use of library websites. Few university libraries were offering innovative web-based services in different sections. They also pointed out, therewas an urgent need to develop dynamic library websites and incorporate relevant Web 2.0 based services including web forms in each webbased library service, apply semantic technologies and ontology and adopt next generation internet and provide multi language support content. Their study also examined institutional characteristics and resources dedicated to web based services.

Svetal & Lalitha (2012)[66] in their study analyzed 173 Indian State Universities for their web presence. They found that some state universities had more visibility compared to other and also found out the ways to get high web links which helped to improve presence on the web. Their findings suggested that should emerge the following tools like blogs, social networking sites for scholarly and scientific communication of universities to their websites. They also advised that Maintaining Institutional Repositories, Open Access, and Collaboration with other universities and Online Communication etc would also help to increase the Visibility of the particular university library on the web.

The study was conducted by Chang Chiao-Chen (2013)[13] to integrate the unified theory of acceptance and usage of technology studying behavioral intentional of 363 undergraduate and graduate students who used library mobile applications in university libraries. He observed it differs from students to students and therefore university librarians should reinforce the efficiency of library mobile applications to influence users' willingness to use such applications.

Omoike & Oke, (2014)[55] discussed some positive effects of OPAC and 239. 50 standards in Nigerian libraries like It allows patrons to use search strategies, hyperlink to search, to search OPAC on the web using common interfaces, timely access to library materials, encourages cooperative collection development and resource sharing. It motivates patrons, equips them with problem solving and information retrieval skills, and provides them with lifelong learning experiences. He also pointed out problems Nigeria libraries are facing while utilization of OPAC like setup and software cost is not affordable, power failure, consistent breakdown, users are abusing copyright, users have technophobia and so it is going difficult to understand and it takes time. Also libraries have inadequate manpower and lack of committed personnel. He also found that most libraries Online Public Access Catalogue fails to provide information in a helpful way to users as it searches only a fraction of the library's resources. And to find much relevant materialthe library patrons those are familiar with sophisticated commercial Web business expect from their library catalogues should work as along withamazon.com's website rather than core functionality.

Bhardwaj (2014)[7] investigated how library and information science professionals working in higher education institutions in India integrate social networking sites (SNS) into their routine work. The findings revealed that information professionals use SNS to socialize, keep themselves up-to-date, find jobs, and acquire information about conferences and seminars in theirrespective fields.

S N Dhamdhere & Egbert De Smet (2015)[20] discussed the current status of various web-based services offered by selecting 14 Five Star University libraries in the USA as per QS World University Rankings 2014 and 28 in India with Higher CGPA (above 3.1) ranked NAAC "A" Grade University Libraries in India to educate their patrons. They also tried to identify best practices followed by another similar kind of libraries for their readers and students. They identified a proper subset of libraries for the USA as a developed country and India as a developing country. They created a list of about 70 identified services offered by these libraries and divided into four main clusters, namely Bibliographical Services, Patron Education Tools, Web-based Best Practices and Web-based publishing platforms for patrons. In the result they found USA libraries offer on average 53 out of 70 services while Indian libraries only offer 6on average. They found that the weakest USA libraries are still stronger than the strongest Indian ones. The ranking the universities by number of offered library web-services do not fit with theirofficial rankings according to the calculated Spearman's rank correlation coefficient for the samplesselected from USA and India. Their findings will be useful to university libraries in developingcountries to diversify their service and change their profiles into more modern information centers withhigher educational potential. The Pearson correlation coefficient of 0.356 for Indian libraries indicates a positive, but rather a low relationship in between the ranking and the number of library services offered. The same coefficient for USAlibrary websites related to their university's ranking is 0.457, indicating a stronger relationship in between the 'quality' of the universities and their libraries as measured by no. of services offered on their websites and found on Google. They suggested Indian libraries could benefit from taking inspiration from the list we drew from the USA university library websites, in order to generally raise the level of such services offered, but also to change the nature into a more diversified spectrum of services offered, showing that modern libraries are closely following the possibilities of the new information web-based era.

Recently in 2016 a comparative study of the use of social media tools by 34 reputed university libraries of the world and 15 top university libraries in Pakistan was conducted by Arslan Sheikh, Kazim Ali Syed & Mirza Naseer[64] and indicated that University libraries in Pakistan are extremely lacking in the use of social media tools compared to world university libraries. They selected top World University libraries from only Canada, Australia, USA, UK and Malaysia and not all countries. The social media tools they shortlisted were Face book, Twitter, LinkedIn, You Tube, Flicker, Pinterest, Orkut, Tagged, MySpace, Google plus, Live Journal, Photo bucket, Picasa, Slide share, Blogs, and RSS. This study clearly indicated that university libraries in developed countries are making wide use of social media tools compared to Pakistani university libraries. From the selected world top university libraries total 89.28% provided links to social media tools on their library web portal. They also found that Face book and Twitter are top social media tools used by top world university libraries. This study was based on only those university libraries who responded. They concluded that Pakistani university libraries are lacking in the use of social media tools and must make effective use of such social media tools for promotion of their library services.

A'dillah Mustafa, et.al. (2016)[2] studied social media promotion tools in one academic library which is equivalent to the university library in Malaysia and found that as web 2.0 applications Facebook and twitter have been widely used in academic libraries since 2009 and recognized as a new communication channel to get user's feedback and insights towards library services and activities.

Adeyinka Tella & Oyegunle John Oladapo (2016)[68] studied 20 university library websites comprising ten top-ranking Nigerian universities and ten top-ranking South African universities for content analysis and use of web 2.0 tools. He found that the South African university libraries are ahead of Nigerian university libraries in terms of the integration of Web 2.0 tools, e-resources and e-databases and provide platforms to their patrons for easy information retrieval. There are more e-resources available on the South African university library websites compared with their Nigerian university library websites. Both countries university libraries gave access to e-Journals are the most available e-resources in the selected university library websites of both countries. Similarly, more academic e-databases are available on the South African university library websites, whereas only a few are listed on the web pages of the selected Nigerian university library websites. Because of the wide variation reported in this study concerning available tools and resources on the university library websites in South Africa and Nigeria, it was recommended that African universities should come up with a standard that will mandate universities to have a certain number of tools identified on their various university websites.

Similarly Vaughan, Liwen& Gao, Yijun (2016)[72] examined the use of microblogs and social networking services by academic libraries in the United States and China. He studies total 200 top university websites and social media accounts and search engines. His findings indicated that the adoption rates of microblogs and social networking services were higher among the U.S. libraries as measured by the number of libraries that had an account in each type of social media studied. However, the number of accounts for the Chinese libraries was increasing faster during his four month study period. The U.S. libraries were found to have started using the social media earlier, but the Chinese libraries attracted more users measured by either the absolute or the relative number of followers of the libraries' microblog accounts.

Moyo, Mathew & Mavodza, Judith (2016)[46] compared the provision of information literacy (IL) skills to university students both at undergraduate and graduate levels in South Africa (SA) and the United Arab Emirates (UAE). Their study will assist policy makers and librarians in the development of appropriate IL programmes in support of teaching and learning.

Most of the studies till date are related to web 2.0 applications in the libraries forgetting basic library services on the web like bibliographical services, patron education services, communication services, research services, publication services, etc and new innovative practices. There is need to apply new services and technology in the library but at the same time there is need to improve basic fundamental library services through web. Considering these issue authors have prepared inventory of maximum services visiting various top university libraries from all over the world to help Indian libraries or developing country libraries to improve their online services to their patron.

UNIVERSITY ACCREDITATION AND RANKINGS

Accreditation process of different countries differs. The quality of a university is evaluated by external bodies (Non Government Organization) in a few countries at the national or regional level and in a few countries universities are evaluated by the Ministry of Education of that country e.g. France, Russia . The criteria or standards defined by these agencies differ from country to country. In Germany 10 certified agencies of accreditation are working, In Canada, Association of Universities and Colleges of Canada evaluate universities. There are few agencies that do ranking of universities from all over the world every year by applying specific criteria and methodology like Times Higher Education World University Rankings, QS World University Rankings, Centre for World University Ranking CWUR World University Rankings, UI Green Metric World University Ranking, Kaggle World university ranking, CWTS Leiden Ranking, University Ranking by Academic Performance (URAP), etc. In few cases university needs to enroll in the ranking system. Many un-enrolled universities are not evaluated in this system. Many countries like India are not reflectedin the top university rankings mentioned above. In QS World University Rankings or Times Higher Education World University Ranking or CWUR World University Rankings or U.S. News Best Global University rankings, Shanghai Ranking all top ranked universities are mainly from USA, UK, Canada, Australia. Therefore, it is observed by the investigator, that idea of selecting top universities from the globe as a sample is not fulfilling with these rankings though they have separated rankings country wise or region wise. The investigator found more suitable ranking system is *Webometrics Ranking of World Universities* which is a initiative of Cybermetrics Lab were selected as the key pillars of what makes a world class university, taking into account a number of factors that are often overlooked in university rankings and other assessments like Research, Teaching, Employability, Internationalization, Facilities, Online/Distance Learning, Engagement, Innovations, Culture, Access and specialist criteria like excellence to claim world Class status.

It is a non-profit company which gives transparency in ranking. It uses link analysis for quality evaluation as it is a far more powerful tool than citation analysis or global surveys. It tries to do the best for not including fake institutions by checking them online or international and foreign branches if they have an independent web domain or sub domain. Webometrics measure not only research output, including both formal (e-journals, repositories) publications and informal scholarly communication , teaching, the scientific impact of the university activities, but also the economic relevance of the technology transfer to industry, the community engagement (social, cultural, environmental roles) and even the political influence.

Total 70 traditional universities out of 11999 World's best university rankings, based on Webometrics Ranking of World Universities, are selected from various areas of the world including World, Brics, Civet, Latin America, Caribbean, Asia/Pacifico, Middle East, South East Asia, Oceania, Europe, Central Eastern Europe, Aftrica, North Africa and Arab World. With this selection investigator covered all top university libraries in the World, Brics Civet, Asia, Oceania, Europe, Africa and Arab World first and then from the regions they covered. The repeated universities from World, Brics, and Civet are excluded in the related area. From each area 5 top traditional university libraries are selected for getting a global view of web-based services offered by these university libraries.

Indian universities are ranked or graded by National Assessment and Accreditation Council, which an autonomous body is appointed by University Grants Commission. Total 39 University libraries out of 53 Accredited as “A” Grade by the NAAC valid from 2009 to 2016 are selected. The criteria to select university libraries used were, according to CGPA score given by NAAC. Traditional universities scoring above 3.0 CGPA were selected and listed state wise.

This chapter gives an idea about what is web, web based services, development and application of web technologies to change traditional libraries into library 1.0, 2.0, and future 3.0 and 4.0. Investigator mentioned the review of literature studied from the library websites came into existence and how libraries started offering various web based services till date. Specific ranking and accreditation system used is also discussed.

Next chapters of this book authors are giving an overview of all the web services and best practices the researcher investigated and searched.

Total of 64 web-based services and best practices offered by different top university libraries, by browsing their website and searching their accounts on various service platforms and through Google. In addition to analyzing the 64 services and practices, the investigator clustered these services in five categories mentioned as below:

1. Bibliographical services
2. Patron education tools
3. Web-based publishing platform for patrons and
4. Web-based Best Practices
5. Single web page university library

REFERENCES

1. 10 people who changed the internet forever (2013). Accessed from http://dsim.in/blog/2013/10/03/10-people-who-changed-the-internet-forever/
2. A'dillah Mustafa, Intan Nurbaizura Zainudin, Sufy Rabea Adawiya & Muhmad Faizal Abdul Aziz (2016). International Journal of Computer Theory and Engineering. 8(3), 260
3. Aghael, Sareh; Nematbakhsh, Muhammad & Farsani, Hadi (2012). Evolution of the World Wide Web: from web 1.0 to web 4.0. International Journal of Web & Semantic Technology (IJWesT). 3(1), January 2012. Available at http://airccse.org/journal/ijwest/papers/3112ijwest01.pdf
4. Arora, J(2001) Availableat http://ir.inflibnet.ac.in/bitstream/1944/105/1/cali_24.pdf
5. Asogwa, Brendan E.; Ugwu, Cyprian I.&Ugwuanyi, Ferdinand C. (2015) "Evaluation of electronic service infrastructures and quality of e-services in Nigerian academic libraries", The Electronic Library, 33(6),1133 - 1149
6. Becker, Danielle A &Yannotta, Lauren (2013). Modeling a Library Website Redesign Process: Developing a User-Centered Website through Usability Testing. *Information Technology and Libraries (Online)*.32(1) (Mar 2013): 6-22. Accessed from http://search.proquest.com/openview/60a4c12c79d7d3f0dfb4a18a2938faf0/1?pq-origsite=gscholar on 1st June 2016 at 3.00pm
7. Bhardwaj, Raj Kumar (2014). Use of Social Networking Sites by LIS Professionals in Higher Education Institutions in India: A Study. The Reference Librarian. 55(1), 2014. Available at http://www.tandfonline.com/doi/abs/10.1080/02763877.2014.855604
8. Bhatnagar, Anjana (2005). Web-based library services. *3rd*

Convention PLANNER -2005, Assam Univ, Silchar, 10-11 Nov., 2005

9. Borasky, Daniellel (1999). Analysis of web based library services. A Master's paper submitted to the faculty of the School of Information and Library Science of the University of North Carolina at Chapel Hill in partial fulfillment of the requirements for the degree of Master of Science in Library Science Chapel Hill, North Carolina December 1999

10. Brower, Stewart M (2004). Academic health sciences library Website navigation: an analysis of forty-one Websites and their navigation tools. *Journal of Medical Library Association,* 92(4) October 2004

11. Chad, Ken & Miller, Paul (2005). Do Libraries Matter? The rise of Library 2.0. (*A Talis White Paper*), Talis. Accessed at http://www.talis.com/downloads/white_papers/DoLibrariesMatter.pdf.

12. Chen, Xu; Fenfei, Ouyang &Heting Chu (2009).The Academic Library Meets Web 2.0: Applications and Implications. *The Journal of Academic Librarianship*.35(4), July 2009, 324–331

13. Chiao-Chen, Chang (2013) "Library mobile applications in university libraries", Library Hi Tech, 31(3), 478 - 492

14. Cohen, L.B & Still, J.M (1999). A comparison of Research University and two-year college library Websites: content, functionality and form. *College Research Library.* May 1999; 60(3), 275–89.

15. Contreras, Paula; Probst, Laura K. &Klimczyk, Linda (2004). Expansion of Web-Based Library Services in Large Research Libraries: A Penn State Case Study. Accessed from https://library.educause.edu/~/media/files/library/2003/1/edu0370-pdf.pdf

16. Chua, Alton & Goh, Dion(2010). A study of web 2.0 applications in library websites. *Library and Information Science Research.* 32(2010), 203-211

17. Curran, Kevin , Murray, Michelle & Christian, Martin , (2007) "Taking the information to the public through Library 2.0", *Library Hi Tech,* 25(2),288 – 297

18. Diaz, K.R. (1998). The role of the library website: A step beyond deli sandwiches. Reference & User Services Quarterly 38(1): 41-43.

19. Dhamdhere, Sangeeta N (2012). Library website: A mirror of the library. *57th All India Library Conference of Indian Library Association on "Knowledge Society: Innovations in Librarianship (ILAKSIL 2012)* at Mangalore. ISBN: 81-85216-45-6 pg.298-302

20. Sangeeta Namdev Dhamdhere and Egbert De Smet (2015). The use of web services for patron education and information by selected top university libraries in USA and India. Journal of Teaching and Education. ISSN: 2165-6266, Vol. 04 Issue 02, pg.175–196. Dora,

21. Farkas, M. (2007). Social Software in Libraries: Building Collaboration, *Communication, and Community Online.* Medford, N.J. Information Today.pp 31&122

22. Getting, Brian. Basic Definitions: Web 1.0, Web. 2.0, Web 3.0. Available at http://www.practicalecommerce.com/articles/464/Basic-Definitions-Web-10-Web-20-Web-30/

23. Guha, T. K. & Saraf, V. (2005). OPAC usability: assessment through verbal protocol. *The Electronic Library*, 23(4), 463-473.

24. Harinarayana, N.S. & Vasantha Raju, N (2010) "Web 2.0 features in university library web sites", *The Electronic Library*, 28(1), 69 – 88

25. Hatua, Sudip (2010). Web Based Library and Information Services. DRTC Seminar. Available at http://shatua.tripod.com/DRTCseminar.html

26. Jasek, Chris (2004). How to design library web sites to maximize usability. Library Connect Editorial Office. Elsevier. Available at http://digital.csic.es/bitstream/10261/2926/1/howtodesign[1].pdf

27. Jeffrey Zeldman. Web 3.0. Available at http://www.alistapart.com/articles/web3point0

28. Jones, M. (2002). Usability testing for library Web sites: A hands on guide. Journal of *the American Society for Information Science and Technology*, 53(13), 1184-1184.

29. Judith Wusteman, (2006) "Realising the potential of web services", OCLC Systems & Services: International digital library perspectives, 22(1), 5 - 9

30. Kataria, Sanjay & John Paul Anbu K(2009). Applications of web 2.0 in the enhancement of services and resource in academic libraries: an experiment @ JIIT university Noida,

India. *ICAL 2009*. Library Services. Available at: http://crl.du.ac.in/ical09/papers/index_files/ical-98_130_287_1_RV.pdf

31. Kate Peterson, "Academic Web Site Design and Academic Templates: Where Does the Library Fit In ?", Information Technology and Libraries, December 2006

32. Khalid Mahmood & Richardson, John V. Jr (2011) "Adoption of Web 2.0 in US academic libraries: a survey of ARL library websites", Program, 45(4), 365 – 375

33. Kimberley, Stephenson (2011). What's really important in library website design. *The Christian Librarian*. 54(2). 89-99

34. Korah, Abe & Cassidy, Erin Dorris (2009). Students and federated searching: a survey of use and satisfaction. *Reference & User Services Quarterly*, 49(4) (Summer 2010), 325-332

35. Kraemer, Elizabeth W.; Lombardo, Shawn V., & Lepkowski, Frank J. (2007). The librarian, the machine, or a little of both: a comparative study of three information literacy pedagogies at Oakland university. *College & Research Libraries*.68 (4), July 2007, 330-342. Accessed from http://crl.acrl.org/content/68/4/330.full.pdf+html

36. Kroski, Ellyssa (2013). 10 Great Technology Initiatives for Your Library:Want to incorporate new ideas into your library's digital strategy? Here are some tips. American Libraries. February 27, 2013. Available at https://american libraries magazine.org/2013/02/27/10-great-technology-initiatives-for-your-library/

37. Kumar, B.V. &Subrahmanya, S.V. (2012).Web Services: an introduction. *Tata McGraw Hill Education Private Limited*, New Delhi. 2nd Ed. ISBN: 978-1-25-900276-2.

38. Kwanya, Tom; Stilwell, Christine & Underwood, Peter (2007). Library 3.0: Intelligent Libraries and Apo mediation. Available at https://books.google.co.in/books?id=QvOiAgAAQBAJ&pg=PA55&lpg=PA55&dq=Kwanya,+Stilwell+%26+Underwood,+2007& source=bl&ots=4c0iyvOK2B&sig=x-hHygib9trvdsYhCur8opdHZQQ&hl=mr&sa=X&ved=0ahUKEwiu687GiJTOAhXDipQKHXW0A9YQ6 AEIJzAC#v=onepage&q=Kwanya%2C%20Stilwell%20%26%20Underwood%2C%202007&f=false

39. Kyle, M., Jones, L & Farrington, Polly-Alida (2011). Word Press as Library CMS: Free and open source technology to

enhance your library's web presence. *American Libraries*, 42(5/6), May/June2011,34

40. Laouar, Mohamed Ridda; Hacken, Richard , Miles, Mathew (2009). "The role of web services in portal design: approaches for an Algerian university library", Library Hi Tech, 27(3), 460 - 479

41. Library 2.0. Wikipedia. Available at https://en.wikipedia.org/wiki/Library_2.0

42. LiLi Li, (2006) "Leveraging quality web based library user services in the digital age", *Library Management*, 27(6/7),390 - 400

43. Liu, S. (2008), "Engaging users: the future of academic library web sites", *College & Research Libraries*, 69(1), 6-27.

44. Madhusudhan, M. &Nagabhushanam, V (2012) "Web based library services in university libraries in India: an analysis of librarians' perspective", *The Electronic Library*, 30(5), 569 – 588

45. Maness, J.M (2006). Library 2.0 Theory: Web 2.0 and its Implication for Libraries. Webology, 3(2). Accessed at http://www.webology.ir/2006/ v3n2/25.html.

46. *Mathew Moyo, Judith Mavodza, (2016) "A comparative study of information literacy provision at university libraries in South Africa and the United Arab Emirates: A literature review", Library Review, 65(1/2), 93 - 107*

47. McGillis, L & Toms, E. G (2001). Usability of the academic library web site: Implications for design. *College & Research Libraries*, 62(4), 355-367.

48. Mehta, J & Trivedi, M (2015). Contents of university library websites of central universities of India: an analysis. *International Journal of Research in Social Sciences*. 5(3), 701-715

49. Moyo, L. M. (2002). Collections on the Web: some access and navigation issues. *Library Collections, Acquisitions, and Technical Services*, 26(1), 47-59. Accessed from http://www.emeraldinsight.com/doi/abs/10.1108/LR-06-2015-0069

50. Nagarkar, Shubada(2011). Web based Reference Services to Bioinformaticians: challenges for librarians. Accessed at http://conference.ifla.org/ifla77

51. Nagarkar, Shubhada & Murari, Durga. Usability testing of library web sites: methods and techniques.

52. Naik, Umesha&Shivalingaiah, D (2008). Comparative Study of Web 1.0, Web 2.0 and Web 3.0. Accessed from http://ir.inflibnet.ac.in/bitstream/1944/1285/1/54.pdf

53. Nithya, S, et. al. Web based services @Bharathisadan University Library: A Pilot Study.Accessed from http://14.139.186.108/jspui/bitstream/123456789/3471/1/scan0006.pdf

54. Norozi, Alireza(2004). Application of Ranganathan'slaws to the web. Webology, Volume 1, Number 2, December, 2004. Available at http://www.webology.org/2004/v1n2/a8.html

55. OmoikeAdenike&Oke T. Akin(2014). Online public access catalogue (OPAC) in Nigerian libraries: a case study of the Kenneth Dike library and university of Lagos library. Ozean Journal of Social Sciences 6(3), 2014. 55-65. Available at http://ozelacademy.com/ojss.v6.i3-1.pdf

56. O'Reilly, T. What Is Web 2.0: Design Patterns and Business Models for the Next Generation of Software. Available at http://www.oreillynet.com/pub/a/oreilly/tim/news/2005/09/30/what-is-web-20.html

57. Poll, R. (2005). Measuring the impact of new library services. World Library and Information Congress: 71st IFLA General Conference and Council: Libraries: A voyage of discoveries, Oslo, Norway). August 2005. Retrieved from http://archive.ifla.org/IV/ifla71/Programme.htm

58. Poll, R (2007). Evaluating the library website: statistics and quality measures. *World Library and Information Congress: 73rd IFLA General Conference and Council:*. 19-23 August 2007, Durban, South Africa. http://www.ifla.org/iv/ifla73/index.htm

59. Preedip, B. B. & Kumar, V (2011), "Use of web technology in providing information services by south Indian technological universities as displayed on library websites", *Library Hi Tech,* 29(3), 470–495.

60. Ranganathan's laws of library science. Available at http://www.jdcc.edu/library/RFL.pdf

61. Rath, Manasa&Rath, Pravakar. Library 2.0 and Its Implications on Library services. Accessed from http://www.liscom.org/postContent/fullPaper/pdf/paper%20presented/P%20O%209%20Library%202.0% 20and%20Its%20Implications%20on%20Library%20services%20manasa.pdf

62. Riddle,P (1998). A comparison of university Websites. [Accessed at http://www.rice.edu/riddle/uniweb/.

63. Sangale, D.B (2015). ICT Applications and Web based services in library and information science. *ASM's International e-journal on ongoing research in management and IT.* 9-14

64. Sheikh, Arslan; Syed, Kazim Ali &Mirza, Naseer(2016).Use of social media tools by reputed University libraries of the world: A comparative study. *Pakistan Library and Information Science Journal.* 47(2), April-June 2016. 45-55.

65. Singh, K.P., Bebi& Gulati, D (2011). Technological march from Web 1.0 to Web 3.0: a comparative study. *Library Herald,* 49(2), June 2011. 146-147

66. Svetal, Shukla &Lalitha, Poluru (2012). Webometric Analysis andindicators of selected Indian state universities. *Informetrics,* 18 (2):79-104.

67. Syed, Sajjad Ahmed. "Managing change to enhance web-based services in the Arabian Gulf libraries", Online Information Review, 26.4(2002):265-70.

68. Tella,Adeyinka &Oladapo, Oyegunle John (2016) "A comparative analysis of available features and Web 2.0 tools on selected Nigerian and South African university library websites", *The Electronic Library,* 34(3), pp.504 – 521. Accessed from http://www.emeraldinsight.com/doi/abs/10.1108/EL-10-2014-0182

69. Tyagi, S. (2012), "Use of web 2.0 technology by library professionals: Study of selected engineeringcolleges in western Uttar Pradesh". *DESIDOC Journal of Library & Information Technology,* 32, 439–445.

70. Vangie Beal. Web-World wide web available at http://www.webopedia.com/TERM/W/World_Wide_Web.html accessed on 22/6/2016 at 2.14pm

71. Vangie Beal. The Difference between the Internet and World Wide Web. Available at http://www.webopedia.com/DidYouKnow/Internet/Web_vs_Internet.asp accessed on 22/6/2016 at 2.17pm

72. Vaughan, Liwen & Gao, Yijun(2016). The use of microblogs and social networking services: a comparison between academic libraries of the United States and China. Journal ofWeb Librarianship. 10(1), 2016. 1-13. Accessed from http://www.tandfonline.com/doi/abs/10.1080/19322909.2015.1118366

73. Virginia Tech University Libraries. Libraries and the web. Available at http://www.lib.vt.edu/help/research/library-web.html

74. Wang, Fr Stephen (2012). Web 1.0, Web 2.0, Web 3.0: What does it all mean and where is it all going? Available on https://bridgesandtangents.wordpress.com/2012/09/25/web-1-0-web-2-0-web-3-0-what-does-it-all-mean-and-where-is-it-all-going/ and accessed on 22/6/2016

75. Wang Zunxin (2005).Study of Evaluation Indicators System for College Library Website. *New Technology of Library and Information Service,2005*,21(3), 60-62

76. Warrier, Nirupama; Shivarama, J & Angadi, Mallikarjun (2015), Role of Library and Information Professionals in Web 3.0 Era. CALIBER 2015: Shimla,HP, Available at http://ir.inflibnet.ac.in/bitstream/1944/1892/1/53.pdf

77. Web. Accessed at https://en.wikipedia.org/wiki/Web

78. Web 2.0. Wikipedia. Available at https://en.wikipedia.org/wiki/Web_2.0

79. White, M.D. (2001) Diffusion of an innovation: digital reference service in Carnegie Foundation Master's (Comprehensive) academic institution libraries, Journal of Academic Librarianship, 27(3). 173 - 87.

80. Wu Xiaoxing. The Evaluation Indicators of Library Website. Accessed at *http://en.cnki.com.cn/Article_en/CJFDTOTAL-XDTQ200404014.htm*

81. Xiang Liling, Dong Xiaoyan and Qu Baoqiang (2005). A Study on homepages of university libraries. *The Journal of the Library Sciene in China.* Available at: http://en.cnki.com.cn/Article_en/CJFDTOTAL-ZGTS805.010.htm

82. Yong-Mi Kim (2011). Users' perceptions of university library websites: A unifying view. *Library & Information Science Research.* 33(1), January 2011, 63–72

83. Younghee, Noh (2015). Imagining Library 4.0: Creating a Model for Future Libraries. *The Journal of Academic Librarianship.* 41(6), November 2015, 786–797

84. Zhao Yuxiang(2007). Study of Evaluation on Information Architecture Usability for Public Library Website. *New Technology of Library and Information Service.* 03. Available at:http://en.cnki.com.cn/Article_en/CJFDTOTAL-XDTQ200703018.htm

85. http://eprints.rclis.org/archive/00012108/

3
Web-based Bibliographical Services Offered by University Libraries: An Overview

WEB-BASED BIBLIOGRAPHICAL SERVICES

According to Wikipedia bibliography is organized listing of books and the systematic description of books as physical objects. As a discipline it is an academic study of books as physical and cultural objects. In traditional libraries, records of books were maintained in card catalogues.

Bibliographical services are services related to the library collection and access to those collections, whether print or online. In modern libraries, these services are provided online through website. In National Library of Philippines there is aseparate technical division for offering bibliographical services which maintains an up-to-date national bibliography and union catalogue, provides online periodical indexing of the serials and special collections, serves as national centre for providing ISSN, ISBN and ISMN numbers, maintains comprehensive and authoritative national bibliographic record for every item of literature issued in the country according to international standards and promotes international networking with other countries to provide inter library loan[5].

The main aim of Nanyang Technological University's Bibliographical services division is to provide users intellectual access to the library's physical and digital resources and assist them in discovering and locating information resources. This division is responsible for the creation and maintenance of catalogues and other metadata records of the library resources in all formats including print, AV and electronic. This department ensures the library material acquired are effectively and efficiently retrieved and utilized. This department manages memberships, subscriptions and keeps up to date with bibliographic utilities for acquisition and creation of bibliographic records. This department also provides metadata consultancy, development and production services across various subject fields and platforms[1]0. Investigator observed that in the USA relatively more emphasis is given to non-traditional services than India, or vice-versa: Indian libraries still mainly focus on more traditional bibliographical services.

Similarly, University of Zimbabwe Library's bibliographical services division caters acquisition, cataloguing, OPAC, online databases and institutional repositories[42]. Cork City Libraries also record maintenance for display on the online catalogue and timely allocation of reading materials to libraries[7]. The Bibliographic Services Council of Penn State University considers matters related to the intellectual access of library materials through the online catalog or other search and retrieval interfaces[24]. Please refer Screenshot 1 given below.

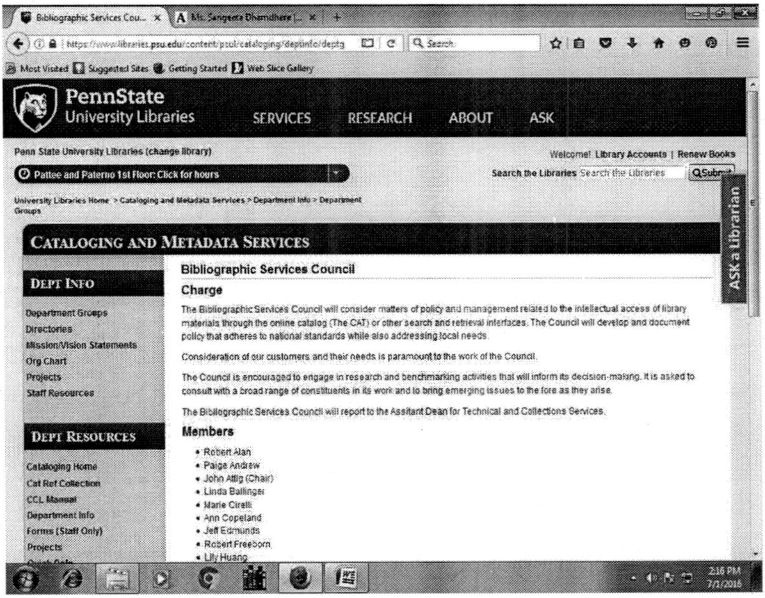

Screenshot 1. Penn State University library's bibliographical services

In this research investigator studied more than 109 university librarywebsite and listed 12 web-based bibliographic services as mentioned here.

Access to web OPAC : One of the most important web based service university libraries are offering since 1990s is a web-based 'Online Public Access Catalogues' means web OPACs (Ramesh Babu & Ann O'Brien, 2000)[27].Using this OPAC of library resources users can search a library catalogue to locate books and other reading material remotely through the web. It is the most important service of any library; this provides a gateway to the library collection (Wikipedia)[22]. Most popular web OPAC interfaces used in UK academic libraries are Talis, INNOPAC, WebCat, Voyager, GeoWeb and ALEPH (Ramesh Babu & Ann O'Brien, 2000)[27].

Below are screen shots of web OPACs of a few selected university libraries like the Puerto Rico, Charles, Jagiellonian and university.

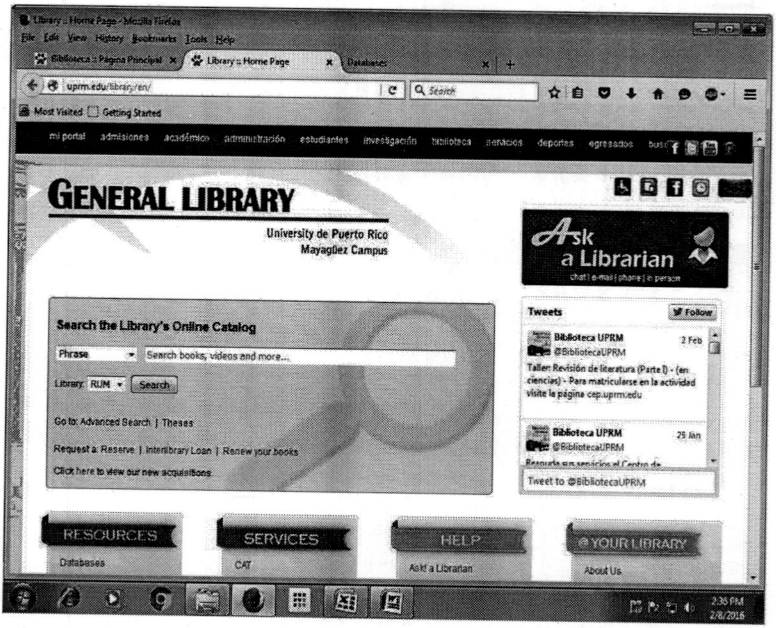

Screenshot 2. Web OPAC of the University of Puerto Rico library

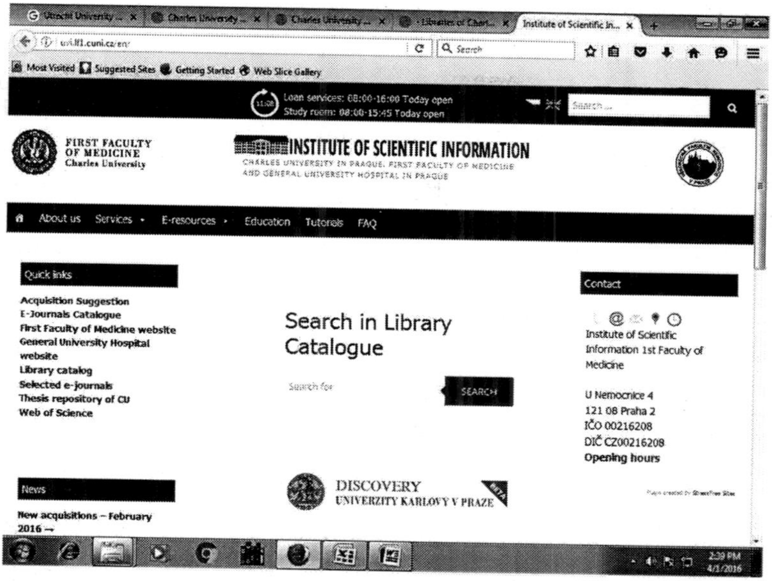

Screenshot 3. Charles university library's online catalogue

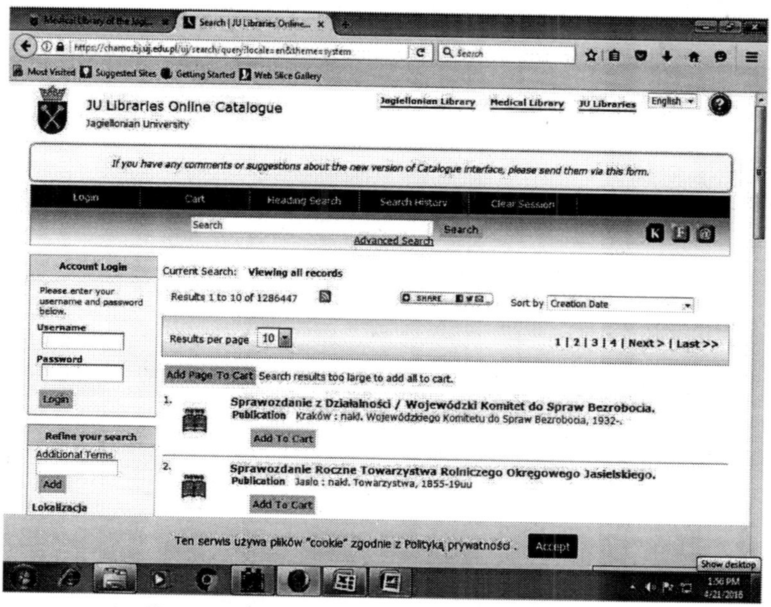

Screenshot 4. Jagiellonian university library's online catalogue

The union catalogue is a database of bibliographic records that are created, maintained and utilized by a group of Libraries (librarynet.com).[40] It is a combined library catalogues describing the collection of member libraries. The union catalogue concept was introduced and implemented long back. The largest print union catalogue was published is the American National Union Catalog (NUC) completed in 1981. With the introduction of computerization and library software this activity was suspended as creation of union catalogues in the form of digital databases has become very easy. OCLC's WorldCat is the world's largest network of library content and services. WorldCat libraries are dedicated to providing access to their resources on the Web, where most people start their search for information (Worldcat.org)[44]. Not all libraries are able to provide Web OPAC to library resources, therefore, to provide Web OPAC to the library collection and to assist in locating and requesting materials from member libraries through inter library loan service many countries are providing such unique platform to all member libraries (Wikipedia)[41].

Below are few examples ofsample university libraries in Egypt and Slovenian countries which are using a single platform for all member libraries for giving Web OPAC or E-Discovery service.

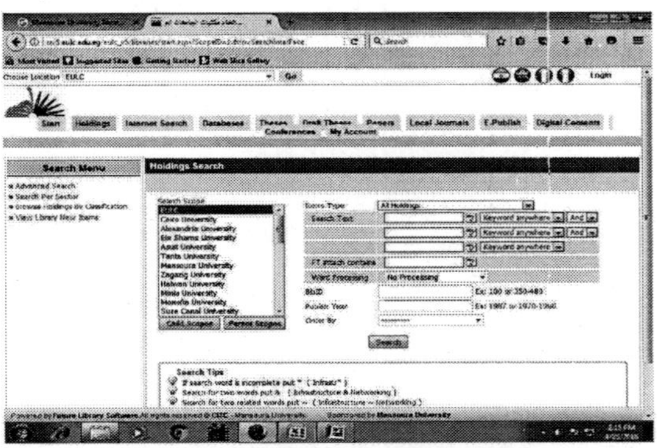

Screenshot 5. Union catalogue of Egyptian universities libraries

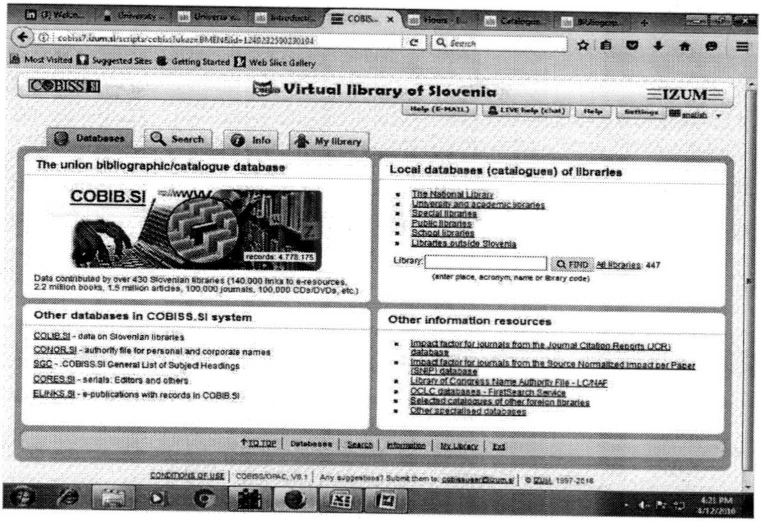

Screenshot 6. COBIB.SI union catalogue of Slovenian libraries

Access to Databases : In traditional university libraries the library databases were in the form of catalogues. Card catalogues were maintained by the libraries to make available information about the library material. With the use of technology, automation and digitization now all library records and digital resources are maintained in the form of databases and made available online to patrons through their website and that is why it is also one of the web based services investigator considered here. According to webopedia[8] a database is a collection of information organized in such a way that a computer program can quickly select desired pieces of data. It is a computerized system that makes it easy to search, select and store information. Databases are used in the library to keep track of library resources[43].

High Plains Library District (2016) a library database isboth an electronic catalog and the access point to information. Library databases provide access to published information sources, both in print as well as electronic form. In libraries various types of databases are maintained and subscribed like e-books, e-journals, articles, newspapers, pictures, videos, manuscripts, thesis and dissertations and other resources. A few databases are subscribed (full text and/or abstract) and few are available freely and library provides access to both.

Here are a few examples of university libraries, giving access to different database via their website. Many libraries from selected universities are giving access to the databases they have subscribed and other free databases on their website. Commonly databases are arranged alphabetically or subject-wise on the library portal. Patrons can search through the databases under title, keyword, subject or author using federated search engine or e-discovery system or tool while few university libraries from different parts of the world including India not given such search facility. Few libraries not even given details of databases they are subscribing or available free of cost on their website. Few libraries do not subscribe online databases.

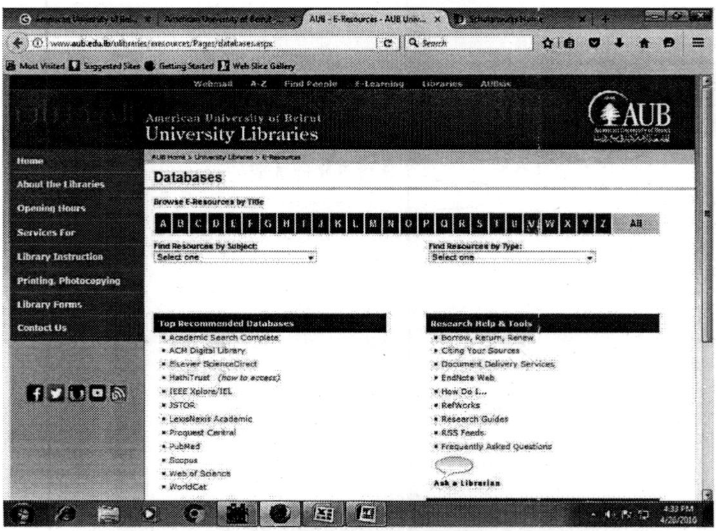

Screenshot 7. American University of Beirut providing access to databases

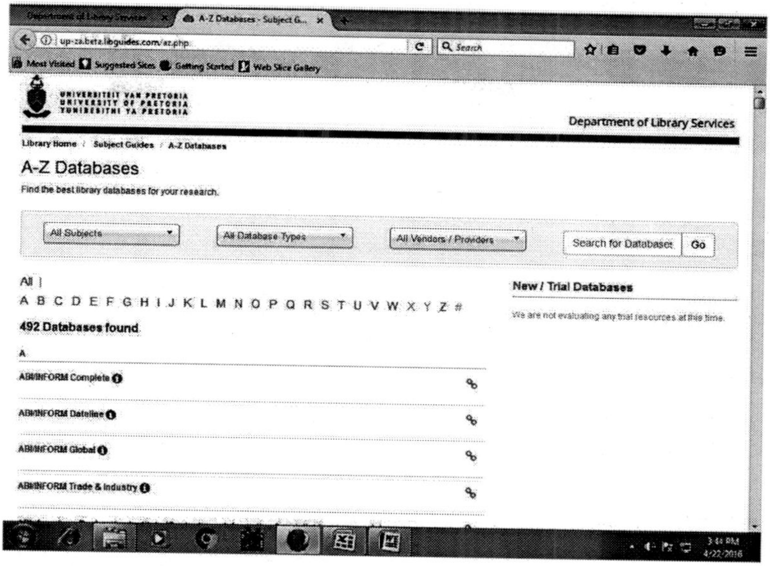

Screenshot 8. University of Pretoria providing access to databases

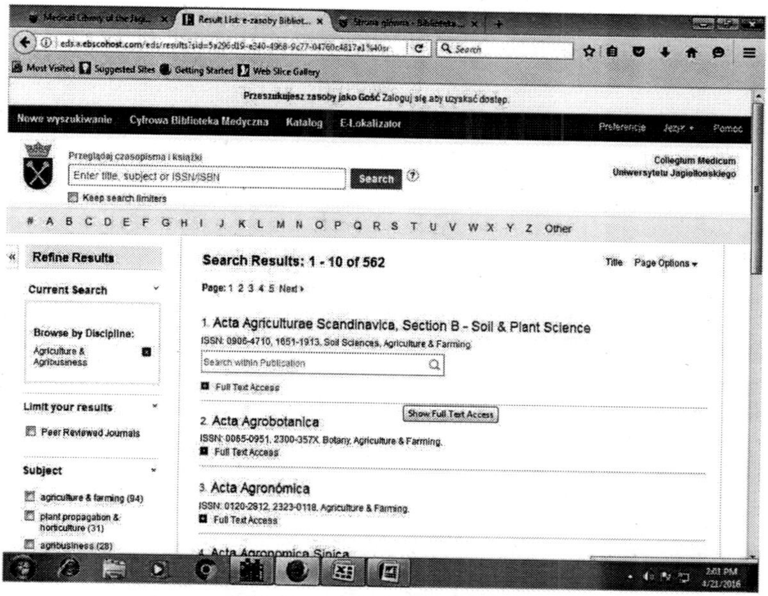

Screenshot 9. Jagiellonian university library providing access to databases

Federated Search/E-Information Discovery Tools : The university library portal contains multiple databases and federated search engine without aggregation at the metadata level. Federated search is an information retrieval technology to search resources from multiple search engines, databases by sending a single query request. (Wikipedia)[10]. To maximize the value, usefulness and easy online access to all library resources both in-housed(catalogue or institutional repository), outsourced and free electronic full text scholarlydatabases many university libraries are using very powerful e-discovery tool (single window access) like EBSCO Discovery services (EDS), Google Scholar, FEDGATE, Mendeley,VuFind, UWIlink, and other in-housed discovery tools, etc.As the cost of high quality e-discovery tools are very high in many countries to save cost all member libraries are using a single e-discovery system(Dhamdhere, 2015)

Few examples of e-discovery search screenshots of the Jawaharlal Nehru university library, Tsinghua university library, Melbourne university library are given below:

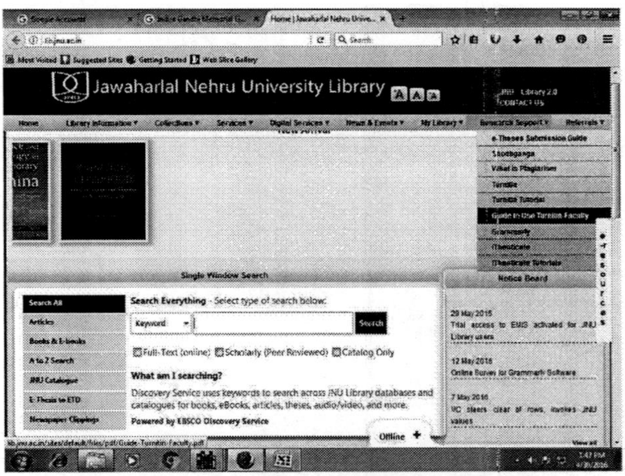

Screenshot 10 e-discovery tool of the Jawaharlal Nehru University Library

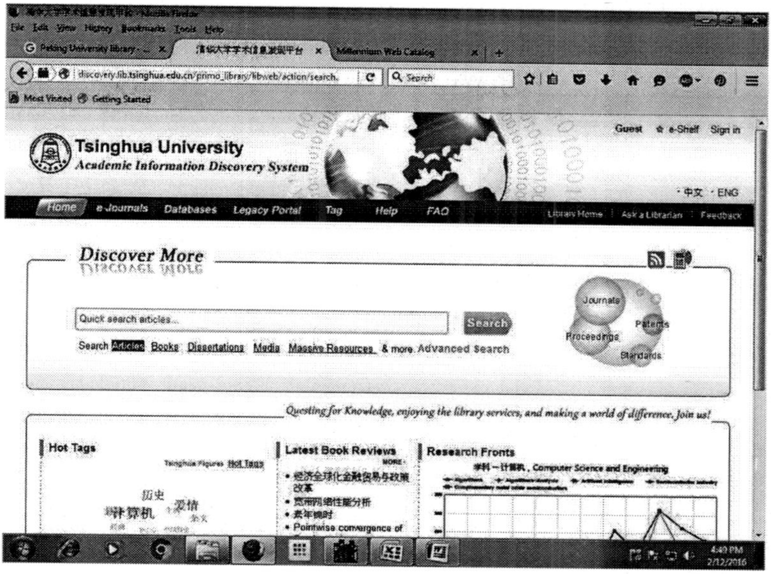

Screenshot 11. e-discovery tools of the Tsinghua unviersity libary

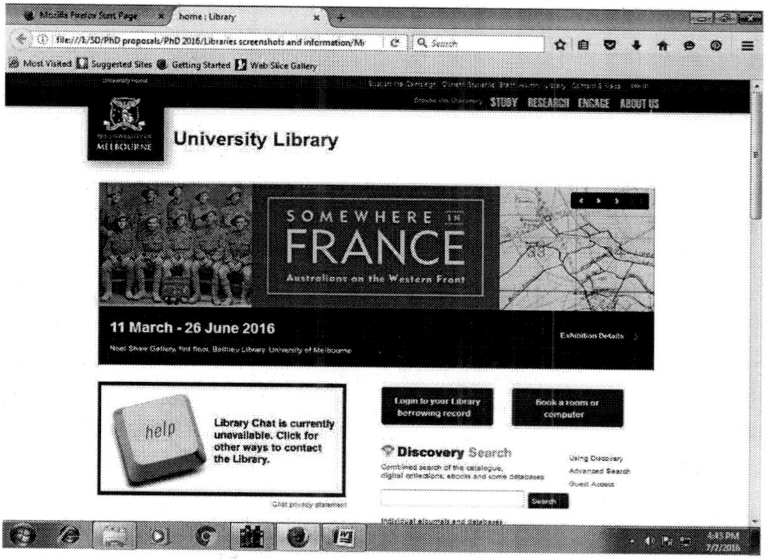

Screenshot 12. e-discovery tool of the Melbourne university library

Datasets : Datasets are nothing but collection of data. According to Margaret Rouse (2016)[29] on whatIs.com, data set is a collection of related, discrete items of related data that may be accessed individually or in combination or managed as a whole entity. Dataset term was originated with IBM. In a database, a data set might contain a collection of business data like names, salaries, contact information, sales figures, etc. The database itself can be considered a data set, as data within it related to a particular type of information. Few of world's top traditional university libraries provide this service along with access to databases. According to Dhamdhere and De Smet (2015) datasets are made available by 14.28% of the USA Libraries but only 3.57% Indian Libraries. Stanford University maintains datasets commonly used in the research activities of the image, video and multimedia system groups at Stanford and made them available. Screenshot 4.13 below shows the research datasets service of Stanford University[35].

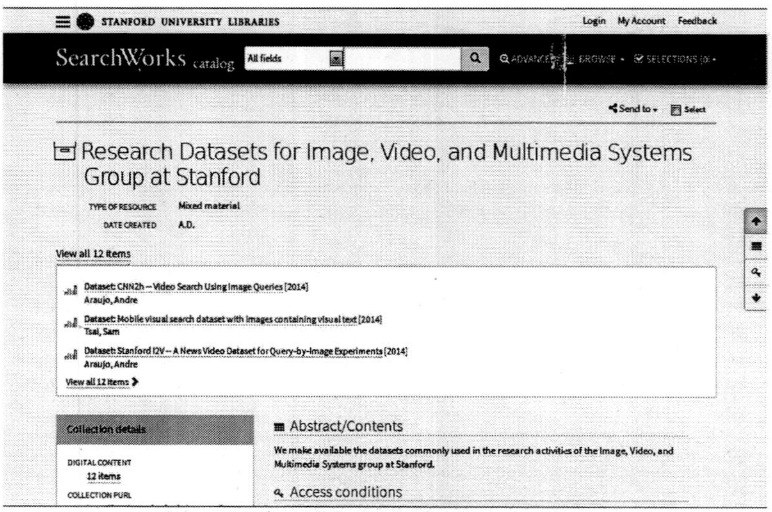

Screenshot 13. Stanford university library's research datasets service

The Berkeley library of California University has a separate data lab for offering consultation services to researchers whose research topic involves numeric data, includes finding and recommends data sources and advises on technical data issues such as file format conversion, web scraping, and basic statistical software related online services.

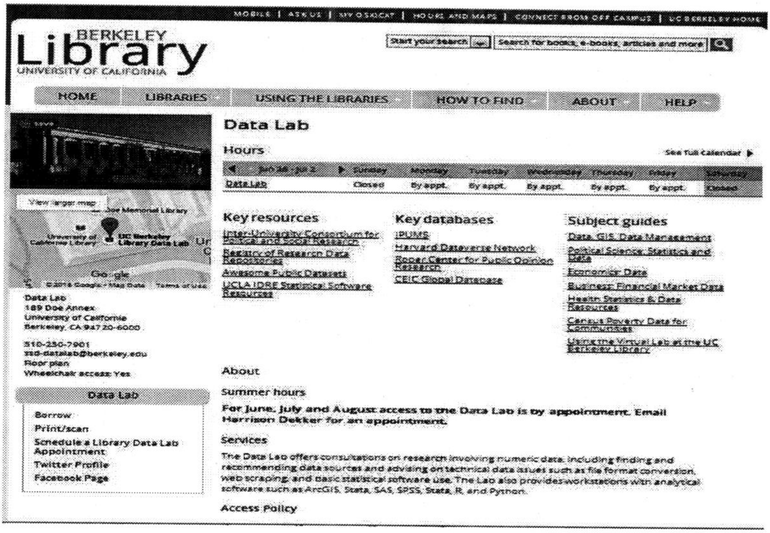

Screenshot 14. Data lab of the Berkeley library

Access to Library Archives/Digital Collection/ Institutional Repository : This is another library web based service in which university library gives online access to collected and preserved archives ordigital collection of intellectual (scientific and scholarly) output created within a university. It is also called as an institutional repository. Itis a set of services to members of its community for the management and dissemination of digital material created by the institution and its community members. In universities repositories are mostly research output and in some cases all university records in digital form. University institutional repository contains digital assets generated by academics such as manuscripts, monographs, eprints of academic journal articles, university projects, test community, electronic thesis and dissertations, pictures, maps, projects, lectures, audio, video files, tutorials, interviews, newsletters, annual reports, speeches of guests, administrative documents, datasets, course notes, learning objects, conference proceedings or other special and rare collection (webopedia)[13]. All these Repositories adhere to an internationally-agreed set of technical standards. They expose the metadata (the bibliographic details such as author names, institutional affiliation, and date, titles of the article, abstract and so forth) of each item in their contents on the Web in the same basic way. In other words, they are 'interoperable'. This common protocol to which they all adhere is called the open Archives Initiative Protocol for Metadata Harvesting (OAI-PMH). The contents of all repositories are then indexed. The self-archiving process in which authors deposit their work in repositories grows the Open Access corpus will represent an increasingly large proportion of the scholarly literature (openscholarship.org)[23].

Some libraries have separate website or blog for such collection and link is given on the main library website. With new digital library software, it is possible to deposit material in an institutional repository and give easy online access. Many university libraries exhibit their special digital collection and made open for all. It is treasure of that university.

Below are few examples of selected university libraryarchives, IRs, special collections.

The main advantages of IR are it opens up the outputs of university to the world, maximizes the visibility and impact of those outputs as a result, collects, curates digital outputs, manages and measures research and teaching activities, encourages collaborative projects and interdisciplinary research, facilitates sharing and development of digital teaching material (openscholarship.org).

Below are screen shots of IR, archives and special collection of few top world university libraries from the sample.

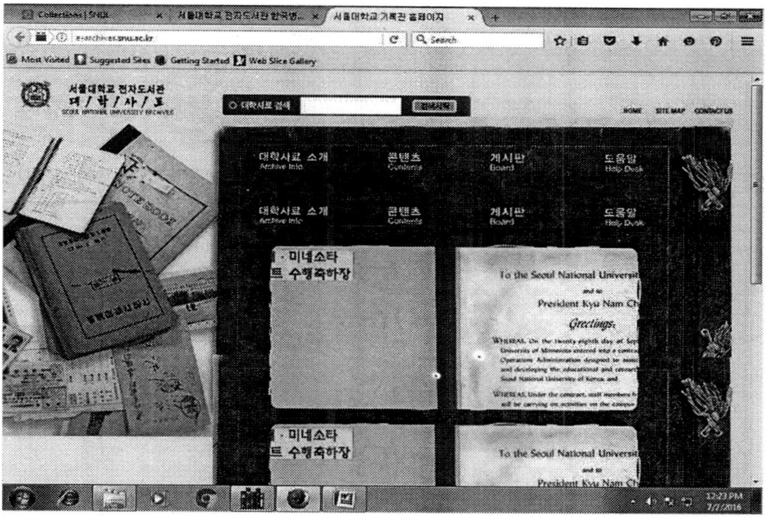

Screenshot 15. An archiveof the Seoul National University

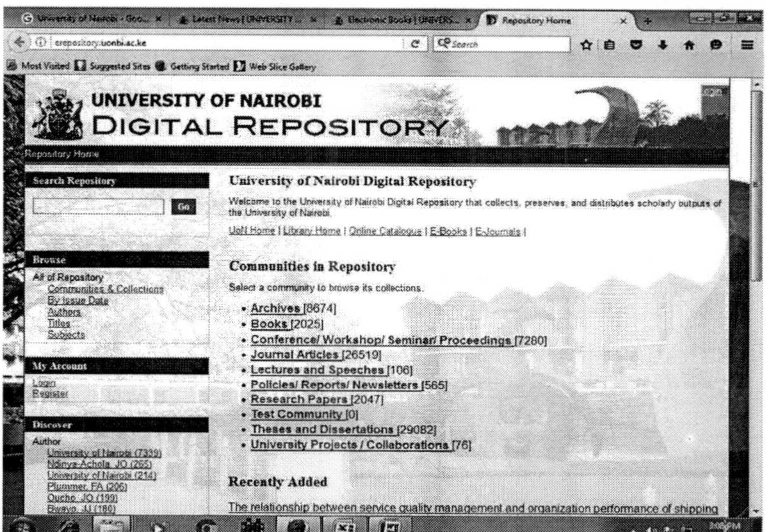

Screenshot 16. Digital repository of the University of Nairobi

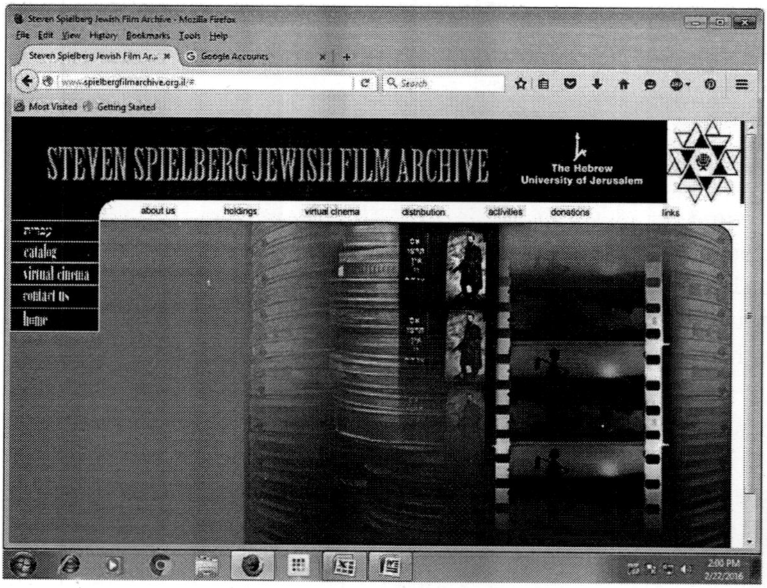

Screenshot 17. Film archive of the Hebrew University of Jerusalem

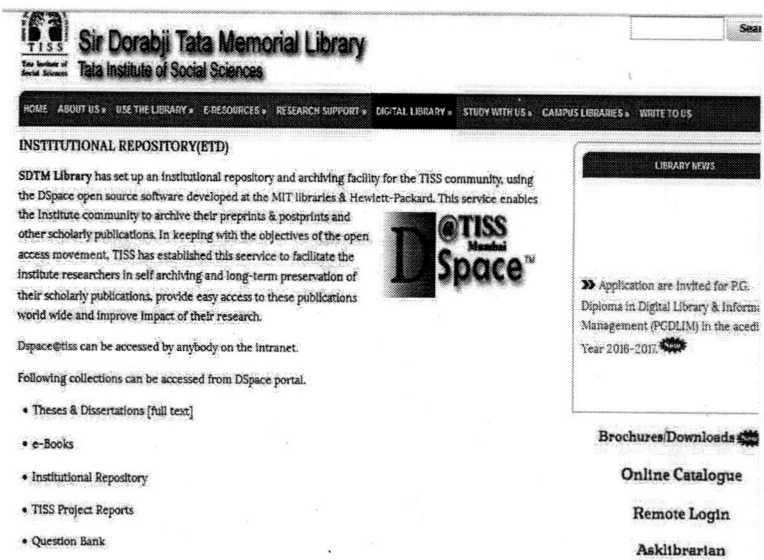

Screenshot 18. Institutional repository of Tata Institutes of Social Sciences library

Access to Audio/Visual databases: The university libraries create or sometimes subscribe audiovisual/ multimedia databases and gives online access to their patrons through library website using in-house or digital library software like Dspace, Drupal, Eprint, etc. This web based service is useful for patrons as they get access to these databases online and from anywhere they can refer these resources. Not all university libraries have multimedia databases or collection of videos, films, music, digital pictures, recordings, animations, graphics together with text data and gives online access.

Screen shots of few prominent universities offering this web based service to patrons are given below.

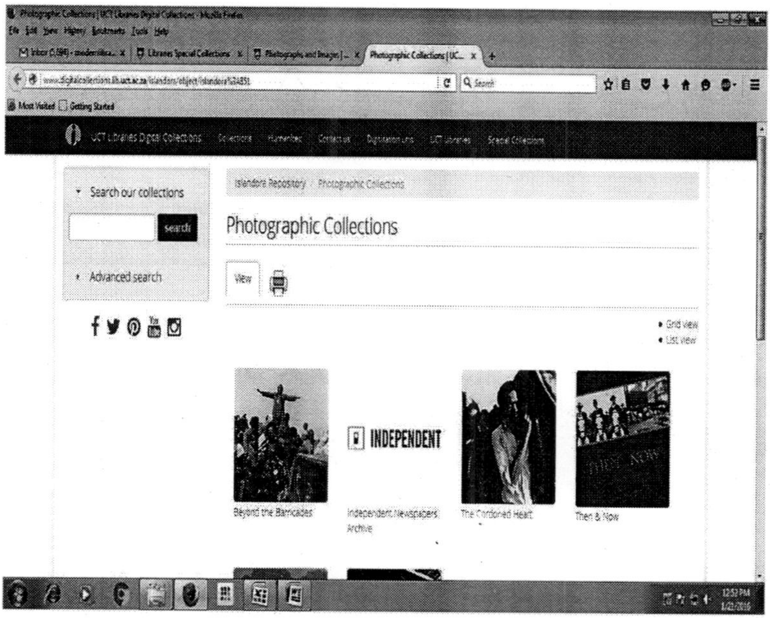

Screenshot 19. Photographic collection of the University of Cape Town

Screenshot 20. Multimedia collection of the National Taiwan University library

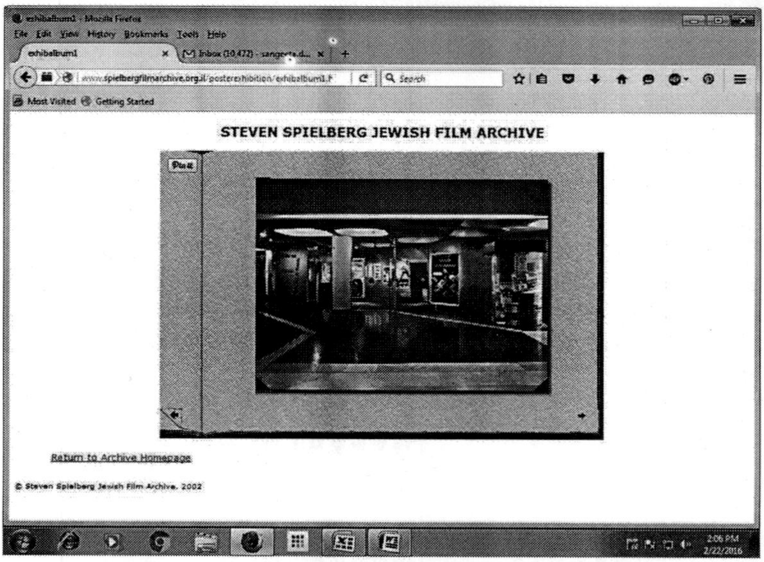

Screenshot 21. Steven Spielberg Jewish film archive

Find a Library : Many top world university libraries are collection of libraries. Department or regional libraries are managed centrally and access to their collection, catalogues and websites are given in the central university library. Because of this central access member libraries get the benefit of resource sharing and inter library loan facility. This find a library web based library features provides access to other sub-libraries. Sometimes all sub-library catalogues are common, but managed separately. Few university libraries give a list of libraries and their links. One can search the library from search box too.

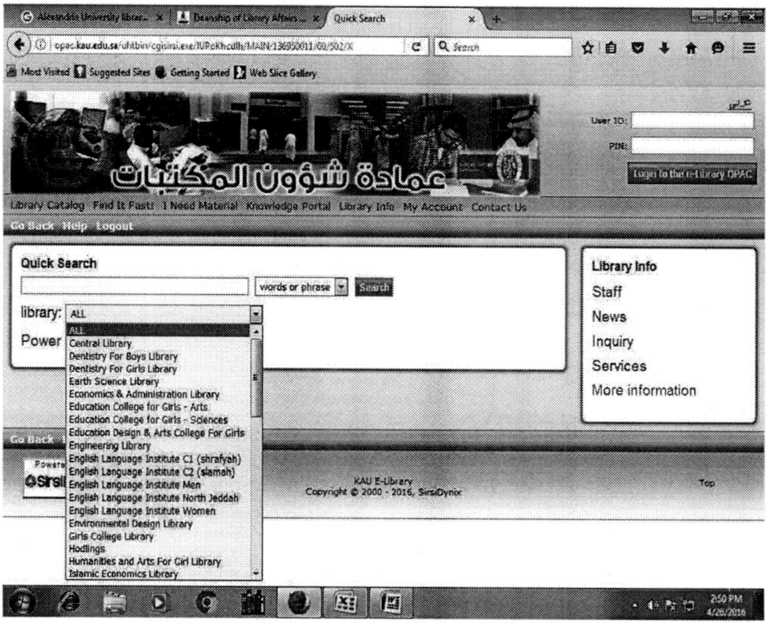

Screenshot 22. Quick search of King Abdul Aziz university libraries

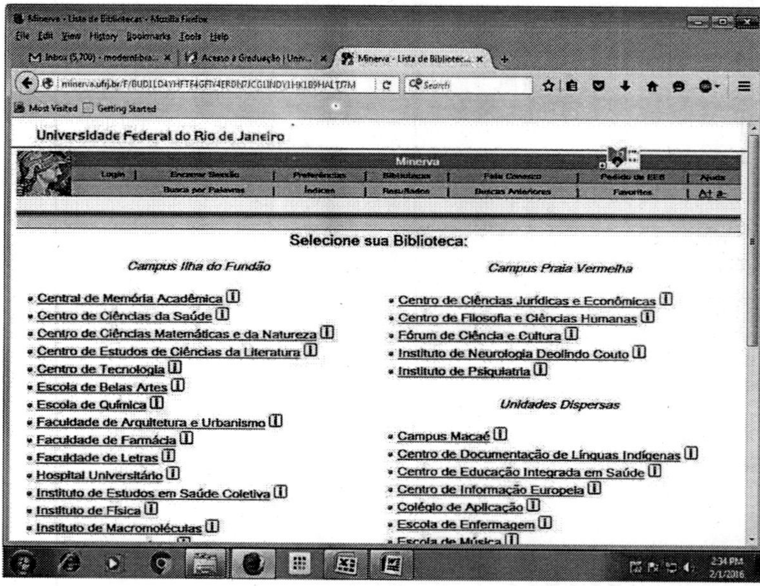

Screenshot 23. Find a library service by Universidad Federal do Rio de Janeiro

Off campus access : Traditional university libraries all over the world give access to resources online. Researchers and teachers can access the electronic information resources like e-books, e-journals, articles and special databases of the library from anywhere in the world using EZproxy system. Users are automatically directed to the *EZProxy* log-in screen. Login and passwords are provided to the users to off campus access to library resources. This web based service is need of time and techno savvy patrons.

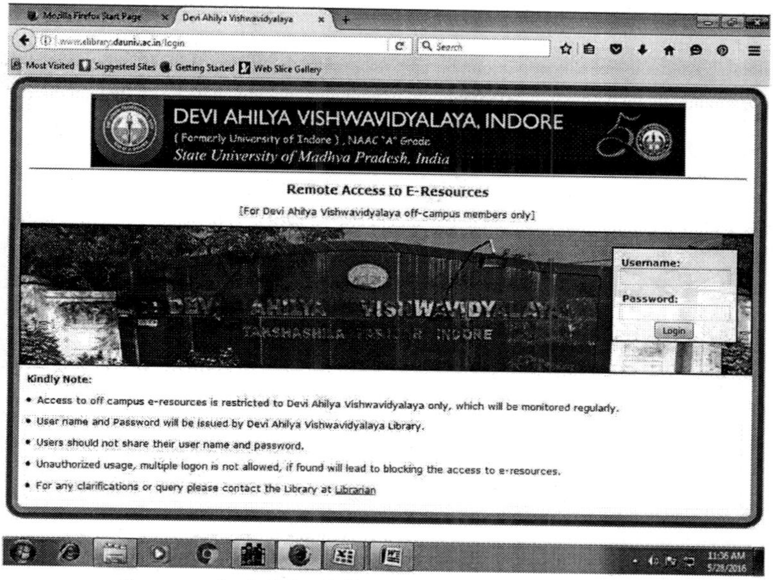

Screenshot 24. Off-campus access service of Devi Ahilya Vishwavidyalaya

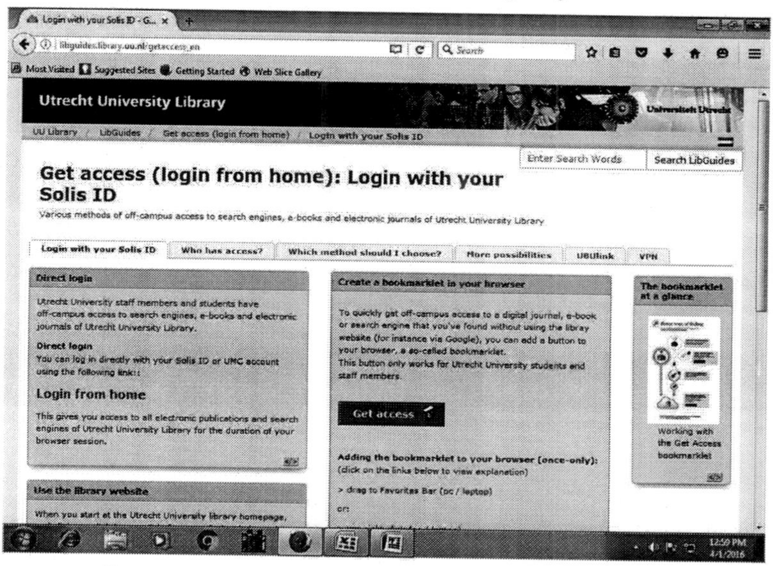

Screenshot 25. Off-campus access service by the Utrecht university library

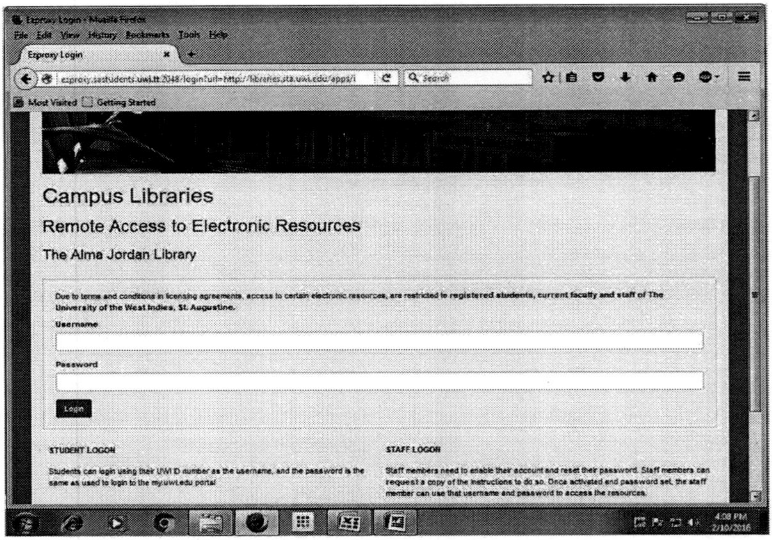

Screenshot 26. Off campus access of the Alma Jordan Library

New Arrivals : Notification of new arrivals has been a current awareness service offered by all types of libraries since long time. In which list of new arrivals or new addition in library collection is communicated to the patron weekly, monthly, bimonthly, quarterly, etc. Using library automation softwares and digital library softwares it has become very easy to share latest updates to patrons daily also. Most of the softwareshave provision to automatically prepare a list and share on the platform assigned. University libraries areproviding these services via email, blog, website, and other web tools.

In below screenshots of new arrival services, cover pages of books are provided along with bibliographical information by few university libraries to attract readers, few libraries give all new arrivals including e-books, journals, databases, CDs/DVDs and other reading materials. Taiwan University library shares these new arrivals on Facebook and other social networks too like Google+.

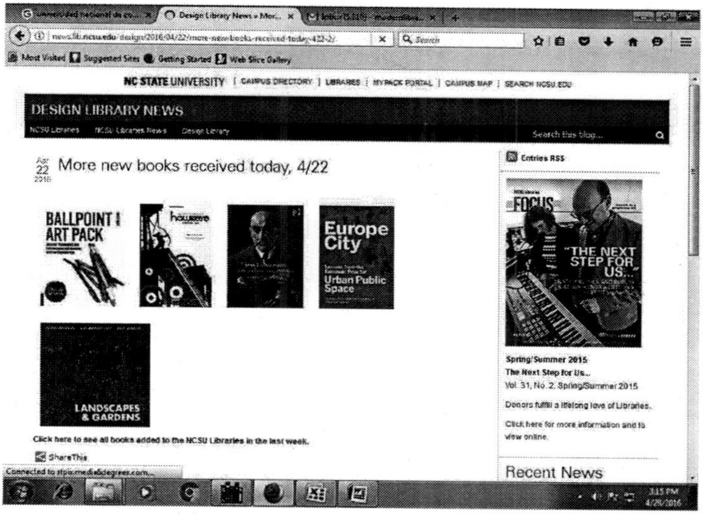

Screenshot 27. New arrival service on NCSU libraries website

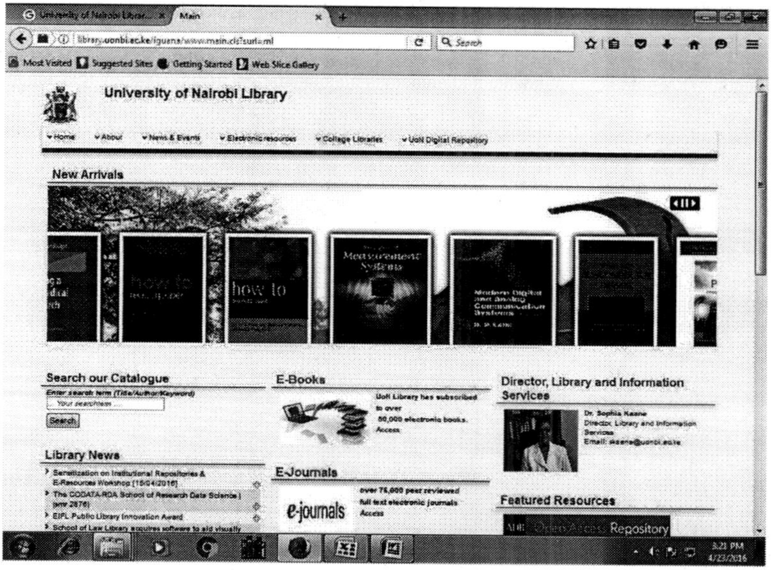

Screenshot 28. New arrivals online displays of the University of Nairobi library

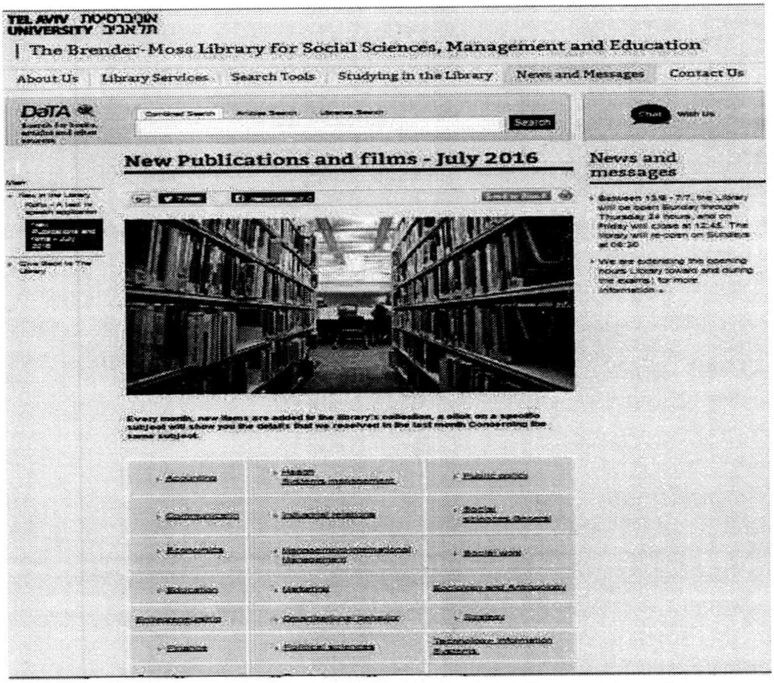

Screenshot 29. Monthly new arrivals services by the Tel Aviv University library

Inter Library Loan : The inter library loan facility is started for resource sharing purpose in libraries. No library in the world is rich with all books, journals and other reading material required by users. In that case a library gives facility to request the required material from the libraries where it is available and make it available to users. Now, because of digitization it has become very easy to get the required material in electronic form too. Now university libraries provide this facility online to their patrons.

Few universities give information about inter library loan, the process, which material is available for loan, etc. on their website. Few libraries providea Google form or pdf forms or word file or request form on the website or invites query via emails. Few universities provide guides,

FAQs, manuals for accessing this web based service as well. In many countries union catalogue or consortia helps to give inter library loan facility to member libraries as they can easily locate the resources through union catalogue.

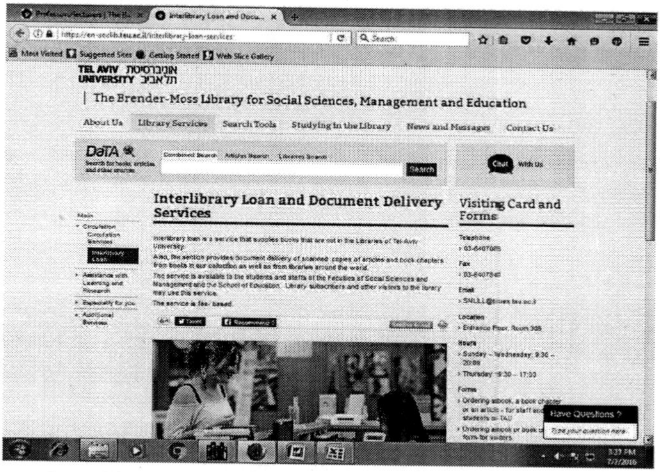

Screenshot 30. ILL service by the Tel Aviv University library

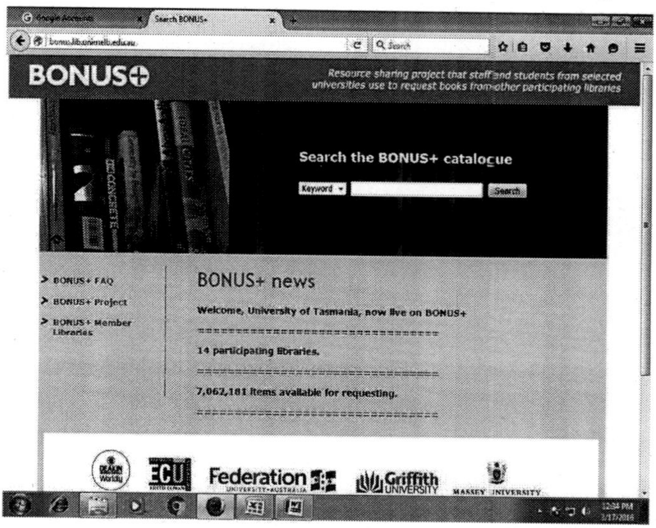

Screenshot 31. ILL service of the University of Melbourne library

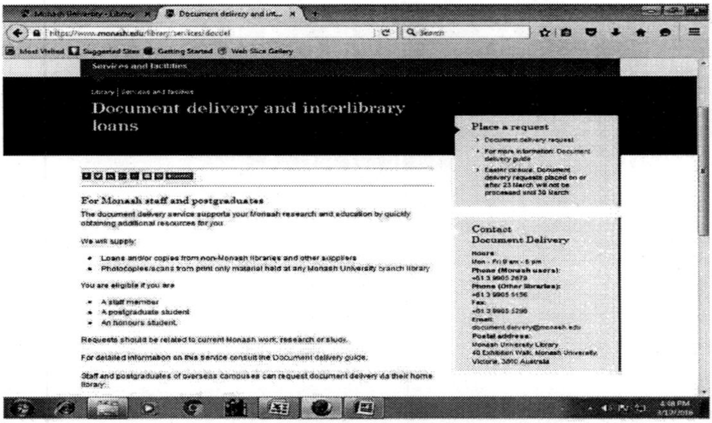

Screenshot 32. ILL service of the Monash University library

e-Document Delivery Service : It is also called digital service university libraries are providing for delivering documents on demand. In traditional libraries in inter library loan only print documents were delivered, but now web technology enabled to deliver documents in electronic forms too. One more reason for providing e-document delivery is now university library has its collection in digital form like articles, ebooks, audios, videos etc.

Screenshot 33. e-document service of the Kasetsart University library

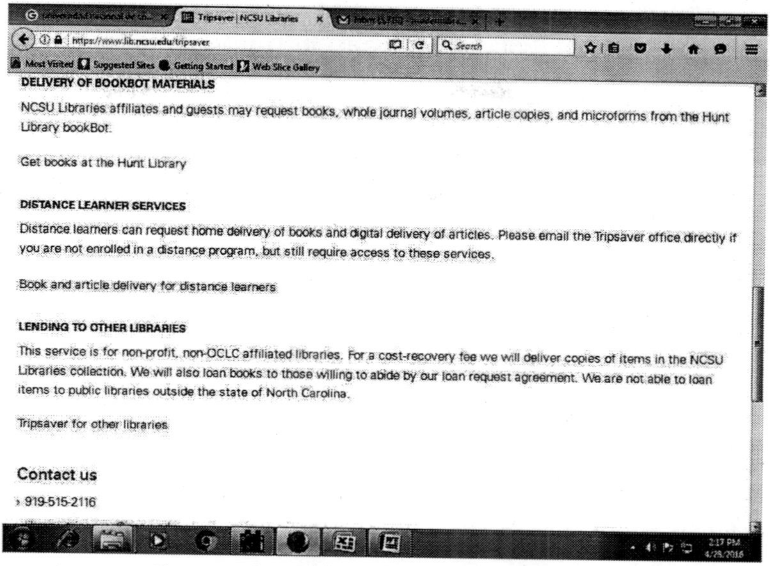

Screenshot 34. e-document delivery service of NCSU libraries

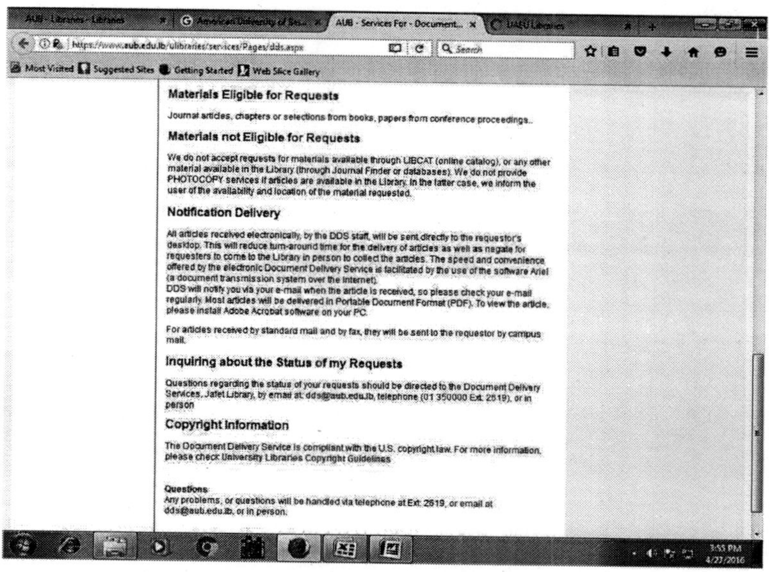

Screenshot 35. e-document delivery service of American University of Beirut

Books Recommendations : Many university libraries provide facility to recommend books and other reading materials like journals, CDs/DVDs, etc. online uses Google form, email or other web platforms. Few universities provide links to publishers or online book shopping sites where users can select the books and recommend to the library. This web based service saves time of patrons and also helps to enrich the collection.

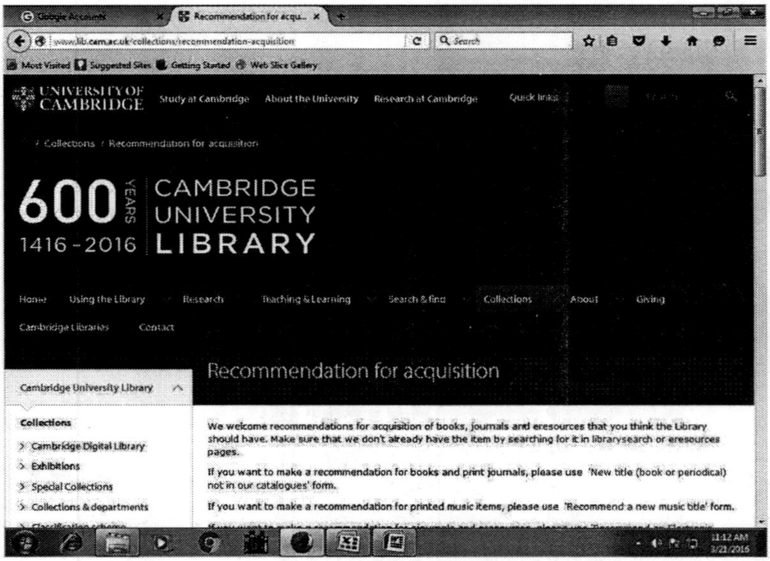

Screenshot 36. Online book recommendation service of Cambridge university

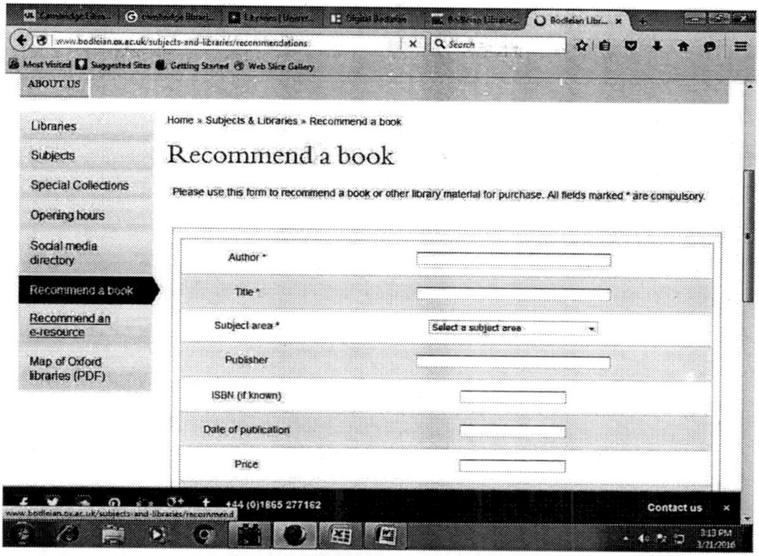

Screenshot 37. Online book recommendation service of Bodieian Libraries

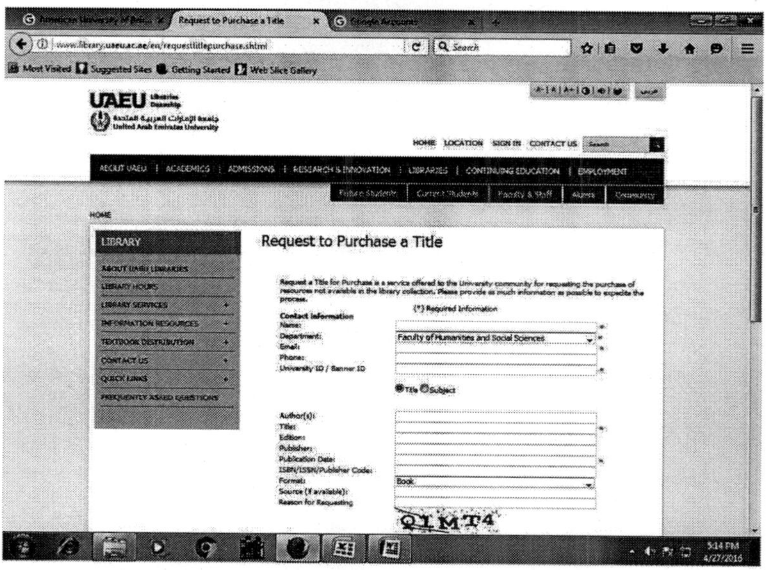

Screenshot 38. Online book recommendation service of United Arab Emirates university

REFERENCES

1. Bibliographic Department. (n.d.). Retrieved from University of Zimbabwe Libraries:http://library.uz.ac.zw/index.php/services/bibliographic-services Bibliography.
2. Bibliographic services. (n.d.). Retrieved from Cork City Libraries:http://www.corkcitylibraries.ie/aboutus/bibliographicservices/
3. Bibliographical Services. (n.d.). Retrieved from http://web.nlp.gov.ph/nlp/?q=node/662
4. Bibliography. (n.d.). Retrieved from https://en.wikipedia.org/wiki/Bibliography
5. Cataloguing and metadata services. (n.d.). Retrieved from Penn State University Libraries: https://www.libraries.psu.edu/content/psul/cataloging/deptinfo/deptgroups/bsc.html
6. Database. (n.d.). Retrieved from Webopedia:http://www.webopedia.com/TERM/D/database.html
7. Dhamdhere, S. N., & Smet, E. D. (2015). The use of web services for patron education and information by selected top university libraries in USA and India. Journal ofTeaching and Education , 4 (2), 175–196.
8. Federated search. (n.d.). Retrieved from https://en.wikipedia.org/wiki/Federated_search
9. Nanyang Technological University. (n.d.). Bibliographic services division. Retrieved from Nanyang Technological University:http://www.ntu.edu.sg/Library/about/staffdirectory/divisions/bsd/Pages/default.aspx
10. Online public access catalog. (n.d.). Retrieved from Wikipedia: https://en.wikipedia.org/wiki/Online_public_access_catalog
11. Ramesh Babu, B., & O'Brien, A. (2000). Web OPAC interfaces: an overview. The Electronic Library , 18 (5), 316-330.
12. Research Datasets for Image, Video, and Multimedia Systems Group at Stanford. (n.d.).Retrieved from Stanford University Libraries: https://searchworks.stanford.edu/view/cm018rf5314 on 2nd July 2016 at 11.46am.
13. Rouse, M. (2016). Dataset. Retrieved from http://whatis.techtarget.com/definition/dataset
14. Union catalog. (n.d.). Retrieved from http://www.librarynet.com.my/librarians/unionCatalog.html

15. Union catalog. (n.d.). Retrieved from Wikipedia: https://en.wikipedia.org/wiki/Union_catalog

16. What is a database? . (n.d.). Retrieved from http://www.bbc.co.uk/guides/z8yk87h

17. What is WorldCat? (n.d.). Retrieved from https://www.worldcat.org/whatis/default.jsp

4

Web-based Patron Education Services Offered by University Libraries: An Overview

In this chapter the author has included all the web based services and tools including social networking sites and other web 2.0 tools used by selecting university libraries for educating and giving instructions to the patrons. With the introduction of new software, resources (print as well as online) in libraries easy access to the internet to all patrons within campus or outside campus, there is a need to educate patrons how to locate the resources and how to search the resources. Sometimes libraries provide many services and facilities, but patrons are not aware about that. So along with personal training it is need of time to educate patrons online as many distance learning programs are run by universities, open education concept is coming forward. In developed country libraries there are special staff for educating patrons online using different tools and platforms, but in Indian university libraries no such separate posts are appointed. Let us discuss how these tools by these libraries to educate and update patrons. It is observed that compared to other country's libraries in India the more widely used tools for patron education in the selected libraries are Notification of new arrivals, photo gallery, news, upcoming events, ask us, Service Directory, Tips for access and use the library resources, tools for discovery, help guides, Map directions, feedbacks, Email, etc. along with other some of the above listed.

News and Upcoming Events : This section of the university library website offers web-based notification of latest library news and list of events library is planning to organize in coming future. Library news can be related to new arrivals in the library collection, events organized, their photos, comments, workshops held, new services, facilities, and other day to day notices library displays on library notice board but in digital form. University libraries conduct many events in collaboration with different departments, publishers, orientation programs, information literacy programs, workshops, conferences, etc. and these events are communicated in advance to the patrons or stakeholders. All news and upcoming events are organized chronologically. Latest news and updates are listed at the top and old news and updates are preserved in archives.

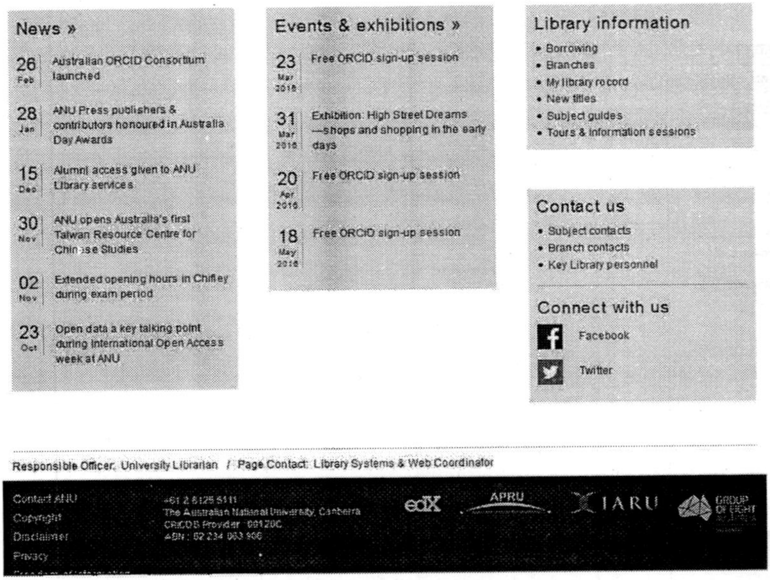

Screenshot 1. News and events service of the Australian National University library

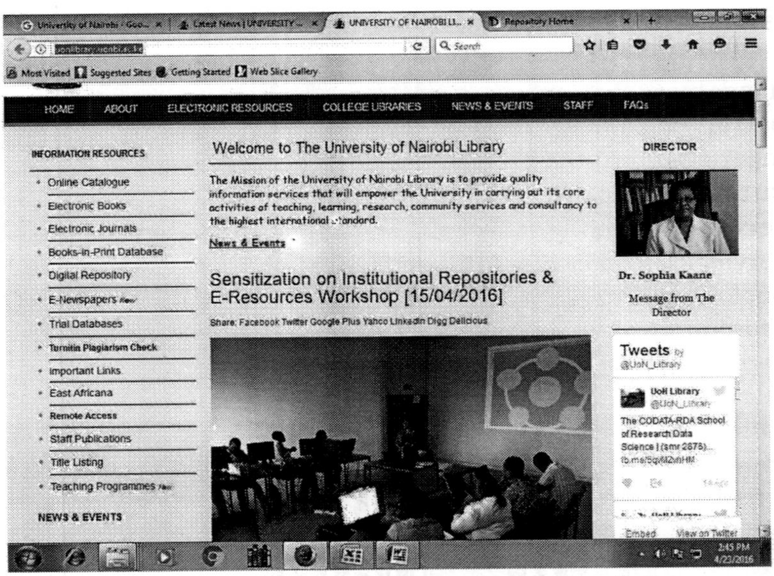

Screenshot 2. News and events service of the University of Nairobi library

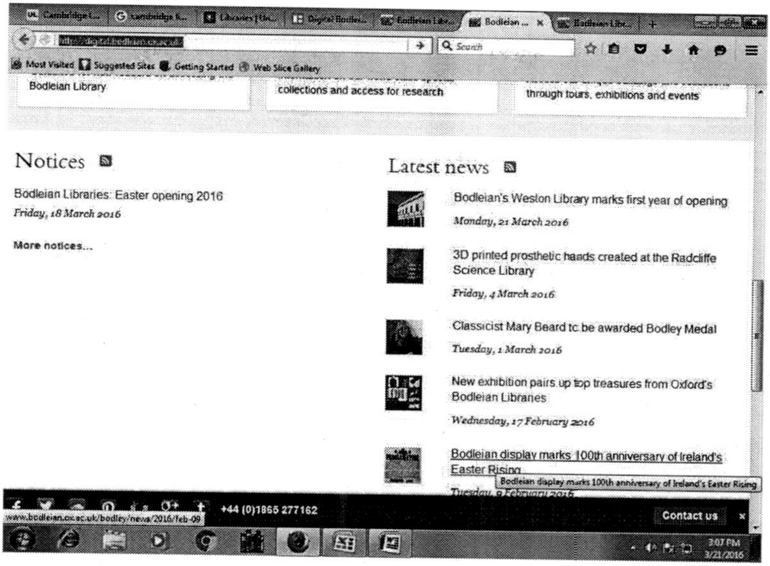

Screenshot 3. News and events service of Bodleian libraries

Weblog : A weblog is an online tool being effectively used by various university libraries in reaching their patron online, to bring their users behind the scene to meet staff, introduce with past and present activities and put them in front of row of events and market their services. The library creates blogs for offering various services like current awareness services about general books, book reviews, selective dissemination information, promoting library services and events, supporting users, highlighting library news, information and resources of interest, preparing subject guides, update new resources, collecting user's feedback or comments, engage community, publishing library newsletter, using as reference desk or library consortia. All posts are organized in reverse chronological order (Dhande, 2014)[4] and users can comment on posts they read. A great library blog requires three ingredients: inspiration, motivation and dedication (Solanki & John, 2015)[12]. The usage of blogs is on higher side among all other web 2.0 applications.

For instance, Universiti Sains Malaysia library (USM) and Universiti Sains Islam Malaysia (USIM) library has created a blog to provide news and events. Few University libraries created blog to update their users on the opening hours, calendar of events, to promote their services, to introduce their liaison librarians, for posting book reviews, events, notifications and library updates or to create official website (Awang, Nor, 2012)[1].

Screenshot 4. The blog of Universidade Federal do Rio Grande do Sul library

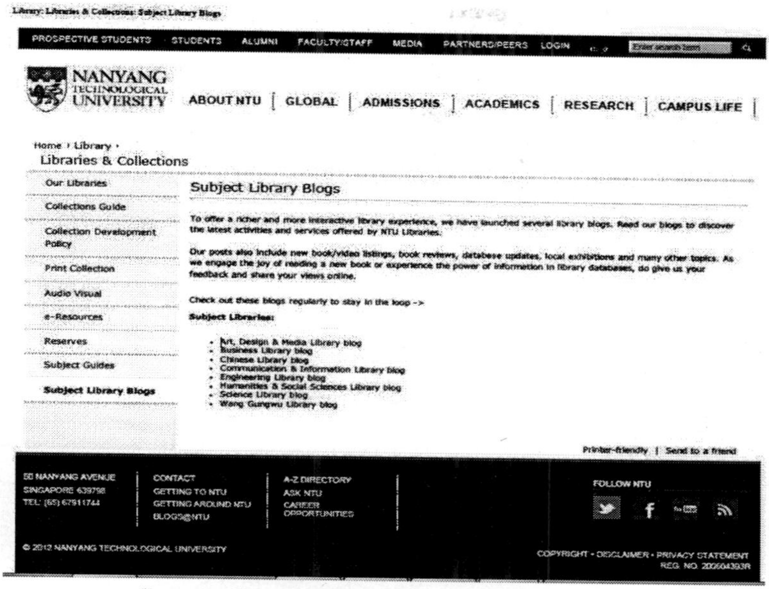

Screenshot 5. Nanyang University Blog

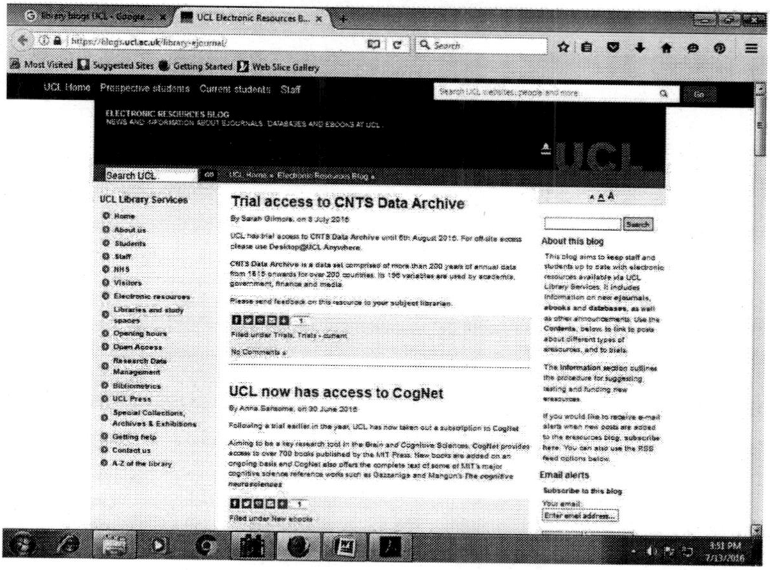

Screenshot 6. The blogs of University College London libraries

WordPress : WordPress is one of the excellent blogging platforms. It is flexible, easy to use, interactive, simple to use and customizable and therefore, since its inception in 2003 thousands of universities using WordPress for the official sites (Joyce, 2013)[6]. In university libraries also it has increasingly gained popularity as a content management system (Singley, Emily, 2013)[10] Few university libraries use WordPress to build official websites too which includes rich contents and WordPress fully supports and meets the requirements like displaying multimedia, integrates static with animated content. It offers a perfect channel to maintain and expand collaboration. In publishing news, information, newsletters, updates university libraries use WordPress.

Screenshot 7. Use of WordPress at the Cornell University library

Screenshot 8: Use of WordPress at the Universidade Federal do Rio Grande do Sul

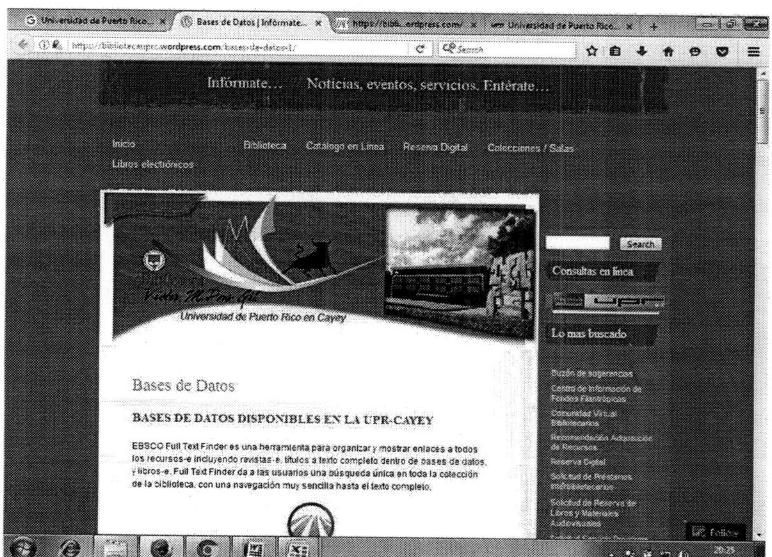

Screenshot 9. Use of WordPress at Universidad de Puerto Rico library

Instant Chat/Messaging : Instant chat/messaging facility on library website provides a platform to interact with on duty librarian and library staff. Patrons do not have to come to the library to ask any help or make an enquiry. Most of the libraries use Meebo, Yahoo messenger, AOL messenger, Skype, Windows live messenger, Google talk, Solo Live, etc. instant messaging web based application to interact with their users (Awang, 2012)[1].Through this service library staff can handle users'inquiries instantly on pre-defined time period irrespective of the user's location. It is also called as virtual reference service desk (Dhande, 2014)[4].

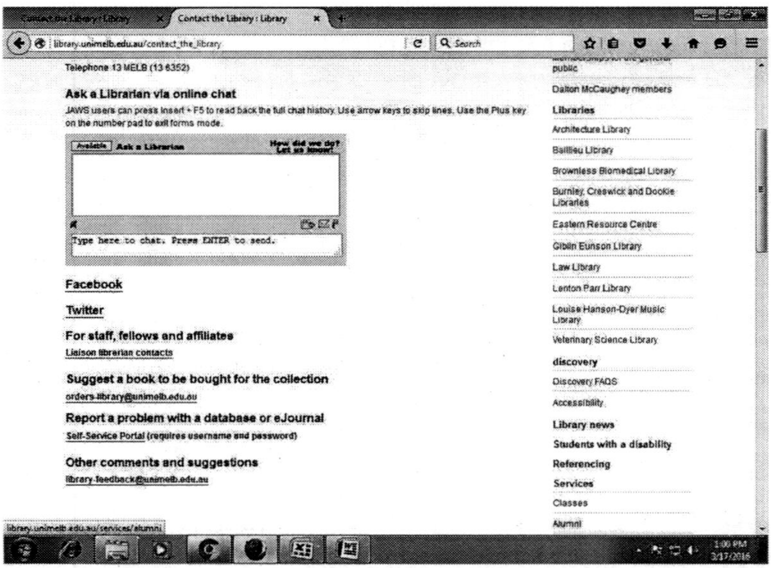

Screenshot 10. Instant Chat/message service of the University of Melbourn library

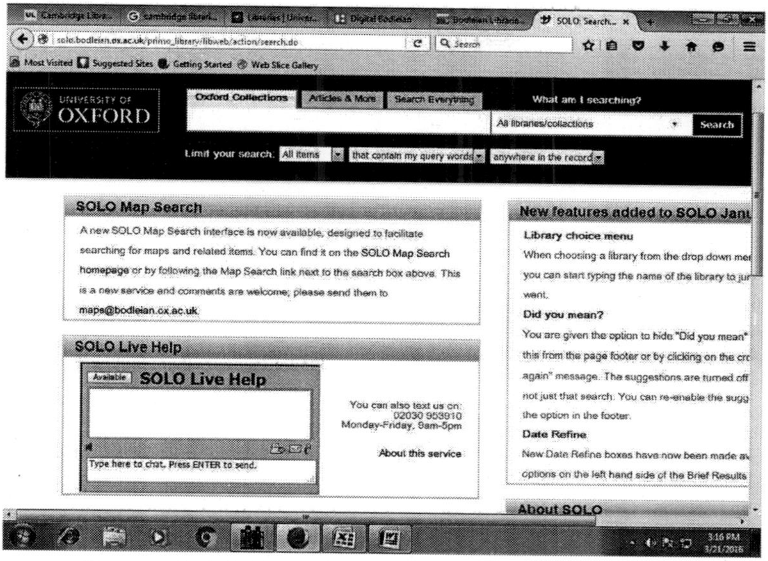

Screenshot 11. Instant messaging service at the University of Oxford library

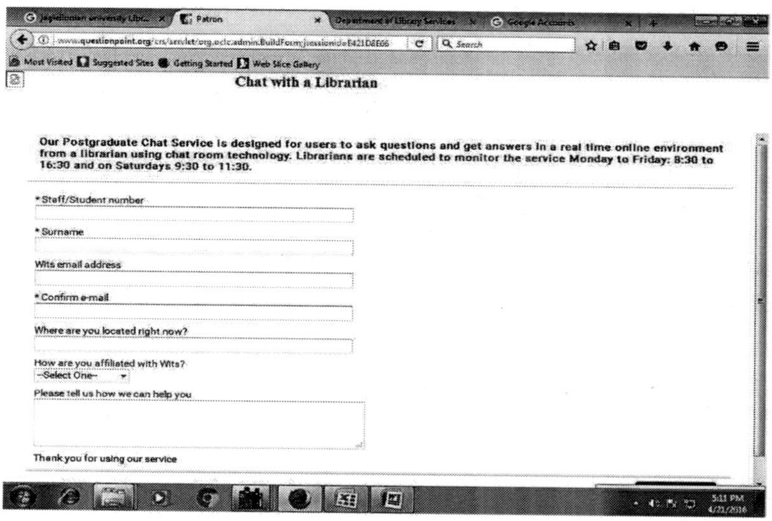

Screenshot 12. Instant Chat service

Ask Us : Is an online consultation service to solve patron's questions or service inquiries. University libraries are using web forms; email, telephone, whatsapp, social networks, instant chat/messaging, FAQs, Fax platforms and details are communicated on the library website.

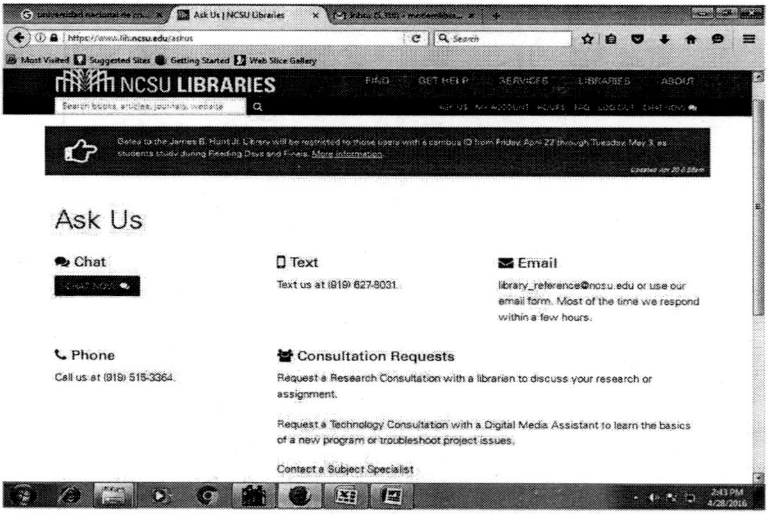

Screenshot 13. Ask us service by NCSI libraries

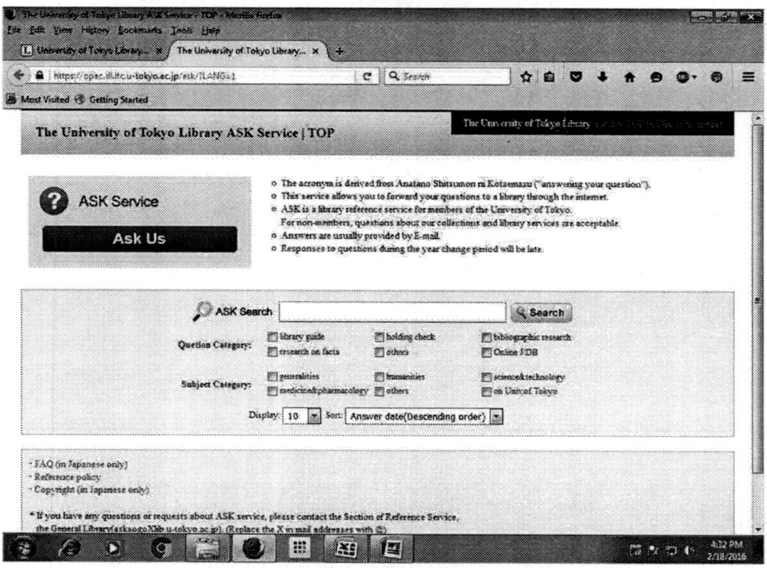

Screenshot 14. The University of Tokyo library's ask us service

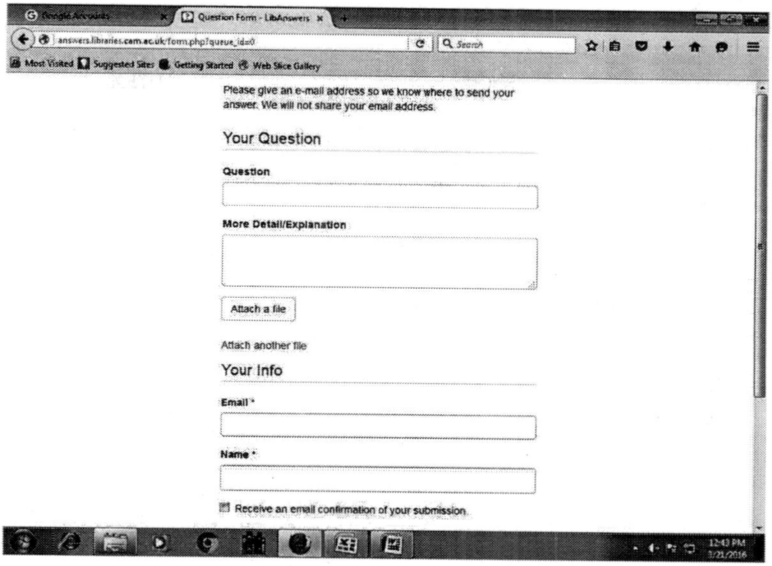

Screenshot 15. Ask us service by the University of Cambridge library

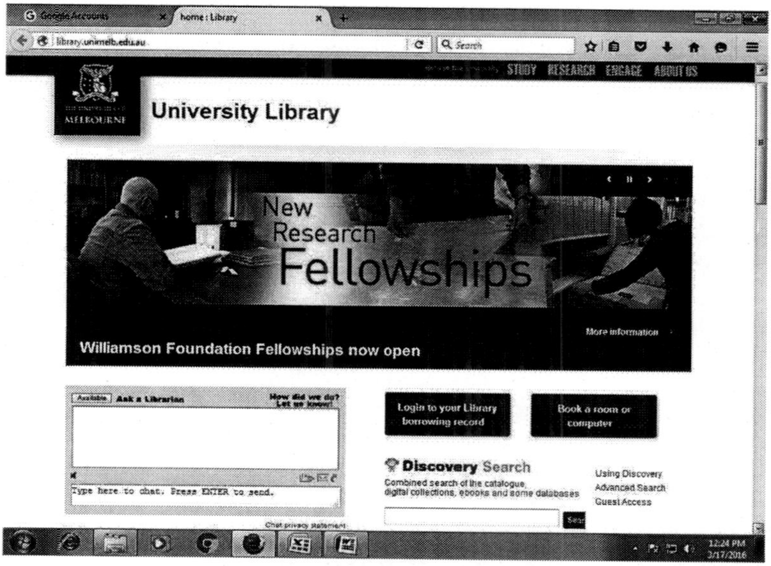

Screenshot 16. Ask us service by the Melbourne university library

Research / Subject Guides : In university libraries, researchers are always asking research support and guidance from library reference section staff. In top university libraries departmental libraries and separate subject librarians are there to manage subject collection and services. University libraries provide active service to researchers by providing them online research or subject guidance called subject guides or research guides. Subject guides are nothing but all information about resources and services for that subject available in the library. Subject librarians compiles list of print as well as online resources in that subject along with research support they are providing like citations, plagiarism, software or help, writing and referencing, news, personal assistance etc. using web technology. For separate subject, separate research portal or pdf file is created or uploaded on the website called subject guides. Subject guide 2.0 is defined as those created by Web 2.0 technologies like multimedia, multi-formats, collaboration, ease of use, global change, search box, browsing, link checking, integration with social bookmarking sites, RSS feed, tagging, interactivity, user input, blog or wiki, and statistics reporting. They have the capability to allow users to bookmark websites directly into their subject guides or to integrate it with major social bookmarking sites. (Yang, S, 2009)[15]. The Murdoch University library has purchased a licensed Libguides from Springshare. Springshare vendor is a pioneer in designing template for libguides or subject to avoid duplication of work. Using this platform library staffs is filling up and updating the contents easily. The Springshare template allows staff to upload specific subject related tutorials, videos, podcasts or slideshows, pdf's, texts, library resources, instructions and online help to researchers in that subject[15] No programming language knowledge is required and library staff can easily publish subject guides on the internet without going through a university server (Chan, H. H. R, 2009)[2]. Springshare integrates Libguides with Facebook and other social networking sites like Twitter and delicious (Springshare, 2009, p.12)[13]. Many university libraries are using such commercial or open source templates like Libdata from University Of Minnesota, MyLibrary from University of Notre Dame, Pirate Source from Eastern Carolina University, Research Guide from the University of Michigan, Subject Plus by Ithaca College and Library Course Builder (Yang, S, 2009)[15] to prepare subject guides and provide research support.

An example of a static subject guide in the form of pdf files by Perpustakaan Sultan Abdul Samad Library of University Putra Malaysia Library is as follows.

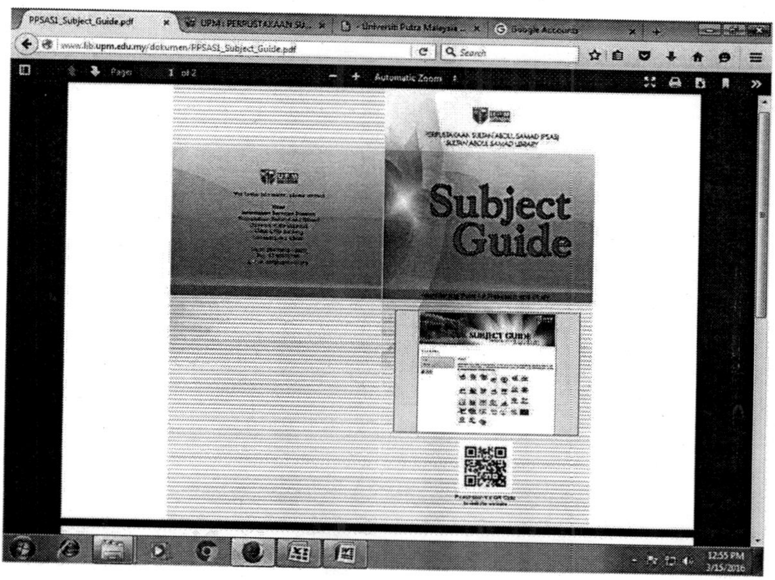

Screenshot 17. Subject guides service of the University Putra Malaysia library

University of Witwatersrand, Johannesburg provides different subject guides which include research support, reference sources, electronic resources, useful web links, ebooks, OPAC and personal help to group of researchers. Normally, all guides are organized alphabetically and category wise. Altogether all guides are called library guides. University libraries in European countries are developing subject gateways to help users to find high quality information resources available on the internet equivalent to search engines or web directories. A subject gateway is the databases of detailed metadata records of internet resources and offers a hyperlink to the resources. Patrons or researchers can search the database by keywords or browse the resources under subject headings (Hatua, Sudip)[14].

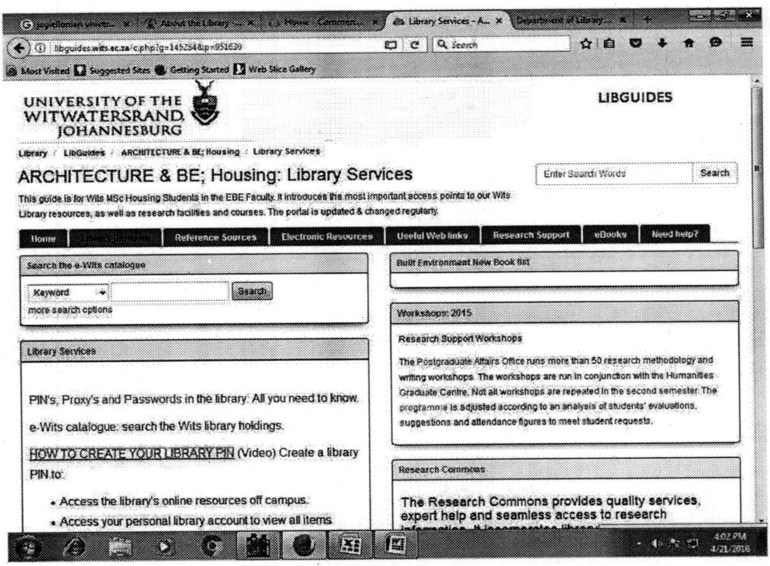

Screenshot 18. Research guides of the University of the Witwatersrand Johannesburg

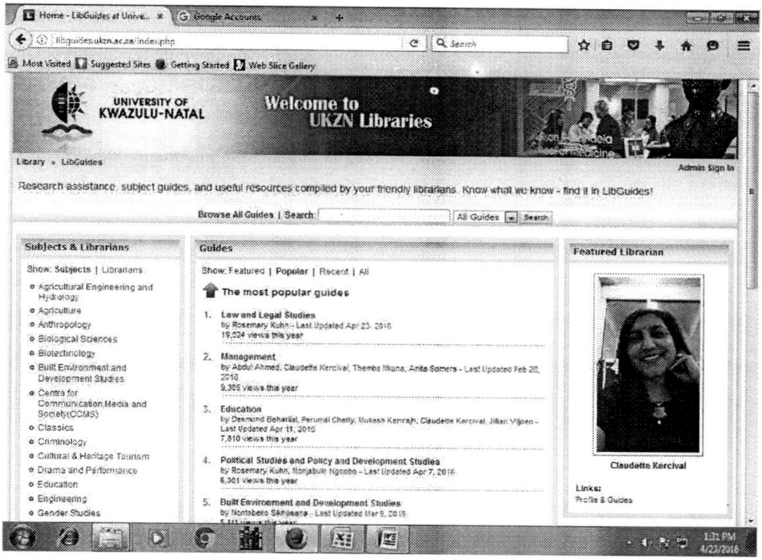

Screenshot 19. Research/subject guides of the University of Kwazulu Natal libraries

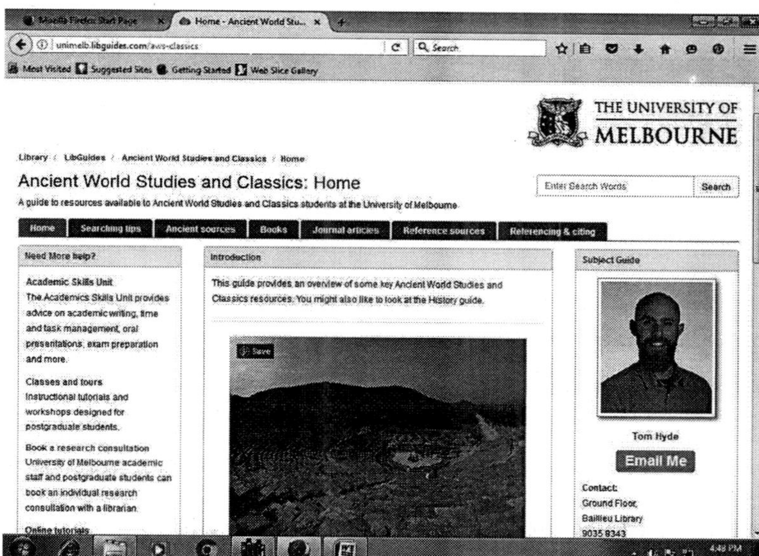

Screenshot 20. Subject/ Research guides of the University of Melbourne library

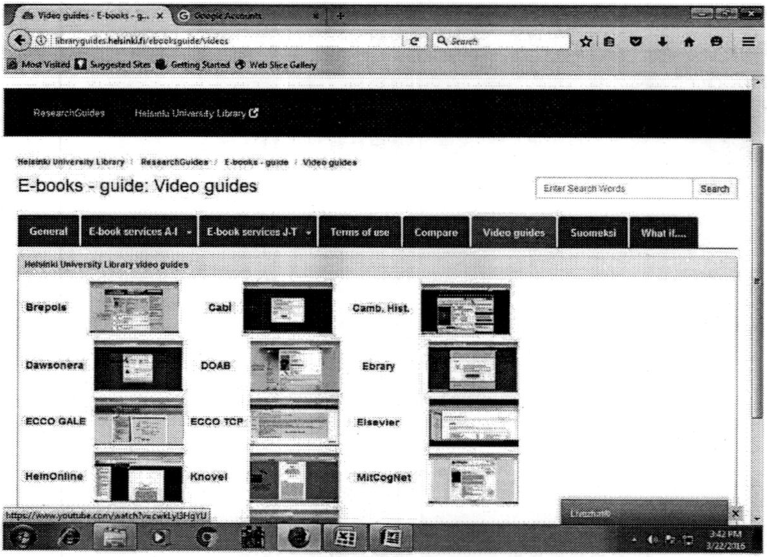

Screenshot 21. E-books guides of the Helsinki University library

Video Tutorials : Library guides or instructions communicating with the patrons in an interactive way using multimedia technology video tutorials are provided by top university libraries. Watching video tutorials are always appreciated and more understandable and catchy than reading the text instructions. Therefore, for giving instruction, orientation, demonstration top university libraries are preparing video tutorials and gives access to them on their websites. Video tutorials are effective learning and teaching media. Sometimes university libraries upload these videos on YouTube or Vimeo platform and then embed these videos on library websites. Sometimes these video tutorials are available on library websites itself. University College London Libraries published a series of short films or videos introducing their library collection and services. In below screenshot library has created short videos to train users on how to search e-discovery tools or OPAC, how to locate library material like books, journals, ebooks, articles, etc. along with how to access various database resources, plagiarism checking software, and various services offered by libraries and how users can get the benefit of those services.

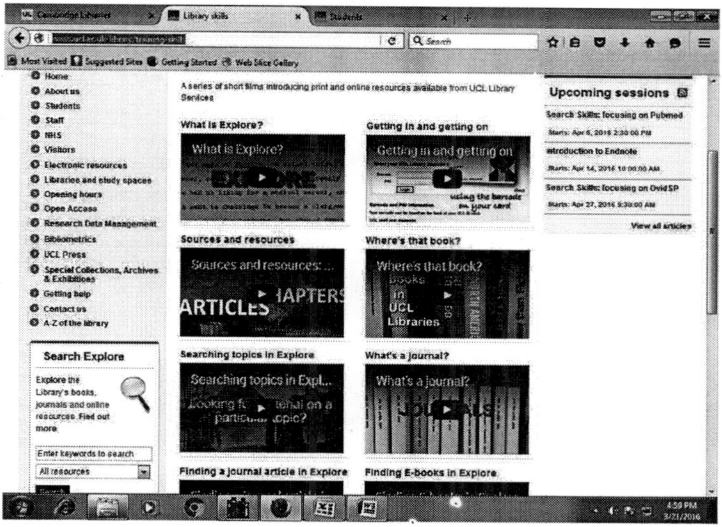

Screenshot 22. Video tutorials of the Cambridge university library

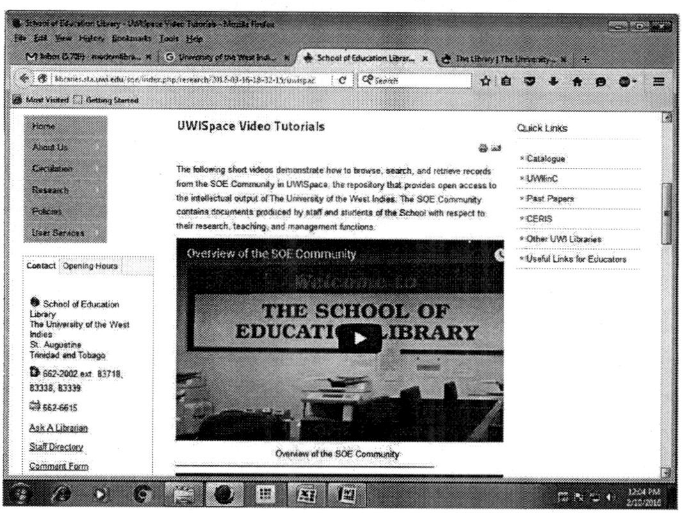

Screenshot 23. Video tutorials of the University of West Indies library

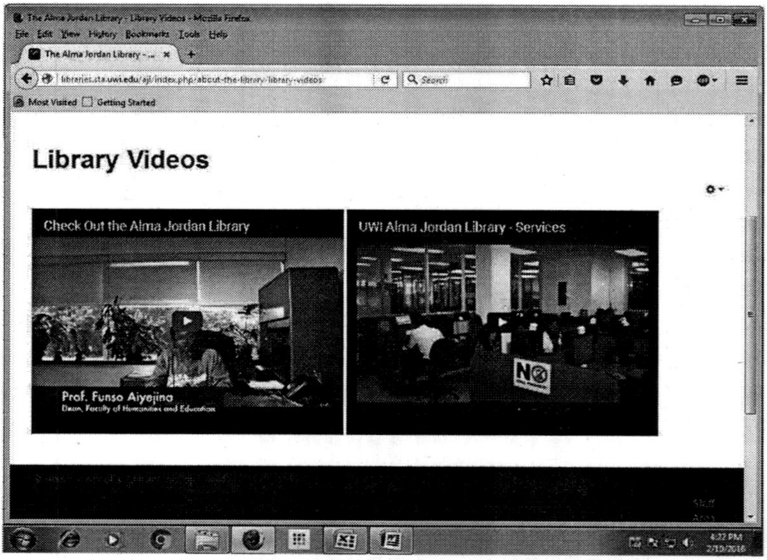

Screenshot 24. The Alma Jorden Library tutorial videos

Screenshot 25. Library tutorials of the University of Pretoria library

FAQs : Newly admitted patrons in university libraries regularly asks many questions about library collections, services, facilities as they are not aware of functioning of the library or any changes made in services. There are many common questions library staff needs to answer to all patrons, so to avoid repetitions to constantly ask questions and to save the time of patrons and staff answers to frequently asked questions are made available on library websites for reference purpose. Patrons do not need to call or email or personal visit library to ask his or her queries. Frequently Asked Questions(FAQs) are a compilation of a list of frequently asked questions by the library patrons and their answers.

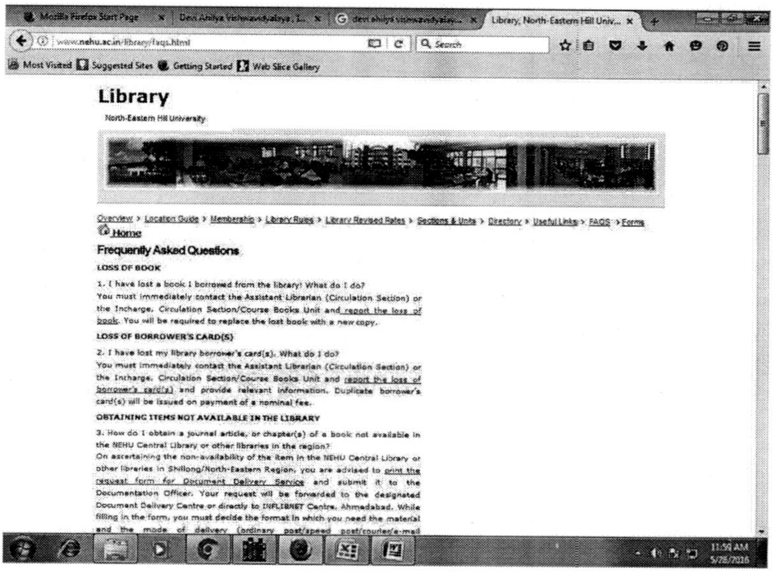

Screenshot 26. FAQ service by the North-Eastern Hill University library

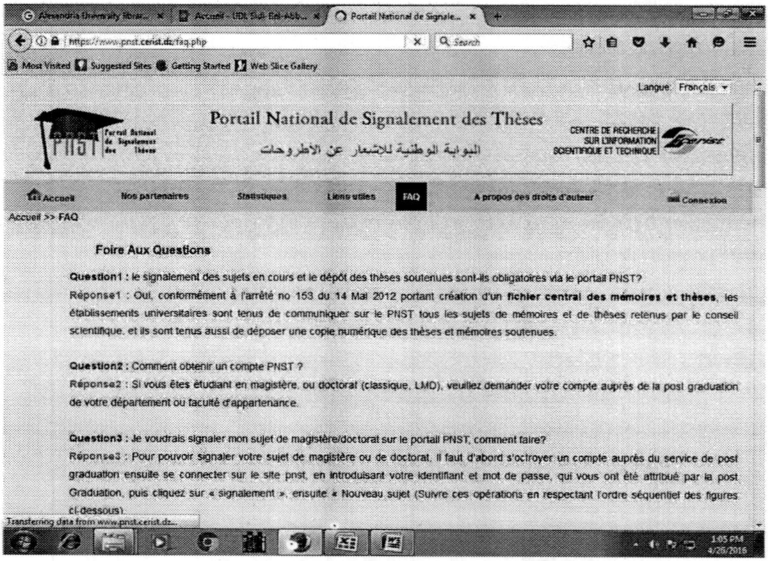

Screenshot 27. FAQ service by the Portail National de Signalement des Theses

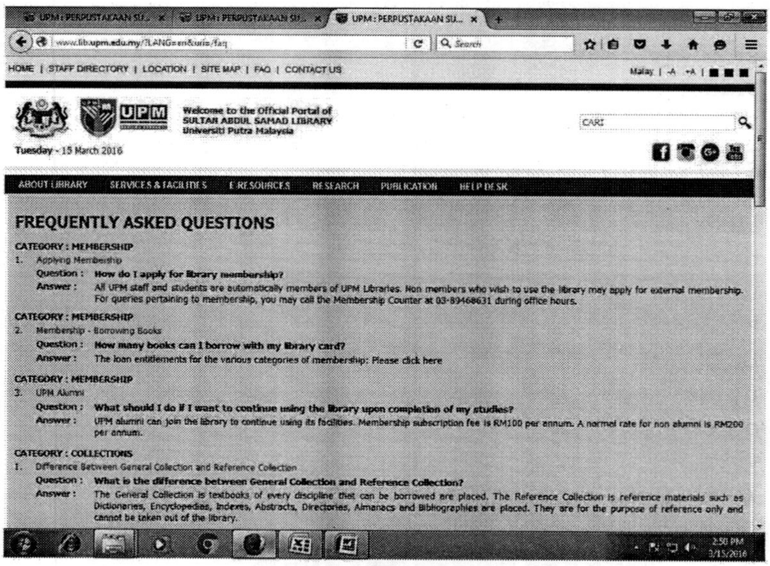

Screenshot 28. FAQ service by the University Putra Malaysia library

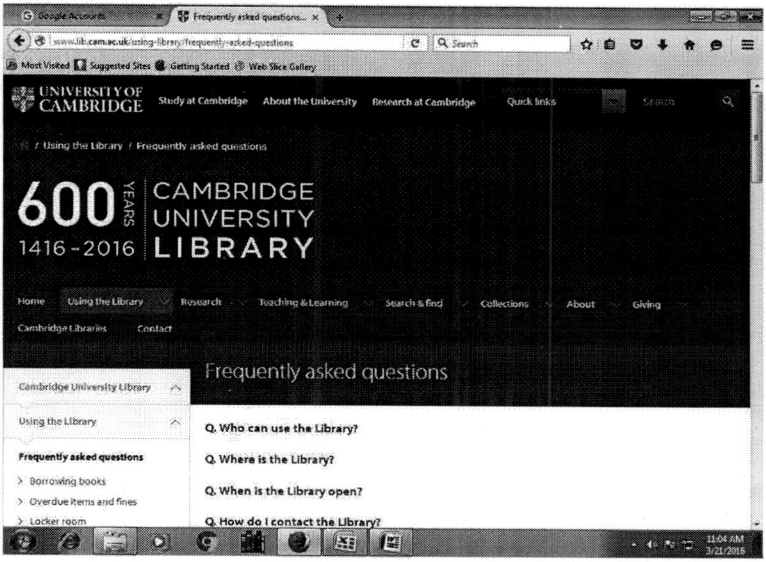

Screenshot 29. FAQ service by the Cambridge University library

YouTube : YouTube application is used for video sharing widely. It allows anyone to post and share their videos, tutorials, recordings publicly or privately. It is a very effective way to deliver or broadcast tutorials of library procedures, to educate patrons and increase use of library resources and promote library services and events. Helsinki university library uploaded video of reading and downloading e-books and e-journals online, *Witwatersrand* university library uploaded video of how to create pin for accessing online e-resources, Indira Gandhi Memorial Library of university of Hyderabad and Brender Library uploaded videos of their laptop zone(Infrastructure or different sections), Tej Aviv university library uploaded video of how to access webopac and e-discovery tool on YouTube.

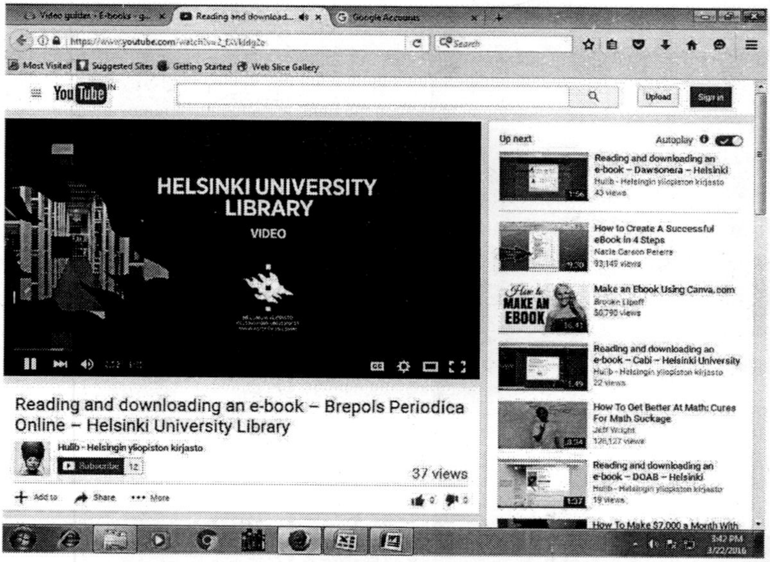

Screenshot 30. The use of YouTube by Helsinki University library

Screenshot 31. The use of YouTube by the University of Hyderabad library

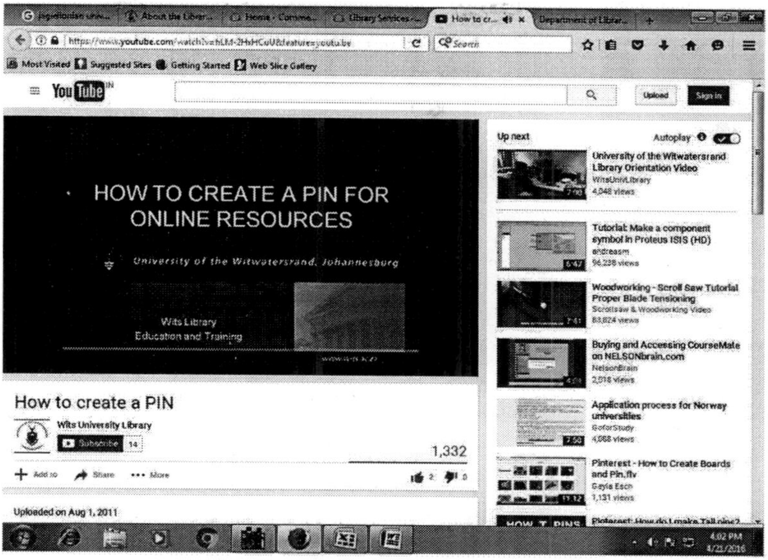

Screenshot 32. The use of YouTube by the University of Witwatersrand library

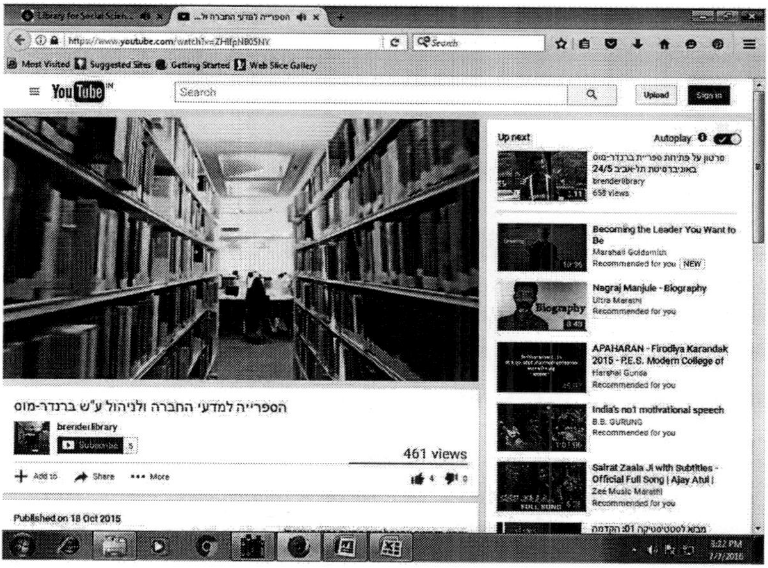

Screenshot 33. The use of YouTube by the Brender library

Service Directory : Under this column university library provides a list or directory of library services and staff.Top world university libraries are collection of libraries centrally accessible. To contact library staff of specific departments or section or service or library this directory helps patrons to reach that staff using details like email ids or contact numbers given in this service or staff directory. Below are examples of the Hebrew university of Jerusalem departmental library

UKZN libraries, King Abdul Aziz Univerity, Nehu library, Tsinghua university library, Australian National university library service directories.

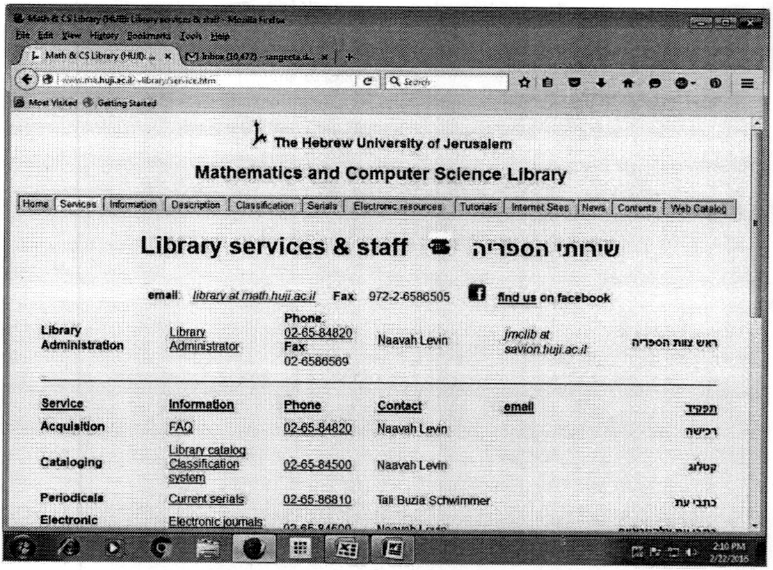

Screenshot 34. Service directory of the Hebrew University of Jerusalem library

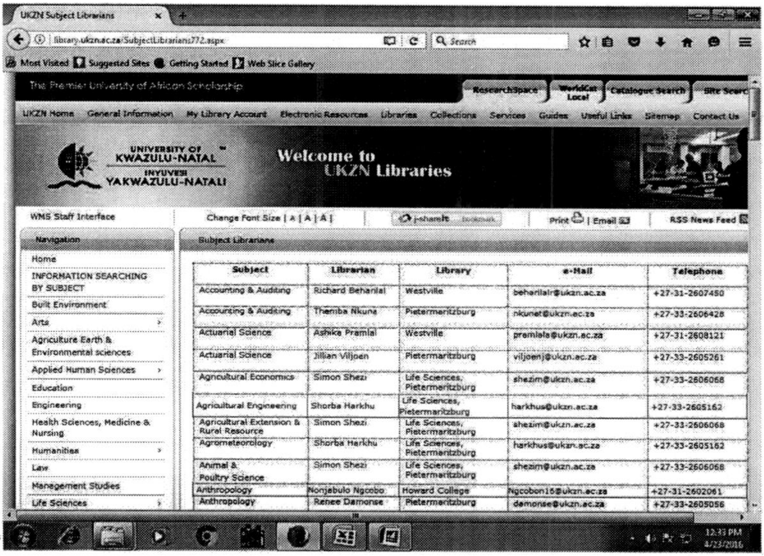

Screenshot 35. Service directory of the University of Kwazulu Natal library

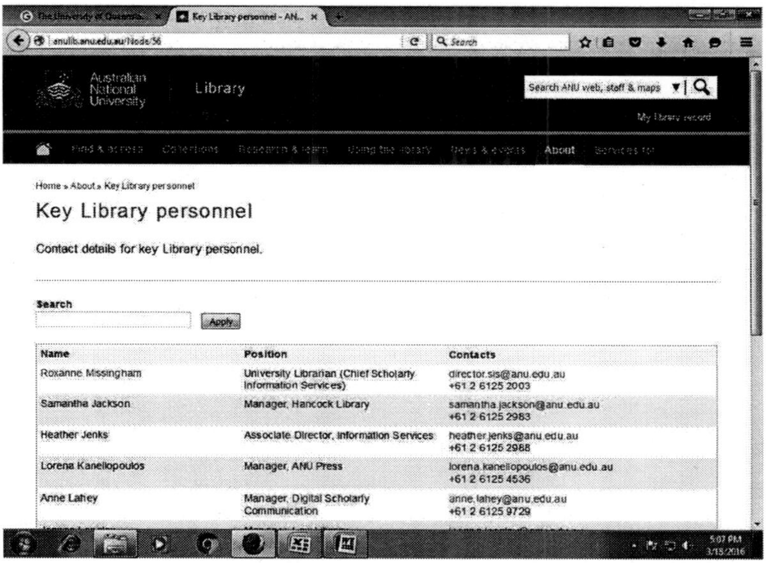

Screenshot 36. Service directory of the Australian National University library

PPTs/PDFs : To educate patrons and give them instructions to access resources, forms, documents and avail the facilities of library many university libraries creates PPTs and PDF files. To upload and give links to presentation and PDF files is very easier task than creating a video or audio tutorial to educate patrons. Below are a few examples of Australian National university library, Universidade de São Paulo library, Universidad de Puerto Rico Mayaguez library, etc.

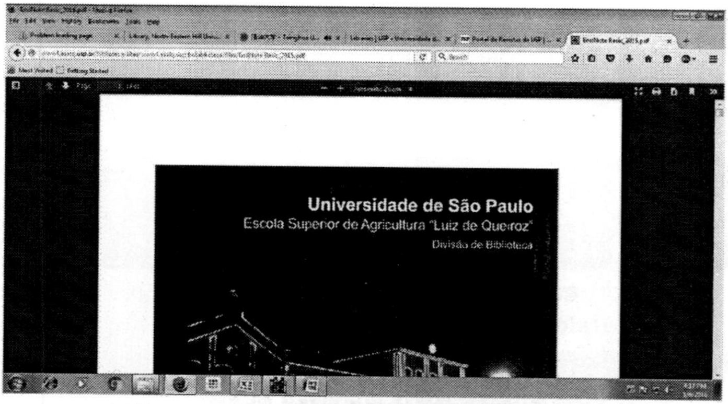

Screenshot 37. The use of PDFs at Universidade de São Paulo library

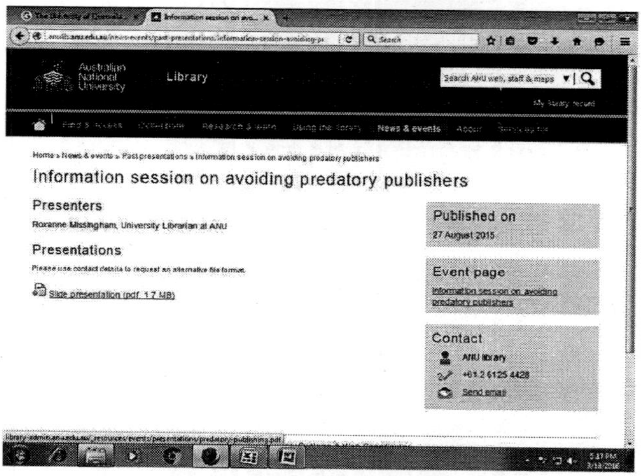

Screenshot 38. Use of PPTs at Australian National university library

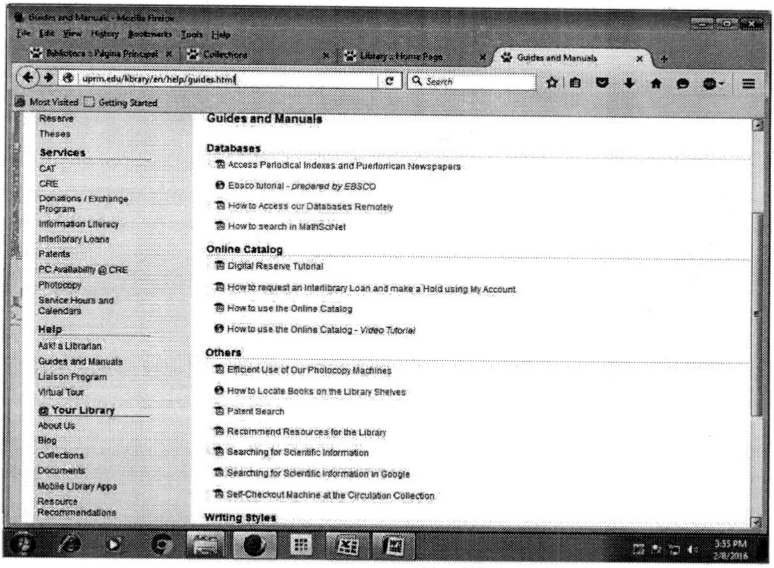

Screenshot 39. Use of PDFs at Universidad de Puerto Rico Mayaguez library

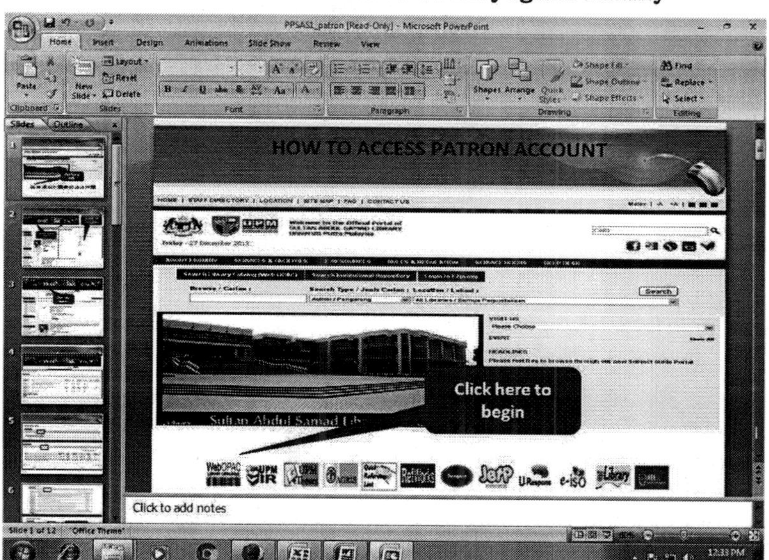

Screenshot 40. Use of PPTs at University Putra Malaysia library

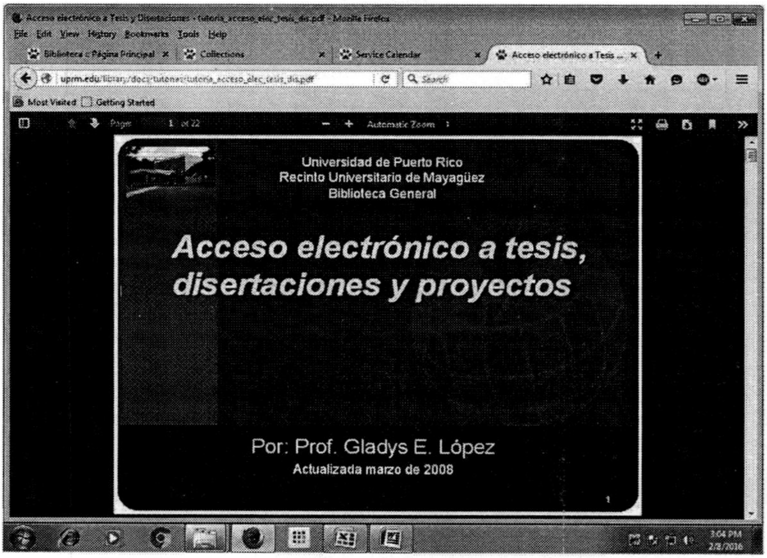

Screenshot 41. Use of PDFs at Universidad de Puerto Rico library

Research Tutorials : The main objective of any university library is to support and promote research. To fulfill these objectives top university libraries providing web based research support and creates tutorials to help researchers about literature search or review, writing research project, reference management and citation, writing research papers, file patents, plagiarism checking software, impact factor, data management and discovery, copyrights, author networks, grants and funding etc. Subject specialists are ready to support researchers online. Research support is provided through social networking sites like Facebook, twitter, etc.

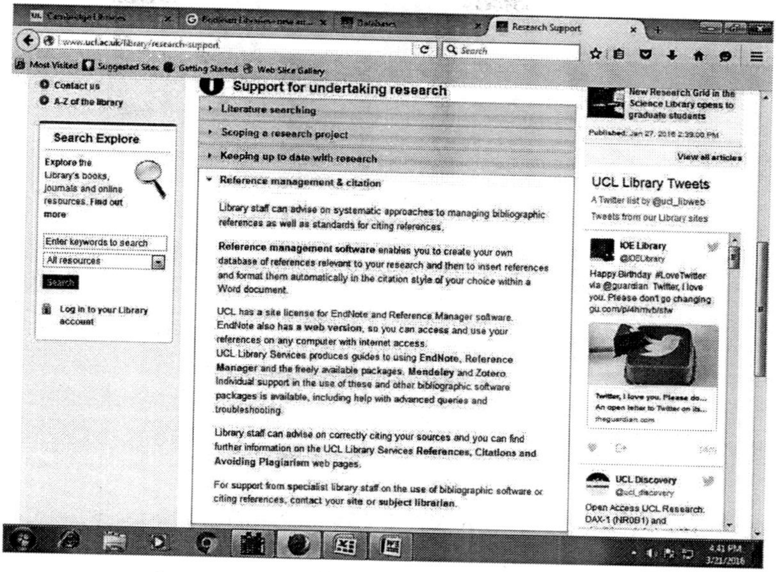

Screenshot 42. Research tutorials of Cambridge University library

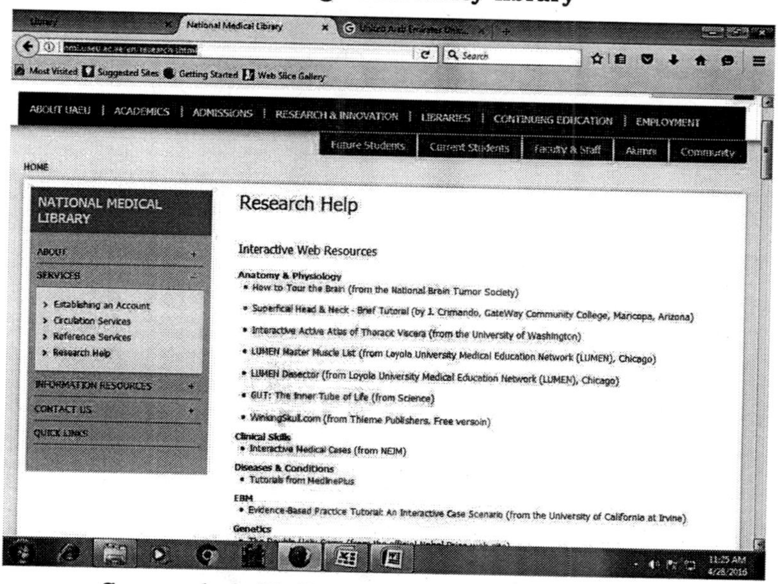

Screenshot 43. Research tutorial/help of the United Arab Emirates University library

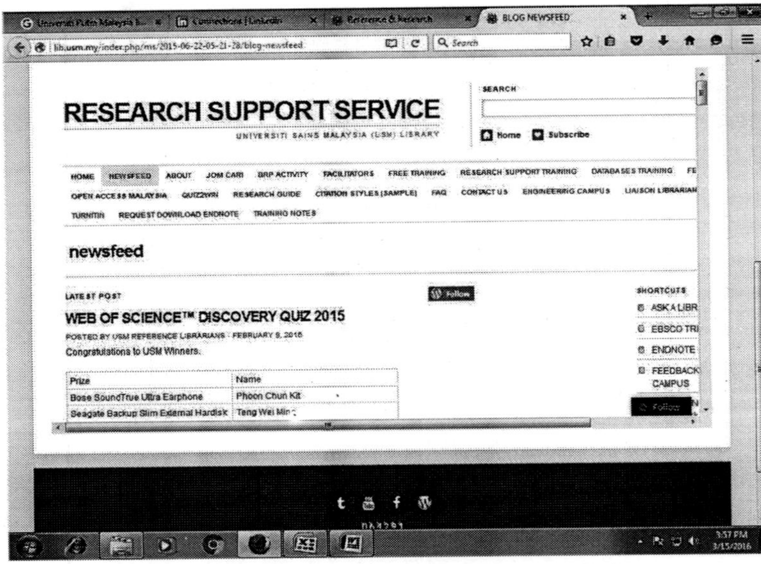

Screenshot 44. Research support of the Universiti Sains Malaysia library

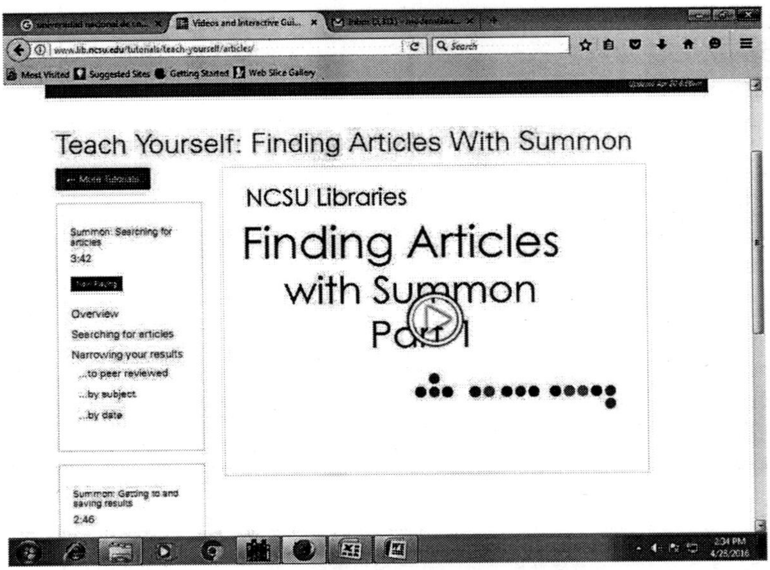

Screenshot 45. Research tutorial of NCSU library

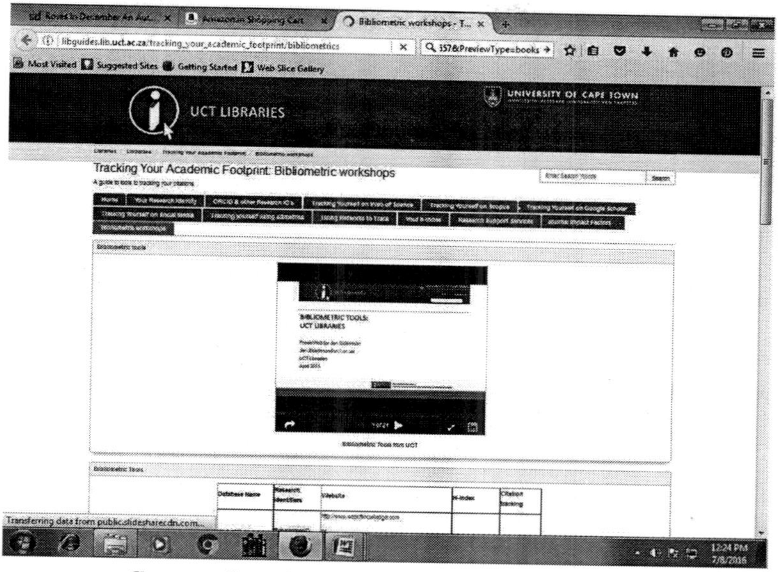

Screenshot 46. Research tutorials of the University of Cape Town library

Tips to Access and Use the Library : Almost all top university libraries provide tips to access and use library resources and services on their website as text or html files.

Newsletter : To offer current awareness service university libraries publishes newsletters or bulletins. In these newsletters and bulletins contains information about library news, pictures of library activities, newly introduced services, sites, new additions, publications of the university, upcoming conferences, workshops, training sessions, fellowship programs, new stories, achievements and future plans of the library. Sometimes newsletter, bulletins involves patrons to contribute their articles, book reviews, etc. Frequency of publishing library newsletters is different for different libraries. African University of Pretoria publishes its library newsletter quarterly, the Tsinghua University library publishes its newsletter monthly, and university of Oxford Bodlian library publishes its newsletter biannually. University libraries publish these newsletters in the blog form or pdf format. These are uploaded on library websites as well as sent by email to all patrons.

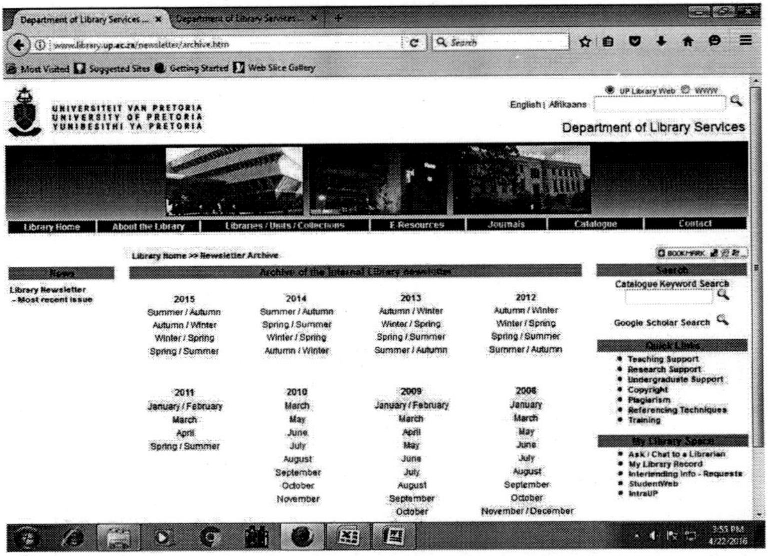

Screenshot 47. Newsletter of University of Pretoria library

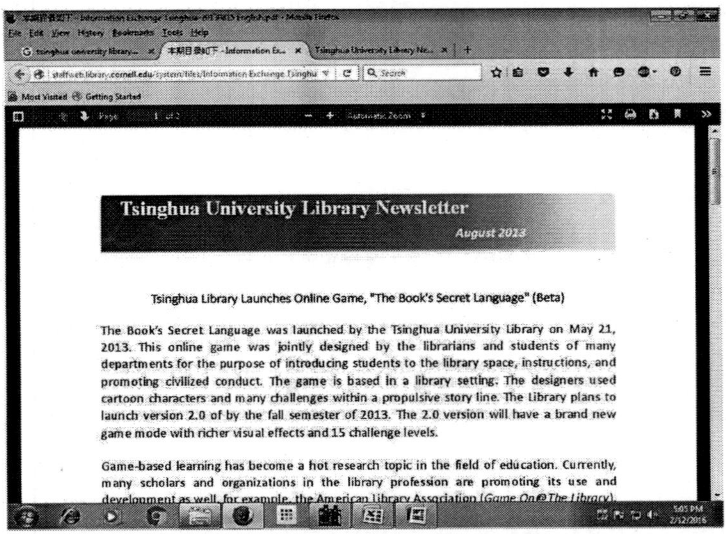

Screenshot 48. Newsletter of Tsinghua University library

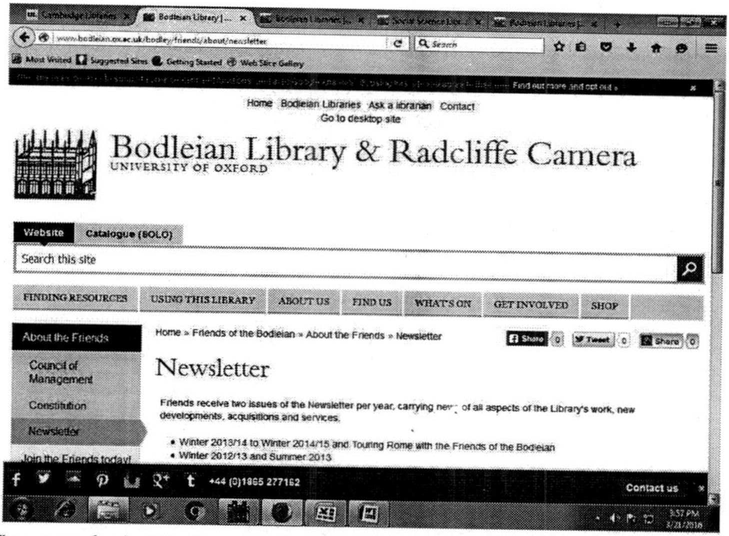

Screenshot 49. Newsletter of the Oxford University library

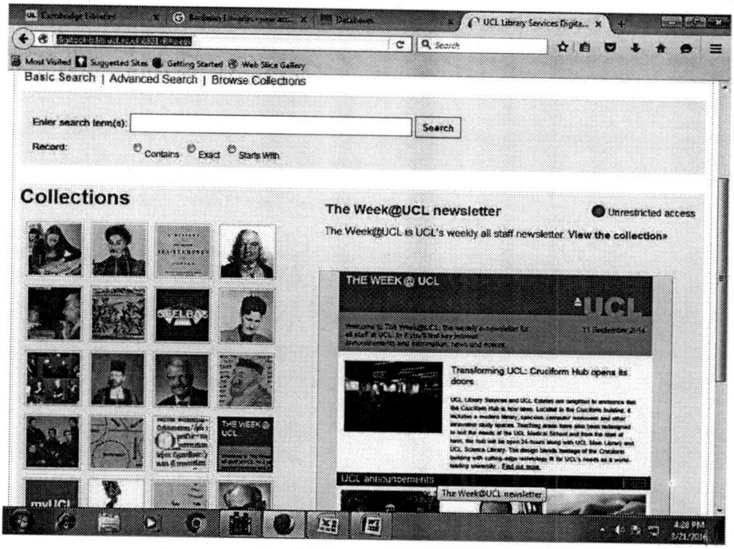

Screenshot 50. Newsletter of the University of Cambridge library

Help Guides/User Guides : These are nothing but manuals or instructions provided by university libraries to patrons. In this chapter, subject guides are mentioned and how they provide support for research. Here these guides are to help patrons to understand procedures, services and the introduction of the library. It is either in PDF file, text file, PPTs, screenshots are used to explain the procedure.

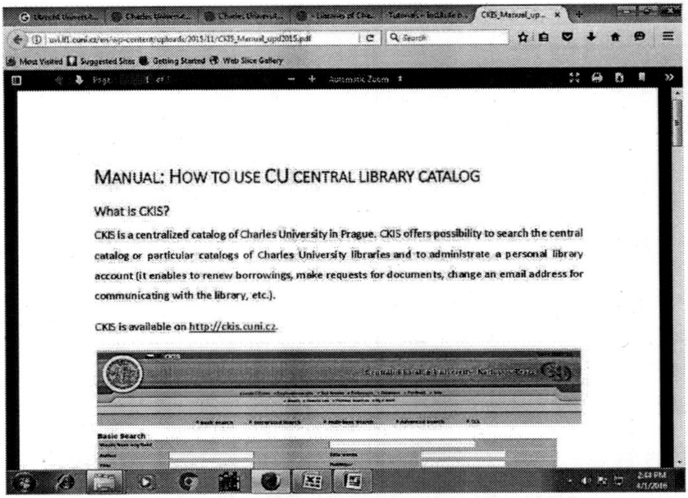

Screenshot 51. Manual/help guide of Charles University of Prague library

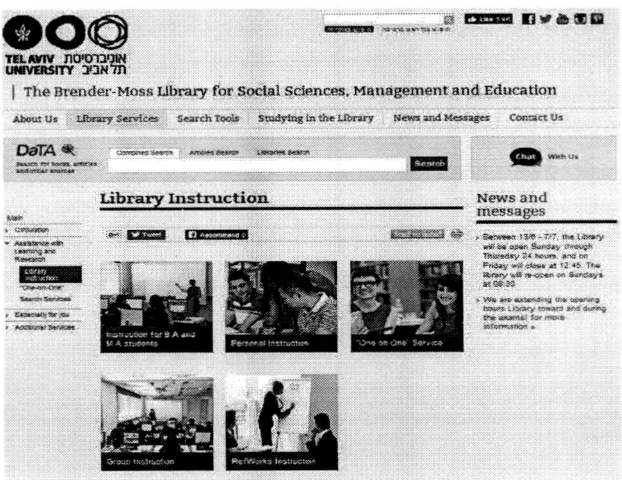

Screenshot 52. Library instructions/help guide of the Tel Aviv University library

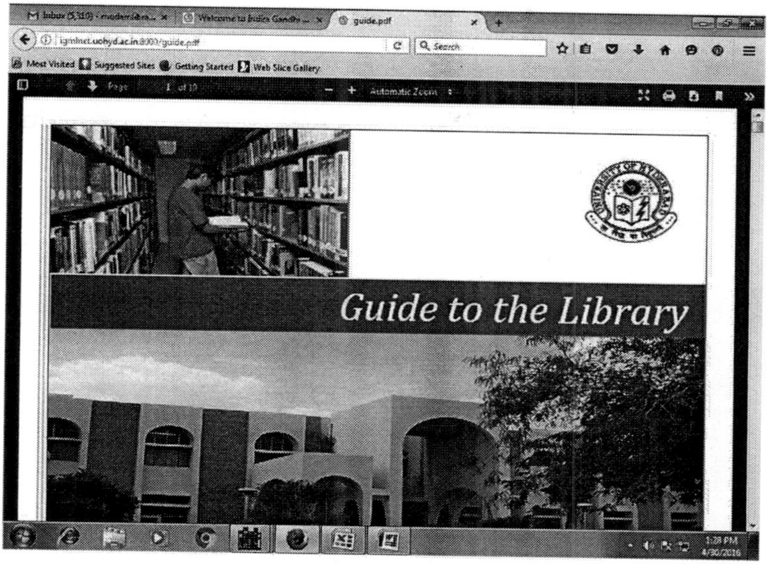

Screenshot 53. Library guide of the University of Hyderabad library

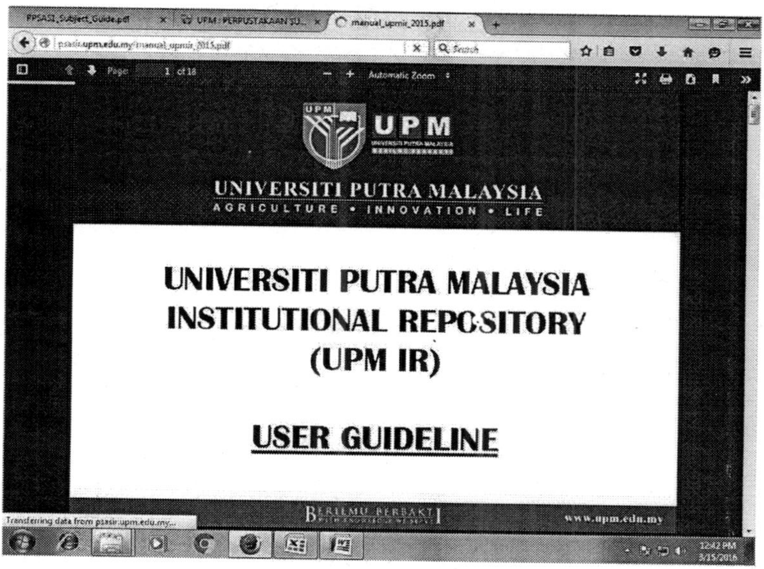

Screenshot 54. User guide of the University Putra Malaysia library

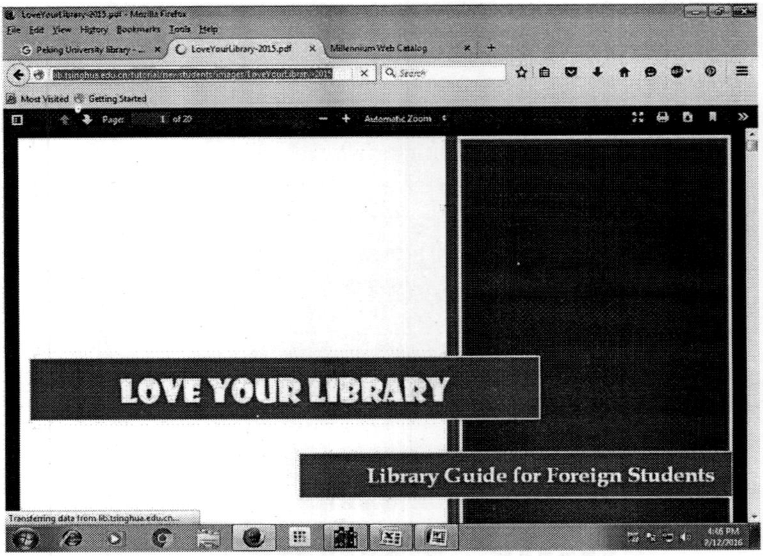

Screenshot 55. Library guide of the Tsinghua University library

RSS Feeds : RSS is most popular and easy web 2.0 tools used in university libraries to give website updates to users in a personal manner without visiting websites (Dhande, S, 2014)[4]. It uses a family of standard web feed formats to publish frequently updated information like blog entries, news headlines, audio, video, etc. (Wikipedia)[9]. The purpose of providing RSS news feeds in university libraries websites or blogs varies from library to library (Awang, Nor, 2012)[1]. RSS feeds enable publishers or libraries to syndicate data automatically. Using RSS feeds patrons can receive timely updates from the library news, SDI, CAS, Bibliographical services, Bulletin board services or websites or blogs automatically if they subscribe to their interested website RSS (Dhande, S, 2014)[4].For instance, Cambridge university library has provided RSS to library news, new resources, notices to readers and job vacancies. Similarly,the Australian National University library provided RSS to disseminate news and updates.

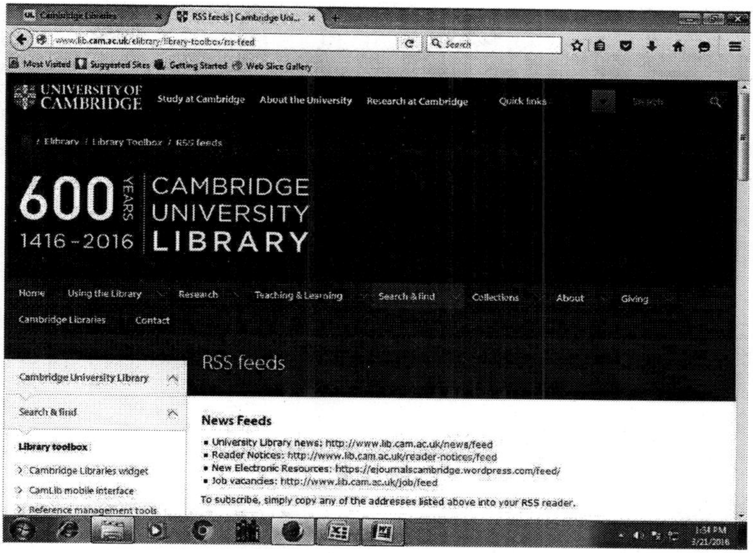

Screenshot 56. RSS feeds of the Cambridge University library

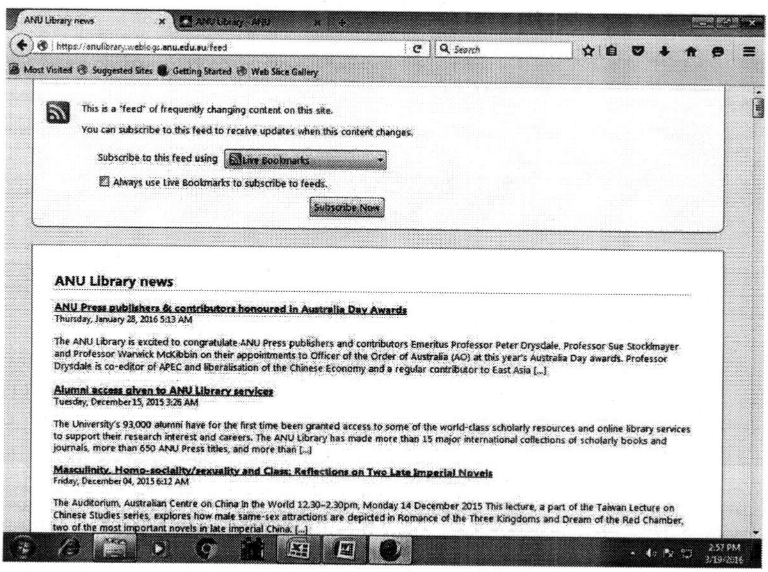

Screenshot 57. RSS feeds of the American National University library

Mobile Application : With increasing use of mobiles among the patrons, university libraries are customizing their webpages and Web OPACs for mobile devices and smart phones to enable users to access library collection and information from their mobile devices. Mobile sites are appearance is little different that actual sites. It is stripped down appearance to make it download quickly and view easily on smart phone's small screen.

Screenshot 58. Mobile interface of Cambridge University library website

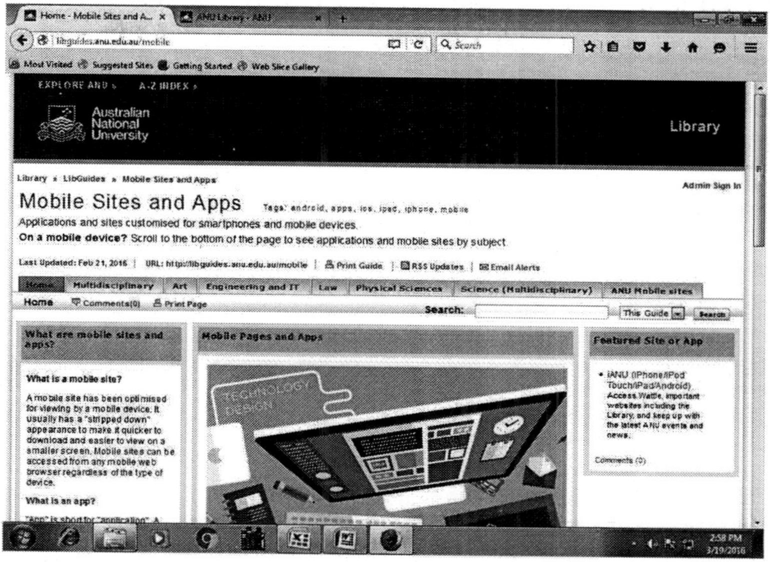

Screenshot 59. Mobile interface for the Australian National University library website

Screenshot 60. Mobile interface of Universidade de Sao Paulo library website

Live/Online Sessions : Many times it is not possible to conduct orientation and information literacy programs for all patrons because university has large number of patrons. On other side students or patrons are sometimes miss the orientation and information literacy programs organized by the library. Therefore few university libraries started to offer live online orientation classes or live sessions for patrons. With these students can attend these sessions from anywhere. The library invites patrons in advance to attend these online classes informing those dates and times. Few libraries keep these online tutorials or classes for future reference too. To attend live sessions helps patrons to clarify their doubts at that time.

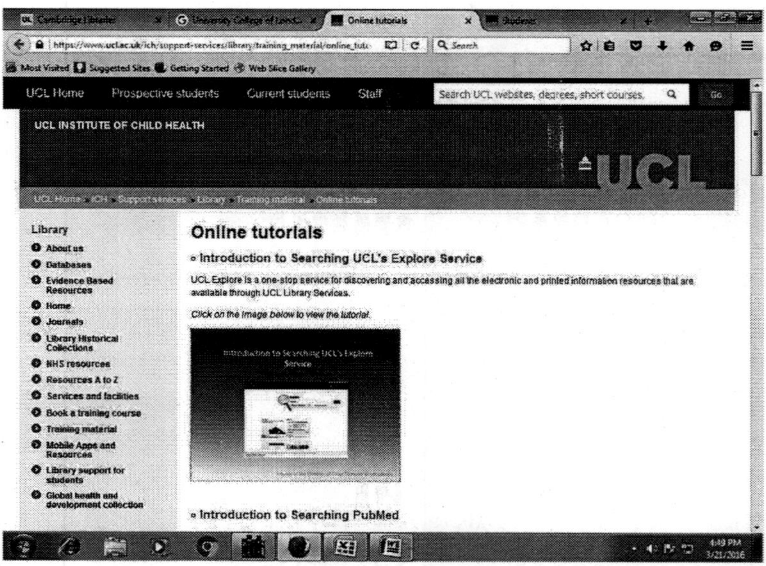

Screenshot 61. Online tutorials of University of Cambridge library

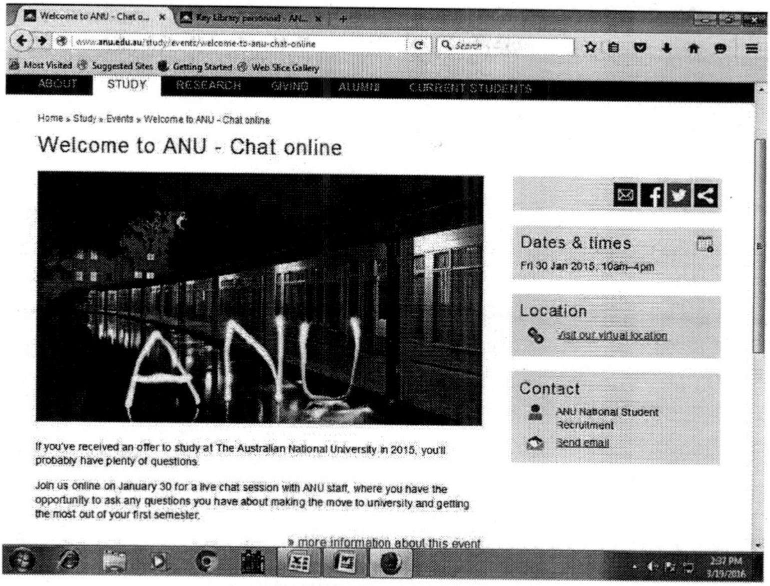

Screenshot 62. Live Chat sessions at the Australian National University library

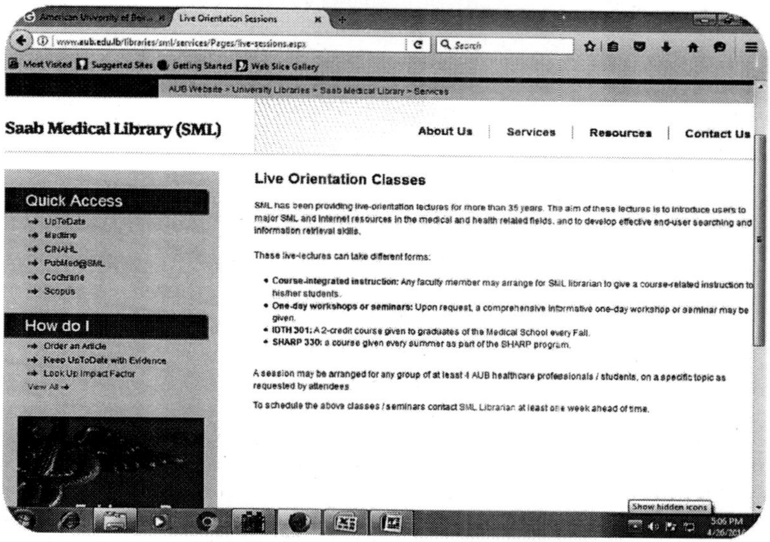

Screenshot 63. Live orientation classes at the American University of Beirut library

Prezi/Slide Share : Slide Share is a Web 2.0 based slide hosting service used widely in academic and research field to share and upload contents in PowerPoint, PDF, keynote or open document presentation format since 2006(Wikipedia)[11]. SimilarlyPrezi is cloud based presentation software developed by Adam Somlai-Fischer as a tool for use in architecture in 2008. In traditional PowerPoint presentations users were able to move from one slide to another slide in a linear fashion, but with Prezi one can produce non-linear presentations where users can move between ideas and highlight key elements in the presentation. It is used to create stunning new presentations that make people remember your message and act on it.User can add data by simply typing text onto the canvas. Prezi bubble menu is used to import pictures, documents (work, pdf), videos, graphs, library guides, maps, web pages for editing and preparing training sessions in university libraries. (Morgan, Jenny, 2012)[7].

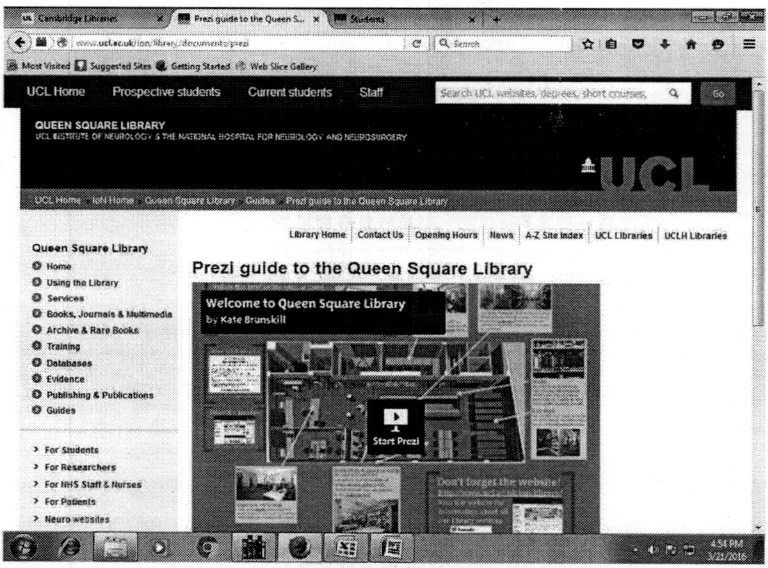

Screenshot 64. Use of Prezi at University of Cambridge's Queen Square Library

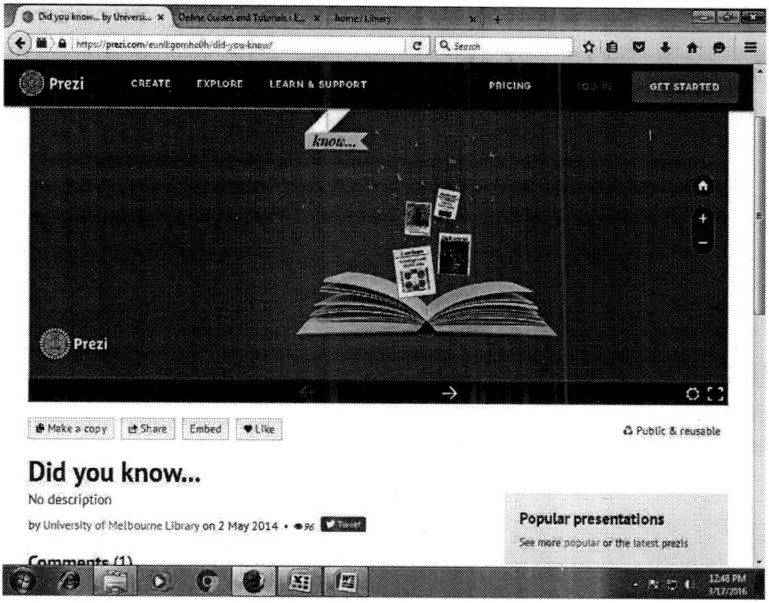

Screenshot 65. Use of Prezi at University of Melbourne library

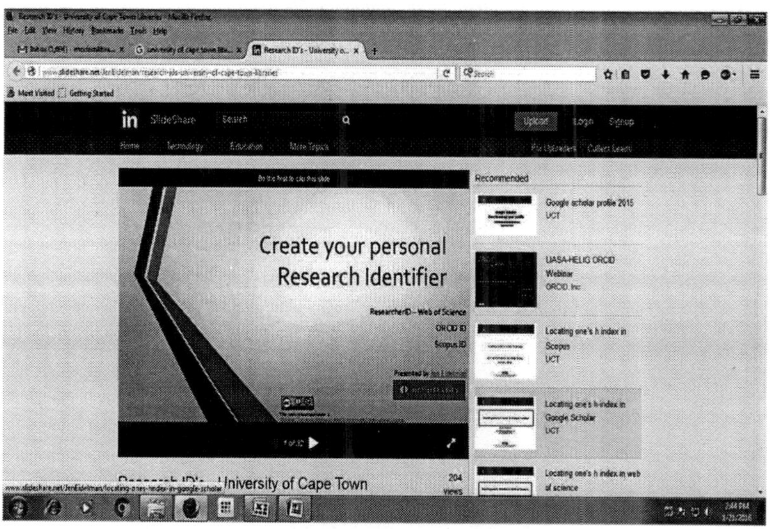

Screenshot 66. Use of SlideShare at the University of Cape Town library

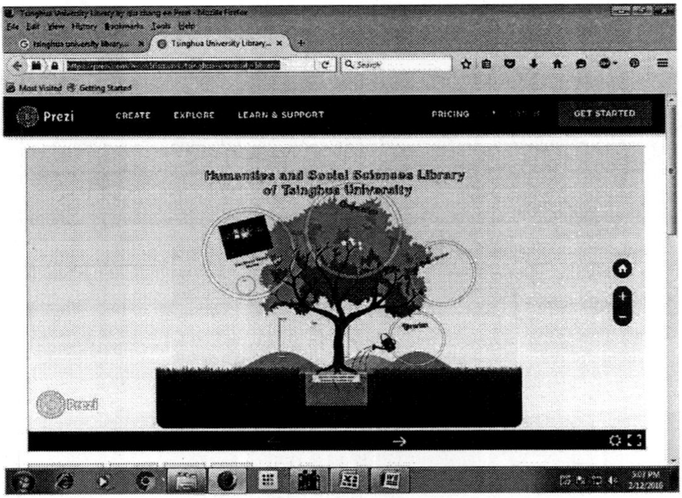

Screenshot 67. Use of Prezi at Tsinghua University library

Audio Tutorials : University libraries use audio tutorials along with video tutorials for patron education. Audio tutorials are easy to prepare and share. Patrons can listen from iPod, mobiles, personal computer, and Mac and learn on their own.

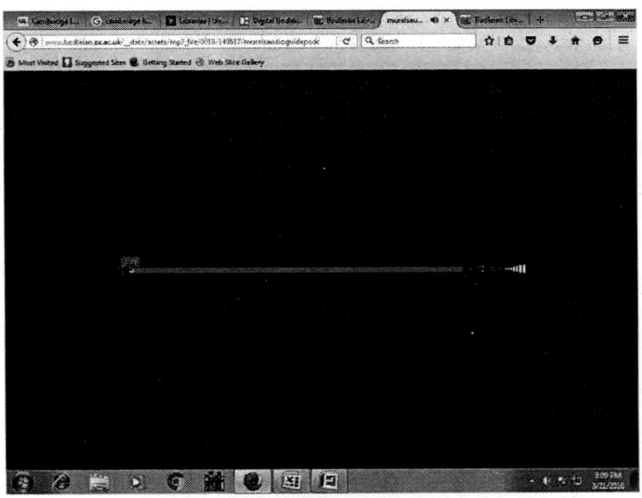

Screenshot 68. Audio tutorials of the Oxford Unviersity library

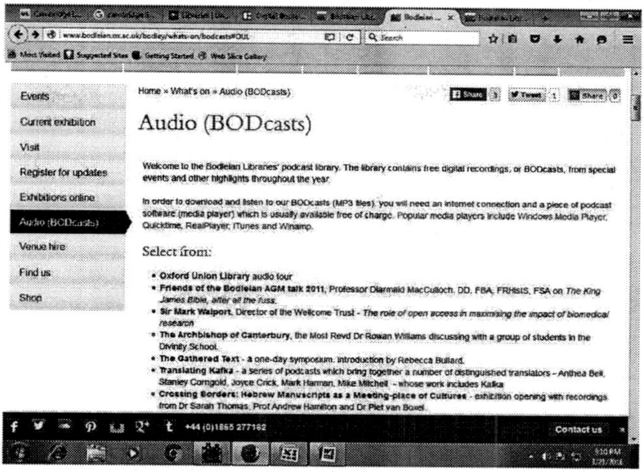

Screenshot 69. Audio tutorials/recodings at Oxford Bodleian libraries

Location maps/Directions : In top universities, libraries are located at different locations within or outside the university premises. Therefore, to help newly admitted patrons to locate their library easily university libraries providing location maps on their website. Few university libraries not only give map of location, but also floor plan and collection maps too.

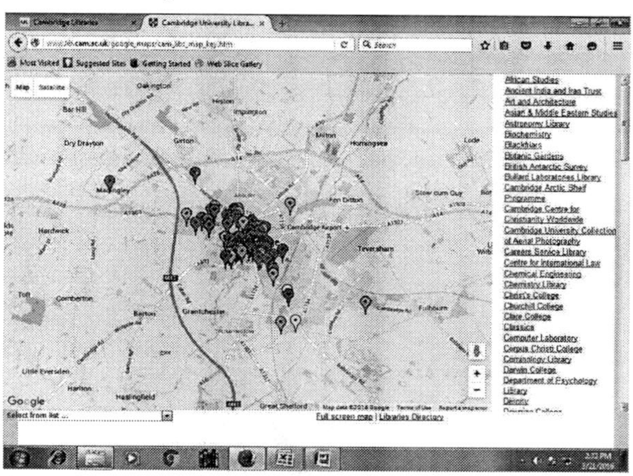

Screenshot 70. Location maps of Cambridge University libraries

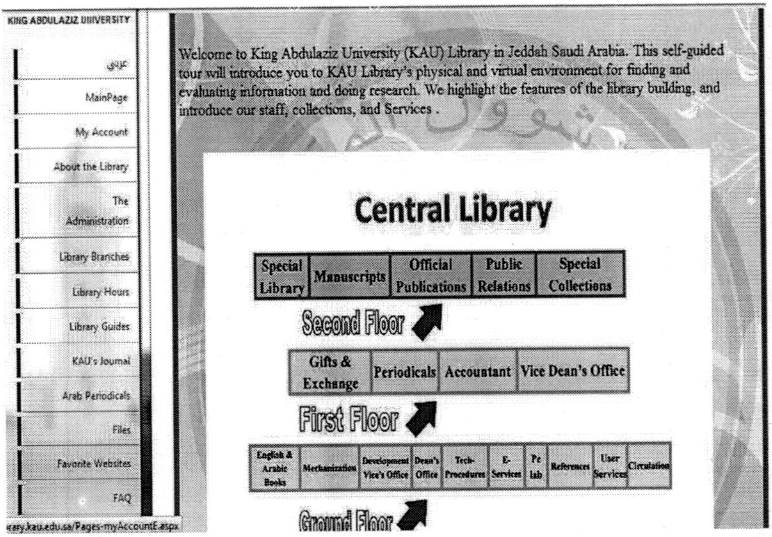

Screenshot 71. Library floor map of King Abdulaziz University library

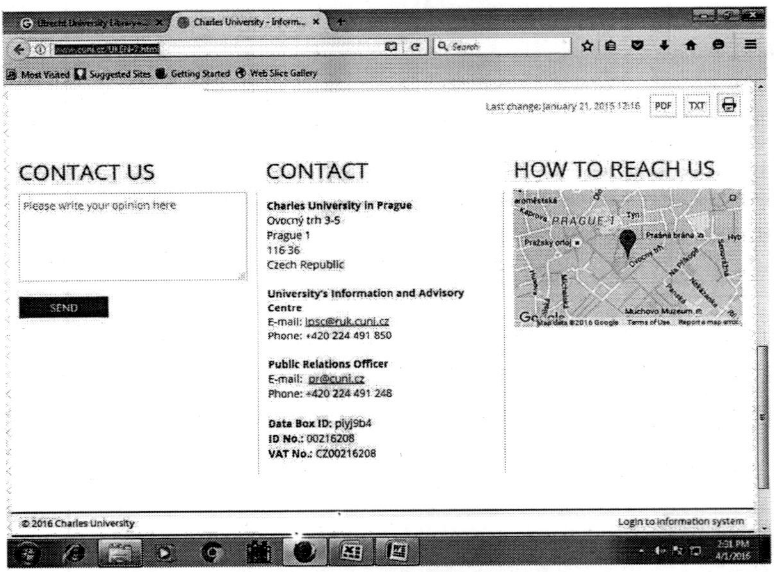

Screenshot 72. Location map of Charles University in Prague library

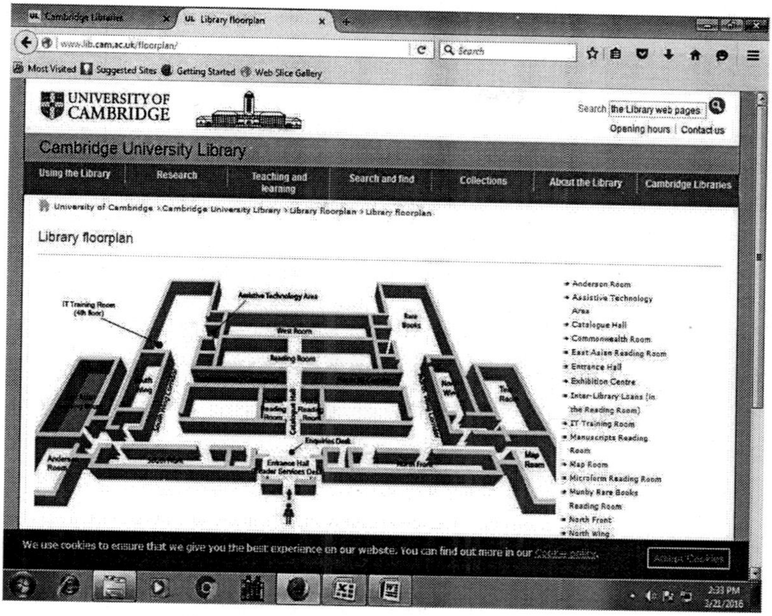

Screenshot 73. Floorplan of the Cambridge University library

Feedback : Feedback is to put things right by taking a corrective action. It is regarded as a strong external stimulus providing positive or negative reinforcement to the behavior. Feedback in higher education must be concerned with developing new ways of knowing stakeholder demands and expectations. Feedback from patrons concerned with looking forward for correction, reinforcement, forensic diagnosis, benchmarking and longitudinal development than concerned with the work already carried out by university libraries (Price, et.al, 2010)[9]. Unlike traditional written feedback from now universities collects feedback online and have database of feedback to work on it. On the library website feedback form is designed and patrons are asked to fill it. It is also called as a suggestion box or it is a survey of user satisfaction. This database of suggestions and feedback helps university libraries to improve their services.

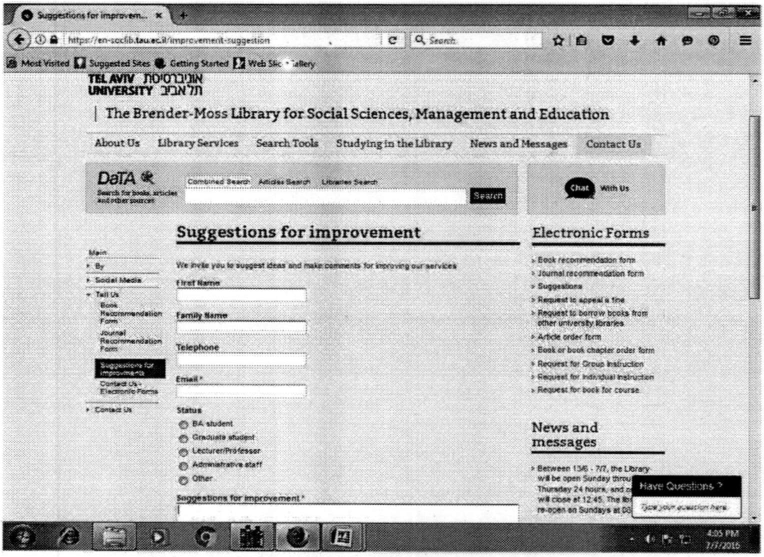

Screenshot 74. Online feedback of the Tel Aviv University library

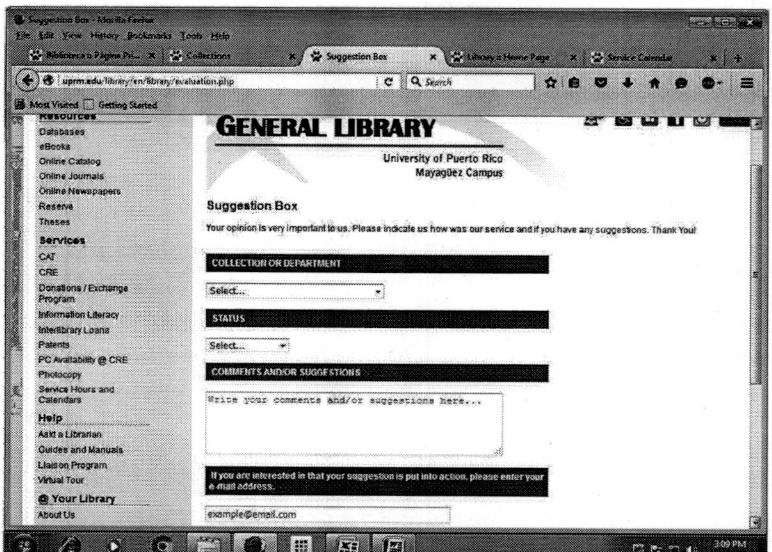

Screenshot 75. Online suggestions of University of Puerto Rico library

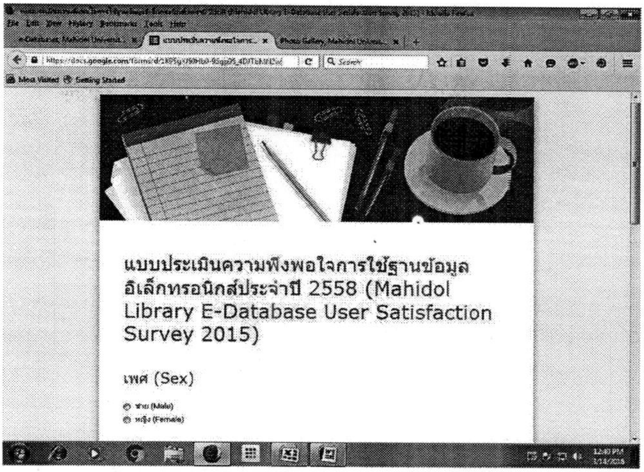

Screenshot 76. Online feedbook of Mahidol University Library

Live/Online Videos Library : Few university libraries give access to live or online videos to educate patron online. To provide current awareness services and updating users this service is provided.

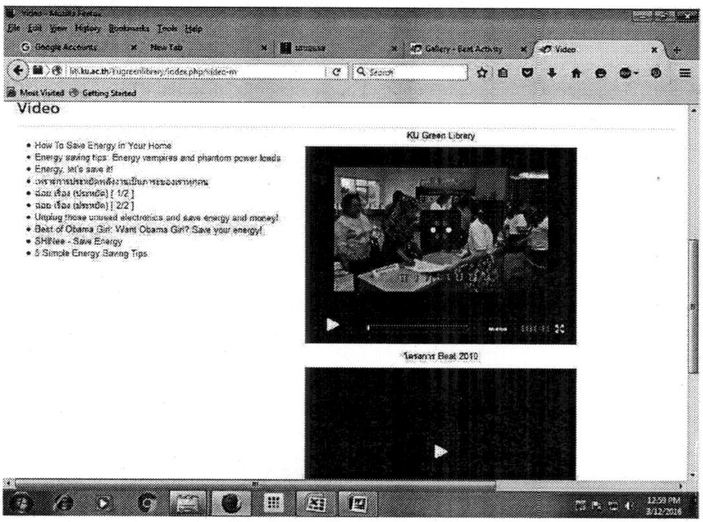

Screenshot 77. Online video library of Kesetsart University library

Library Calendar : Online library calendar is nothing but the preplanned tentative event planner and updated library opening hours during the week, month and year. Libraries update the event and working hours time to time on their website. On the main university library website all connected libraries of that university are also listed. Below is an example of the American University of Beirut mentioned department wise of branch libraries timings and holidays.

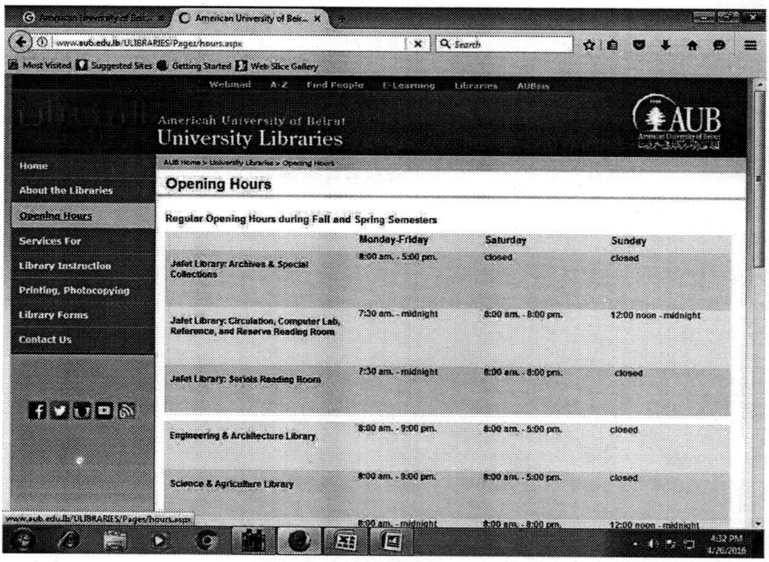

Screenshot 78. Library calendar of The American University of Beirut

Screenshot 79. Library calendar of Kesetsart University

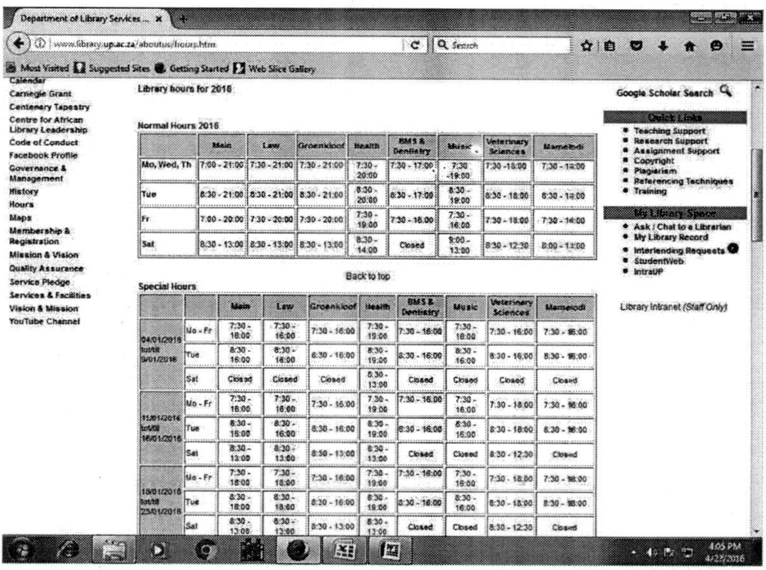

Screenshot 80. Library calendar of University of Pretoria

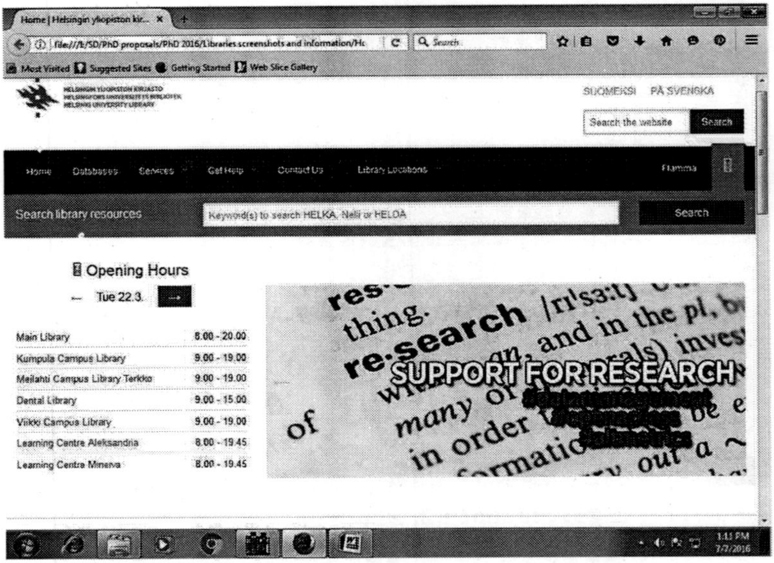

Screenshot 81. Library Calendar of Helsinki University

Photo Gallery : University libraries provide photos of library infrastructure, different sections, events, etc. in the form of an album or scrolling photos. Displaying photos of services and sections are more attractive, catchy and easy to understand by, the patrons than giving description in text form. It also helps to market library services and attract readers. Many university libraries publish albums of events they organized in the library on their website.

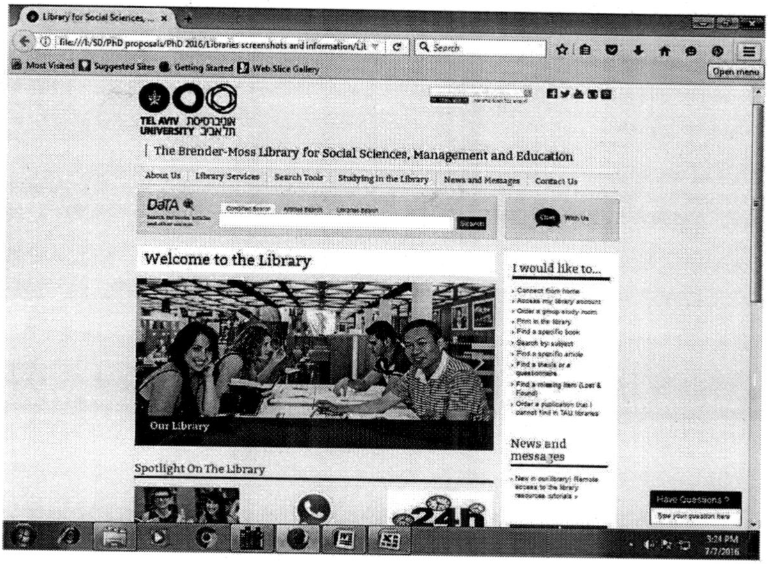

Screenshot 82. Photo gallery of the Tel Aviv University library

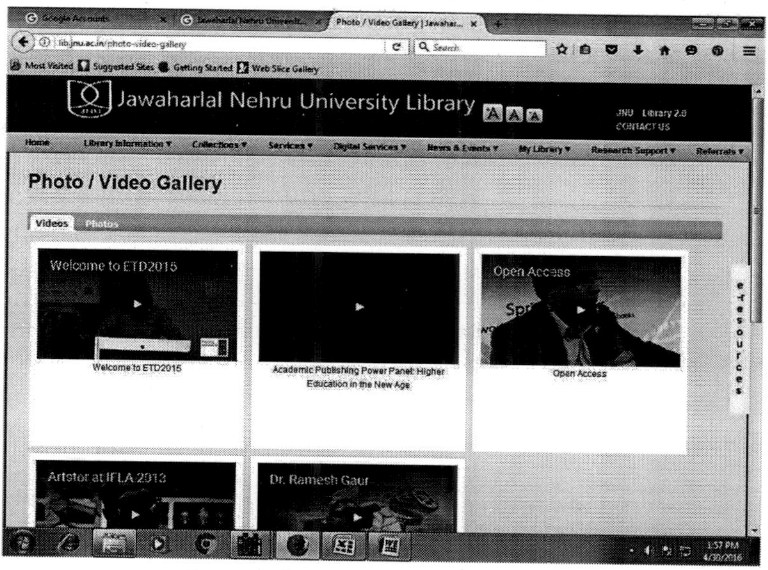

Screenshot 83. Photo gallery of Jawaharlal Nehru University library

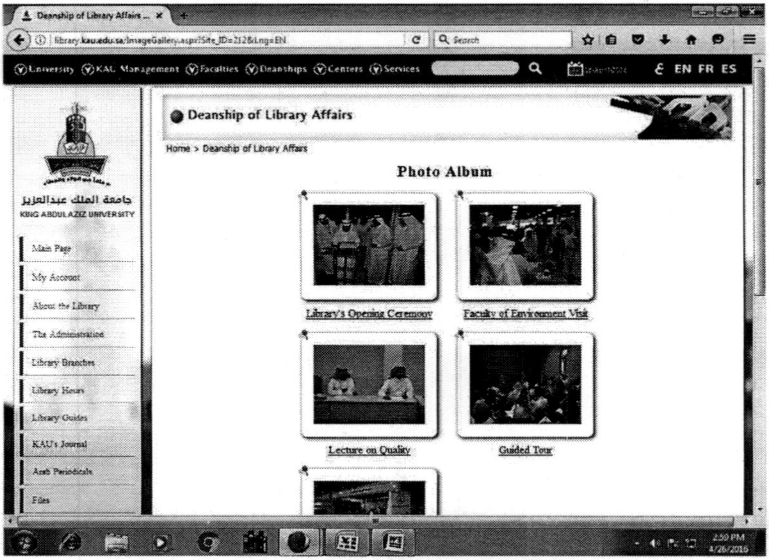

Screenshot 84. Photo gallery of King Abdul Aziz University library

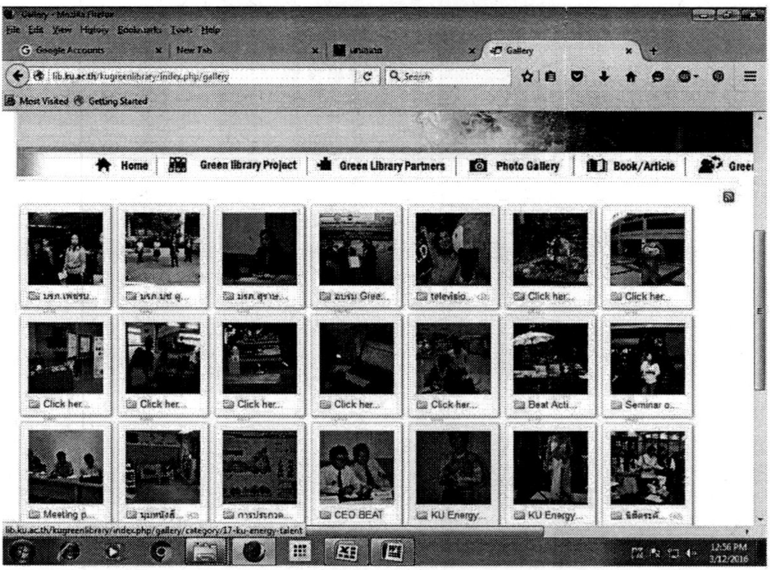

Screenshot 85. Photo gallery of Kesetsart University libary

Text Instructions : This is very simple and basic way of providing information about library rules and regulations, timings, user guides, services and facilities in text html form. University libraries provide video and audio tutorials, pdf, ppts and along with in detail they explain the procedure also to educate patrons. Below is example of University of Nairobi stating rules and regulations of that library.

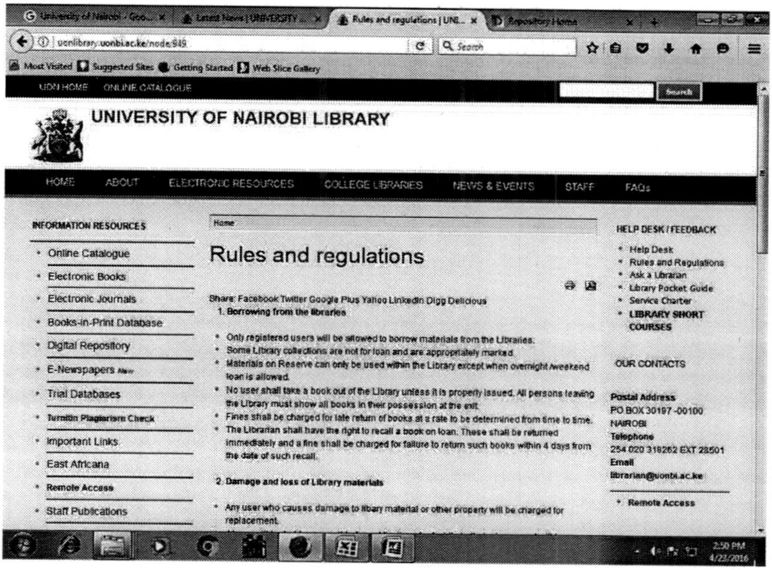

Screenshot 86. Instruction (rules and regulations) of University of Nairobi Library

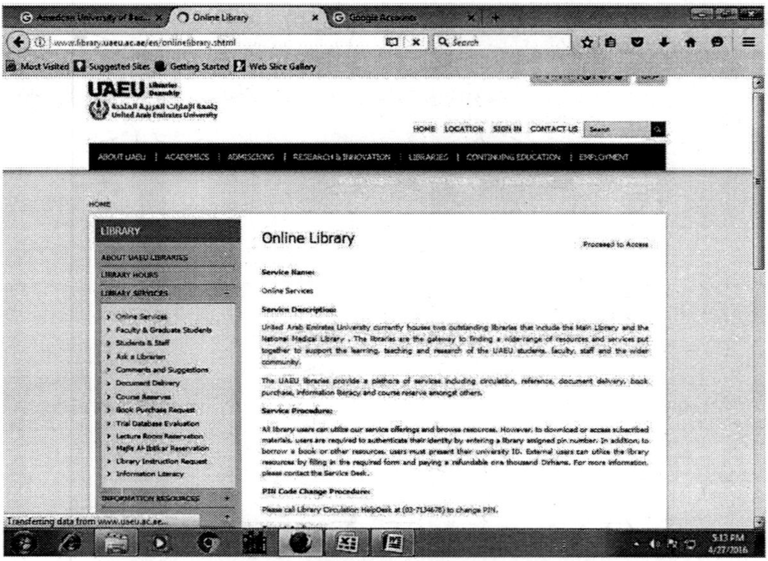

Screenshot 87. Library instructions on United Arab Emirates University library website

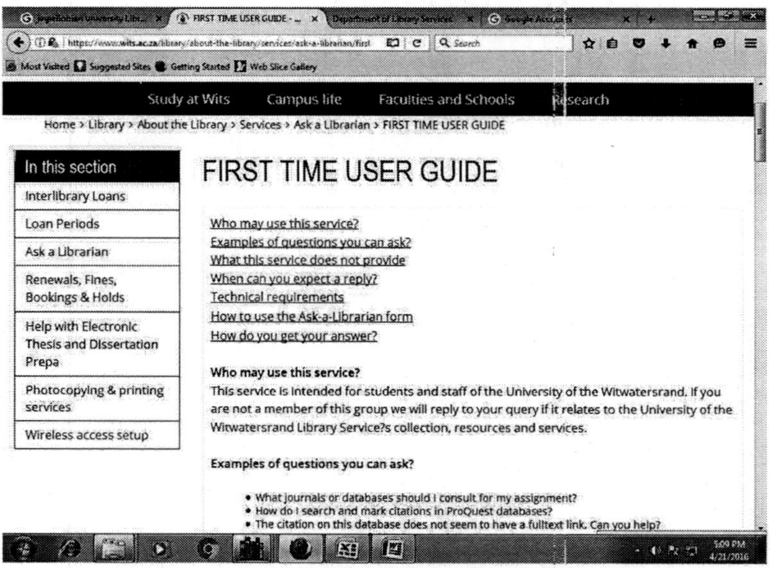

Screenshot 88. Library instructions on the University of Witwatersrand website

REFERENCES

1. Awang, N. (2012). Towards library 2.0: The adoption of web 2.0 Applications in Academic library websites in Malaysia. International Conference on Libraries: Transformation to Humanized Libraries. Kota Bharu.
2. Chan, H. (2010). Murdoch University Library: A Web 2.0 Journey. ALSR 2010 Academic Librarian 2: Singing In The Rain. Hong Kong.
3. Database. (n.d.). Retrieved from Webopedia: http://www.webopedia.com/TERM/D/database.html
4. Dhande, S. (2014). Web 2.0 applications in library. New Delhi: EssEss Publications.
5. Hatua, S. R. Web based library and information services. DRTC Seminar. Institutional repository. (n.d.). Retrieved from https://en.wikipedia.org/wiki/Institutional_repository
6. Joyce. (2013). Top 10 universities using wordpress. Retrieved from https://whatswp.com/top-10-universities-using-wordpress/
7. Morga, J. (2012). The use of Prezi for customer journeys and customer service excellence. 56, pp. 40-42.
8. Price, M., Handley, K., Millar, J., & O'Donovan, B. (2010). Feedback: all that effort, but what is the effect? . Assessment & Evaluation in Higher Education , 35 (3), 277–289.
9. RSS. (n.d.). Retrieved from Wikipedia: https://en.wikipedia.org/wiki/RSS
10. Singley, E. (2013). Academic libraries using WordPress CMS. Retrieved from http://emilysingley.net/academic-libraries-using-wordpress-cms/
11. SlideShare. (n.d.). Retrieved from Wikipedia: https://en.wikipedia.org/wiki/SlideShare
12. Solanki, V., & John, K. (2015). Blog: a tool for online library services. International Journal of Research in Library Science, 1 (1), 45-50.
13. Springshare(2009). (n.d.). LIbGuide Features. Retrieved from Springshare: http://www.springshare.com/libguides/features.html
14. What is a database? (n.d.). Retrieved from http://www.bbc.co.uk/guides/z8yk87h
15. Yang, S. Q. (2009). Subject Guide 2.0: A Dream or Reality? Journal of Library and Information Science , 35 (1), 90–98.

5

Web-based Patron Communication Services Offered By University Libraries: An Overview

WEB-BASED PATRON COMMUNICATION TOOLS

The second cluster was related to services, tools and techniques used for patron education through the web. This third cluster is formed to know which better communication tools are being used by top university libraries in the world. Most of the previous studies are done on social networking sites and web 2.0 technologies covered the uses of these tools in libraries. This cluster contains uses of Facebook, Twitter, email, Tumblr, Stumbleupon, Linkedin, Flickr, Pinterest, iTunes,

Instagram, Delicious, Google+, Foursquare and WhatsApp social communication tools in the selected university libraries. Below are given details along with examples.

Facebook : The use of social networking site/ web 2.0 application Facebook is becoming more popular and widely used in university libraries as percentage of patrons using Facebook is very high and they can easily connect with libraries through Facebook. Building a network of patrons has become very easy because the university has patron database. University libraries are using Facebook for disseminating information, opening hours, notices, new arrivals, online current awareness and reference services, library facilities, updates of events, and to educate patrons. It also helps university to create a discussion forum and collect feedback from patrons, share book reviews, event photos, videos, links, and attract patrons towards library and market library services. Awang, Nor (2012)[1] this application helps to forge relationships among library users.

Screenshot 1. Facebook page of the University of Petroria

Screenshot 2. Facebook page of the Jagiellonion Library

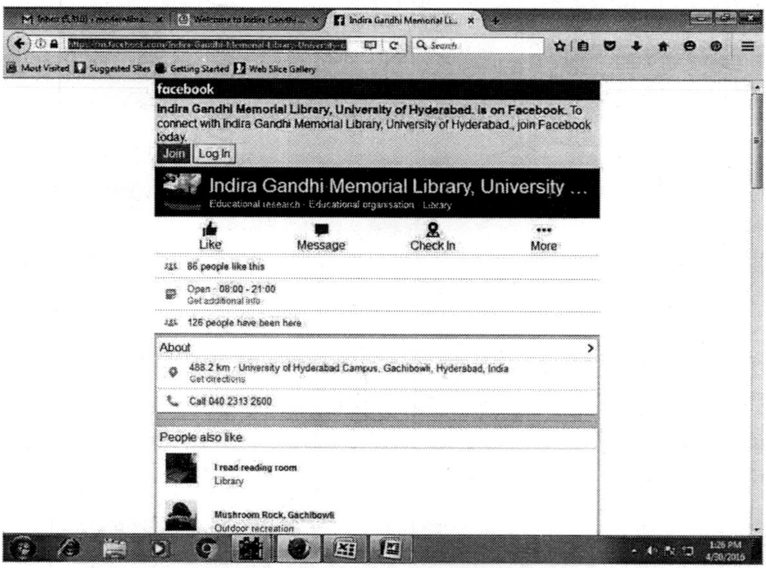

Screenshot 3. Facebook page of University of Hyderabad library

Twitter : Twitter is a real-time information network that connects users to the latest updates, ideas, opinions and news about what patrons find interesting. It allows patrons to re-tweet, reply, like and open the tweet (Awang, Nor, 2012)[1]. As it is a free service to send or receive short messages (max 140 characters) via the web or SMS using mobile phone, libraries can make good use of this service without spending much time or effort to connect with patrons(Milstein, Sarah, 2016)[6]. University libraries use this web platform to send short messages about news and events they organize like readings, lectures and book sales, new arrivals with cover pictures, changes in library hours or links to new interesting stories about literacy, to share videos or information about new as well as existing library services and facilities (Dhande, 2014)[2]. Twitter feeds are broadcasted on the home page of library website or virtual learning environment (Helen Loughran &Carly Miller, 2012)[5]. Different sections of library offers services related to their section on twitter, e.g. about research support or platform, opening hours, archives, exhibitions, notification of upcoming conferences, seminars, workshops, etc.

Screenshot 4. Twitter account of Nanyang Technological University libraries

Screenshot 5. Twitter account of the University of New South Wales library

Screenshot 6. Twitter account of the University of Cambridge library

Screenshot 7. Tweets of the University of Witwatersrand website

Email : Communication plays important role in delivering web based library services. Email is a web based media to provide current awareness services to patrons. Almost all university libraries inform email id of concern department or service staff to the patrons on their website. From a service point of view providing contact details of staff must be available to all in case of emergency service. Patrons can contact staff by email or phone if they need any information or have questions about library services or facilities or want to give feedback. Librarians need to be more prompt to reply the email queries. University libraries have different Google groups for providing CAS to different categories of patron (Hatua, S.)[3]

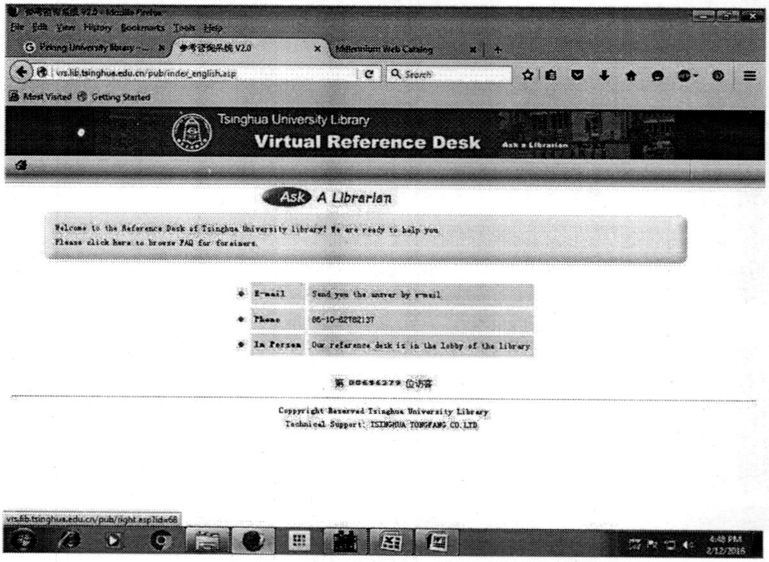

Screenshot 8. Email service of Tsinghua University library

Tumblr : Tumblr is a blogging platform and can extend the virtual reach of a library website and, services by sharing archival resources, digital collections, books, and special event notices. It can increase the diversity of the audience accessing these university resources via social media accounts. To post pictures of library infrastructure, different sections this tool is used in many university libraries. It helps external audiences to discover library collections and communicate with library representatives on the other side, it helps libraries to publicize services and resources and harness the power of social media to connect patrons to collections, people, and resource. Recently since 2014 university libraries are started using this platform (Welch, 2014)[10].

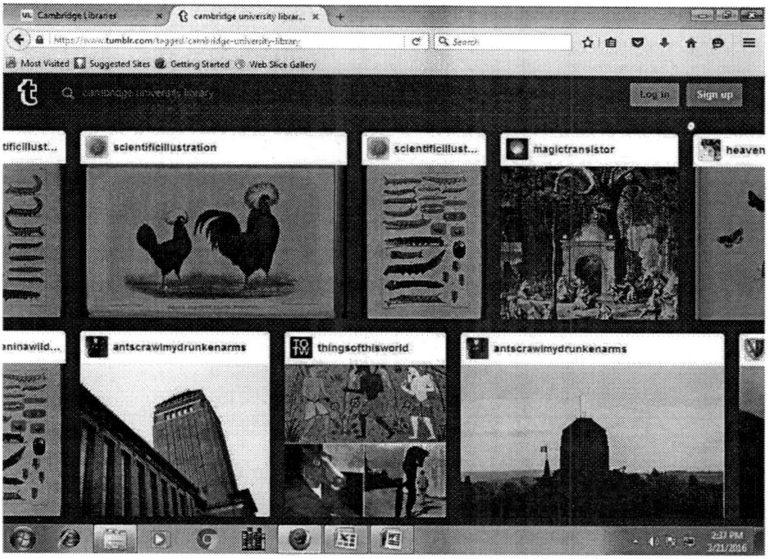

Screenshot 9. Tumblr account of the Cambridge University library

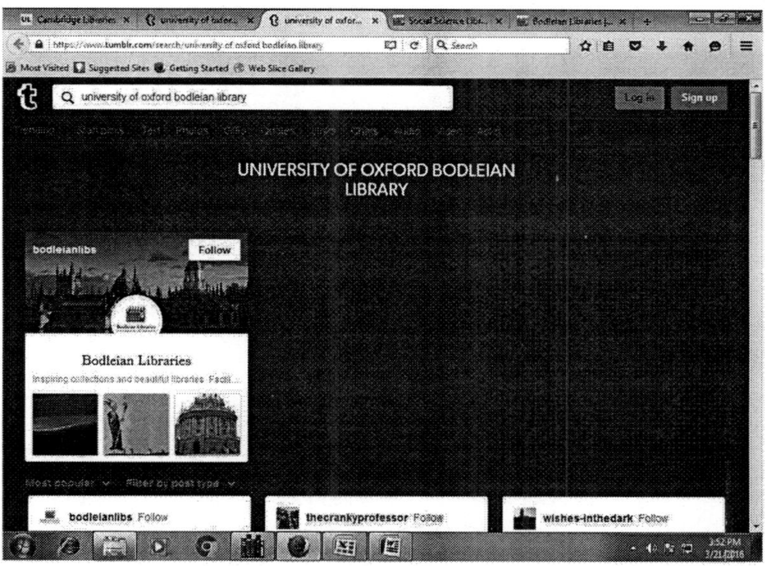

Screenshot 10. Tumblr account of the University of Oxford library

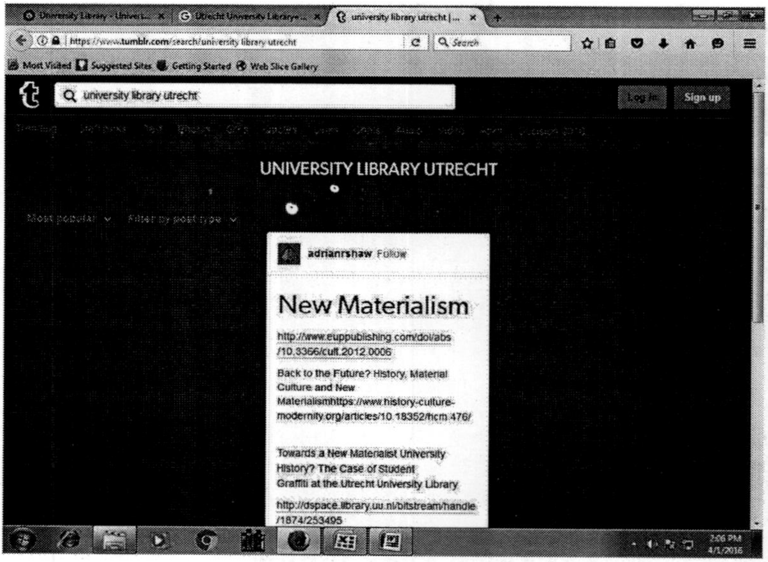

Screenshot 11. Tumblr account of the University of Utrecht library

Stumbleupon : StumbleUpon is a discovery engine that finds and recommends web content to its users[8]. It's a powerful way to discover our favorite web content like web pages, photos and videos that are personalized to their tastes and interests using peer-sourcing and social-networking principles (Wikipedia)[7] University libraries are using this platform to share photos, videos, article, quotes, news, location maps, resources, websites, blog, news-letters etc. to rate them and make them best content to refer by the world and patrons.

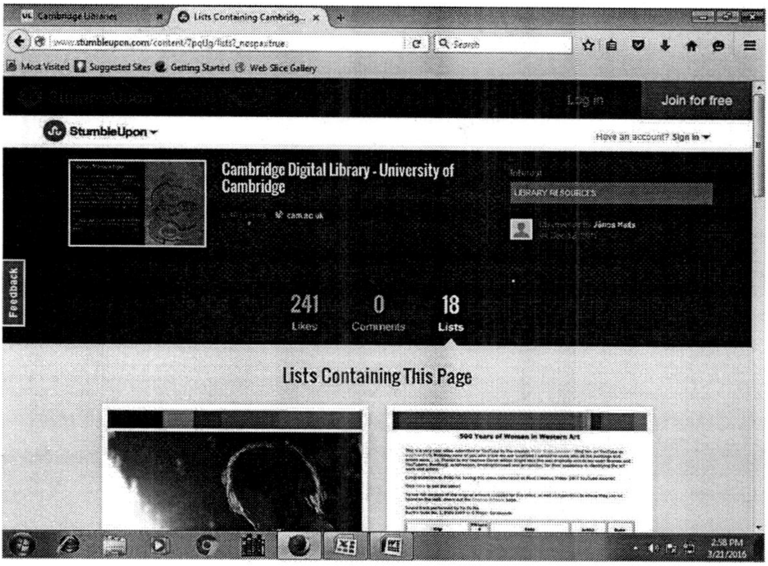

Screenshot 12. Stumbleupon account of the Cambridge University digital library

Linkedin : LinkedIn is the world's largest professional network with more than 433 million members in 200 countries and territories around the globe launched in 2003. The main mission of LinkedIn is to connect people to make them more productive and successful. University library staff creates their professional profile on LinkedIn and communicates their activities and connects with professional globally. Also, they connect with their staff and students. Many university libraries created groups on LinkedIn.

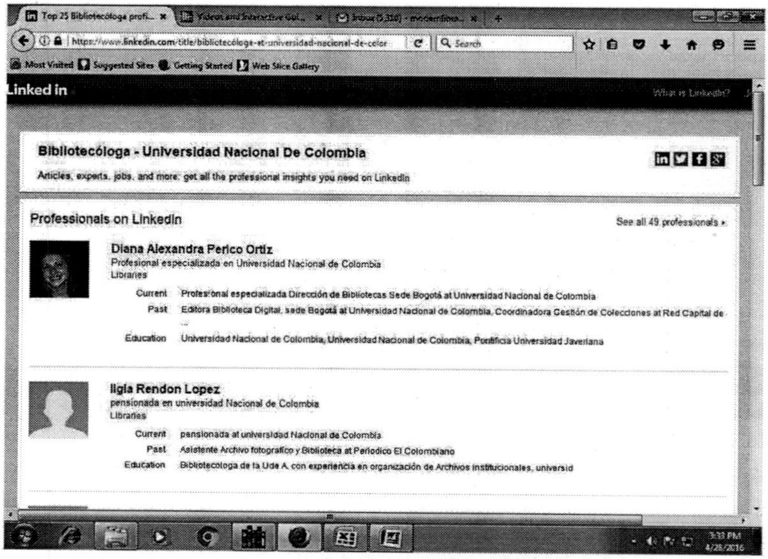

Screenshot 13. Linkedin profile of library staff of Colombia University

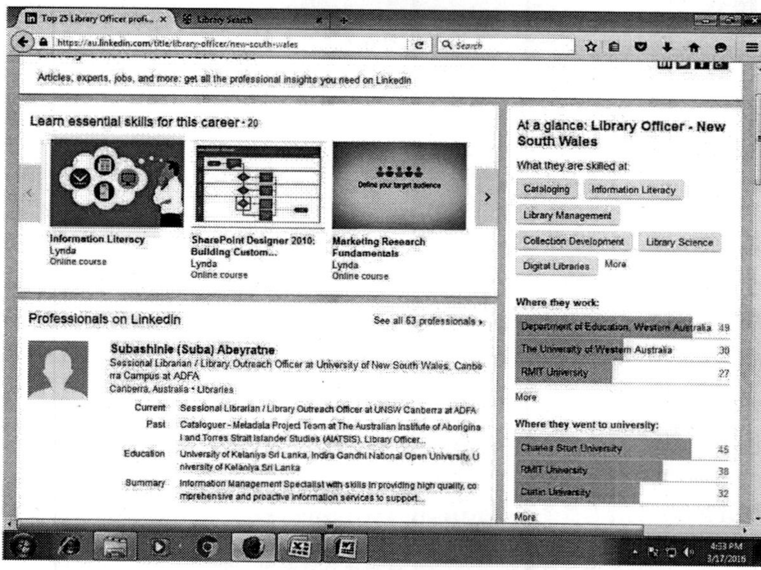

Screenshot 14. Linkedin profiles of library staff of University of New South Wales

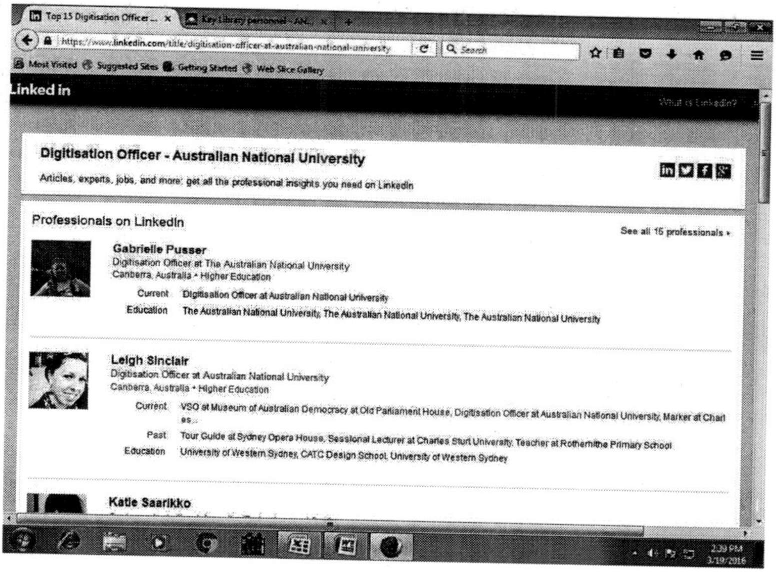

Screenshot 15. Linkedin profiles of libray professionals of the Australian National University

Flickr : University libraries are using Flickr to market their services and upload pictures of different sections and surroundings of libraries to demonstrate library collection and resources. Sometimes Flickr tags publicly held photography too. Flickr highlights library current events, historical photos of libraries and its collection and displays visual library visit or tour, etc. Libraries can get feedback or comments too on Flickr. In below Cambridge university Flickr showing reading room and different sections of library, university of West Indies library and the Monash university library uploaded pictures of events they organized and Bodleian libraries uploaded its archive of rare collection of manuscripts.

Screenshot 16. Flickr account of Cambridge University library

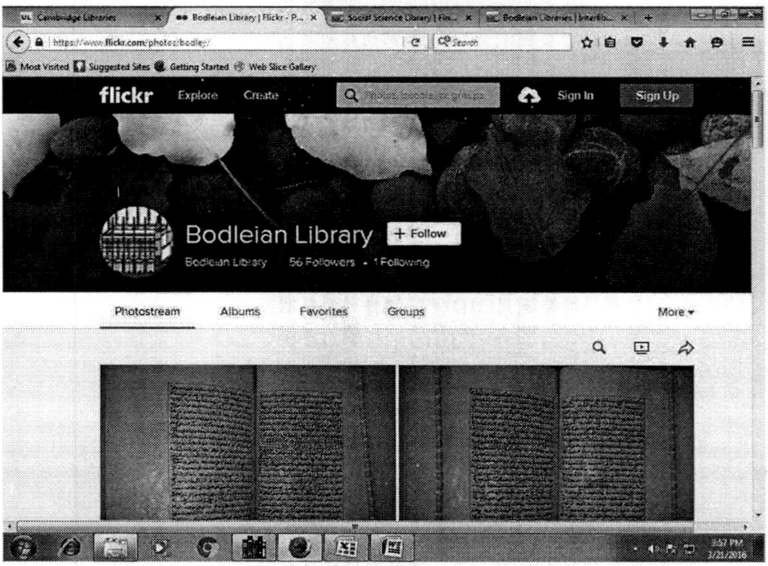

Screenshot 17. Flickr account of University of Oxford library

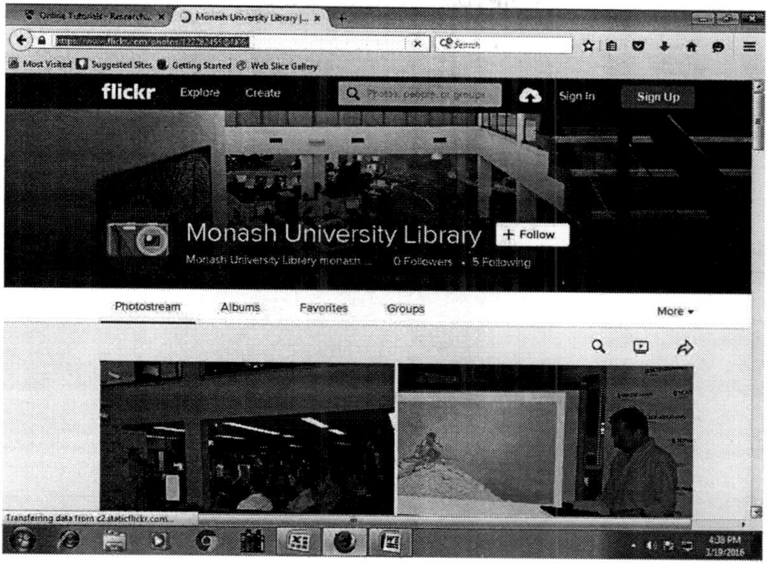

Screenshot 18. Flick account of Monash University library

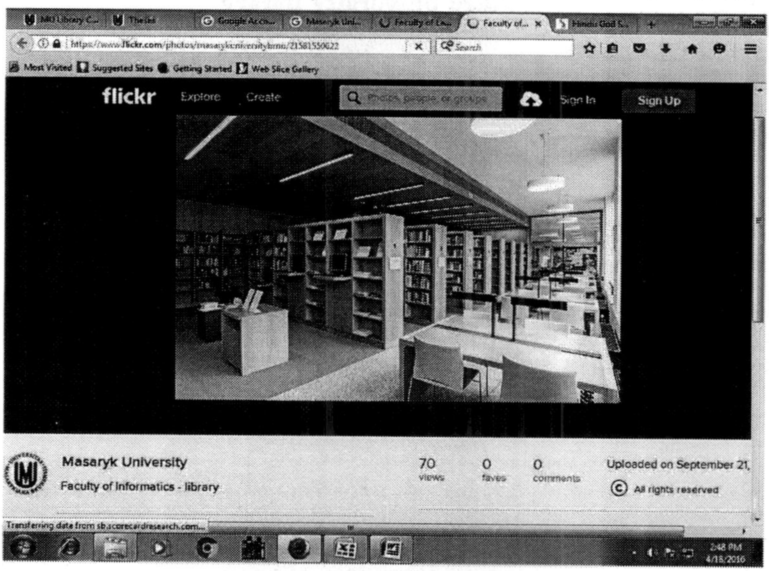

Screenshot 19. Flickr account of the Masaryk University library

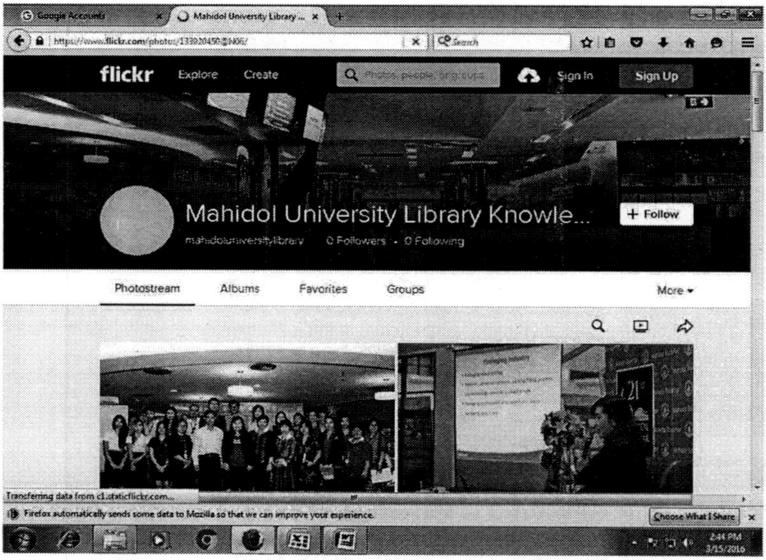

Screenshot 20. Flickr account of the Mahidol University library

Pinterest : It is a pin-board style photo sharing website that gives the libraries an opportunity to create images collection depending on the theme like library events, special collection, library infrastructure photos, etc. It is one of the web based marketing service used by top university libraries to showcase their services and collection for their users.

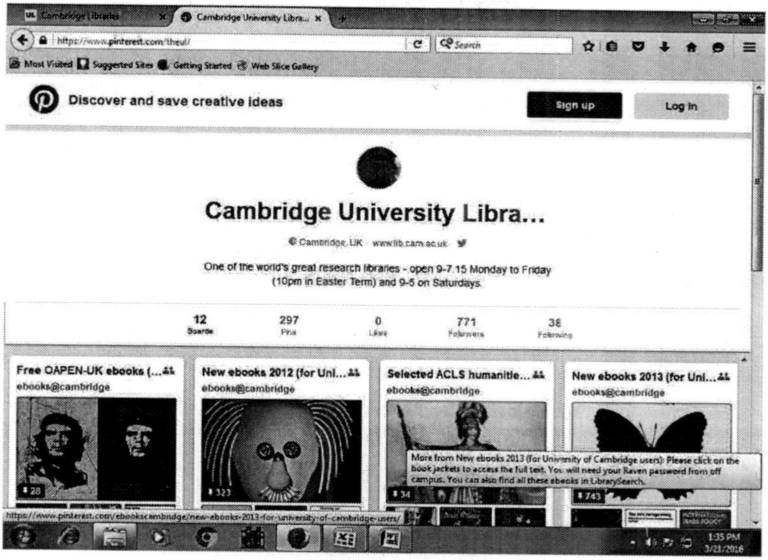

Screenshot 21. Pinterest account of the Cambridge University library

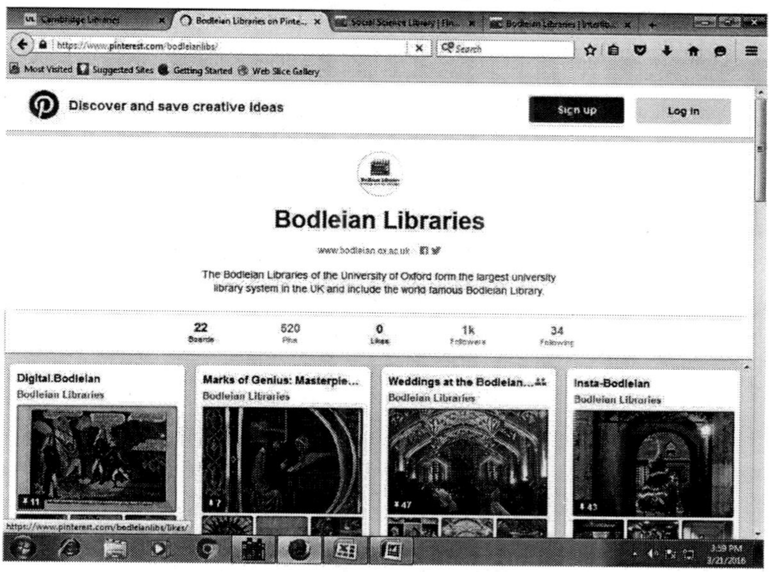

Screenshot 22. Pinterest account of the Bodleian libraries of Oxford University

iTunes : TheiTune is designed as a service for university libraries to organize, manage their audio, videos and PDF content, pictures, screenshots, lessons, audio books and make it available easily and quickly to their users. It is an innovative way to engage and empower patrons to accommodate the digital lifestyle and personal learning needs. Patrons can listen and view the audio or video tutorials and other audio learning material on their computer, iPod or smart phones[14]. Library staff shares audio or video tutorial they prepared to train and to give instructions to patrons, services and collection to patrons to learn on their own and gets review on them. For example Bodleian libraries which shares free digital recordings, audio tour of the library, events, exhibitions and other highlights throughout the year. University of Cambridge and University of Cape Town libraries provides library services and introductory video on iTunes.

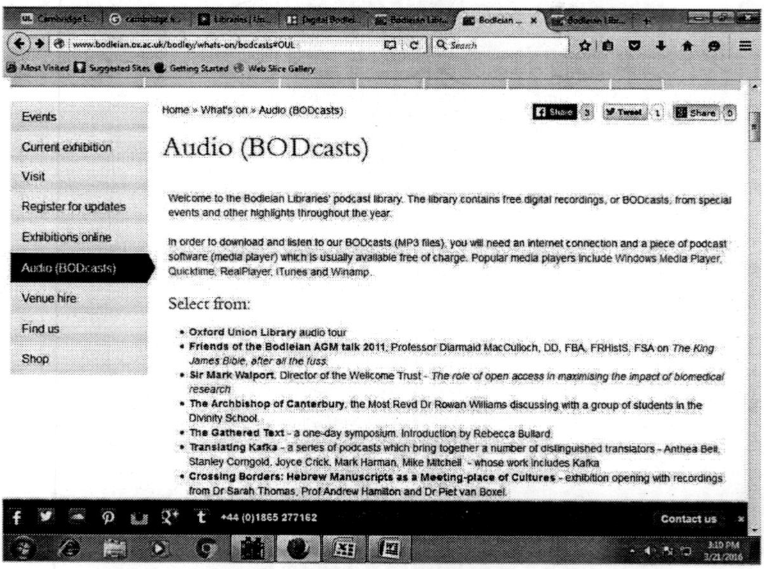

Screenshot 23. Use of iTunes for audio files at Oxford University library

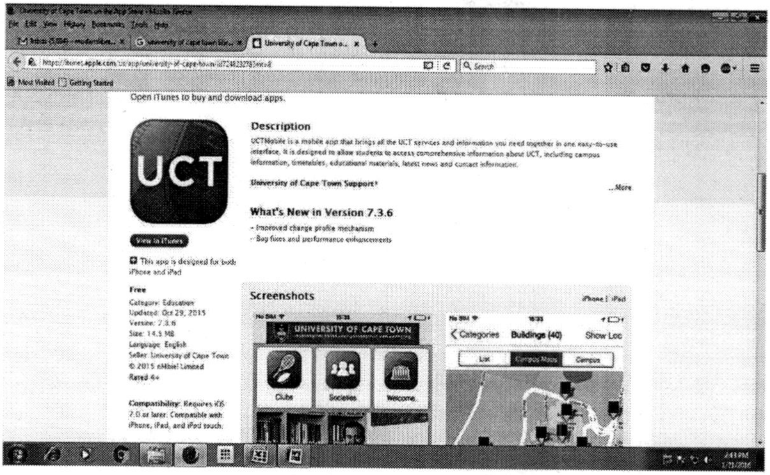

Screenshot 24. Use of iTunes at University of Cape Town library

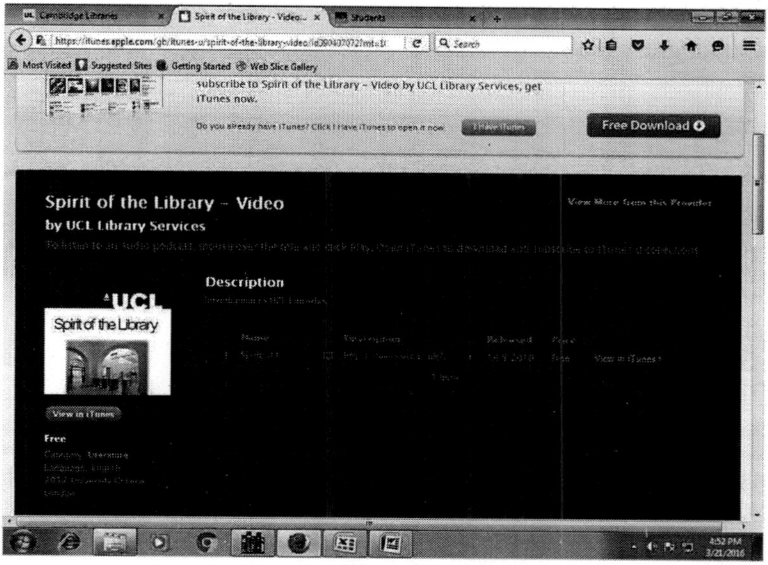

Screenshot 25. Use of iTune for audio files at University College London library

Instagram : It is a simple photo application free of cost allows libraries to document and share their photos. This application launched in 2010 to make taking mobile photos in a simple, fast and beautiful way to social network(Tekulve & Kelly, 2013)9. University libraries use this application to showcase upcoming events, activities, success stories and outreach to patrons.

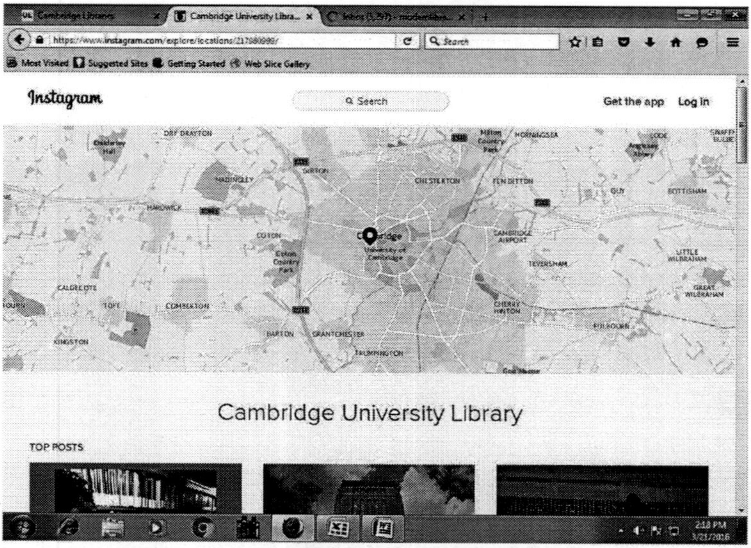

Screenshot 26. Cambridge University library on Instagram

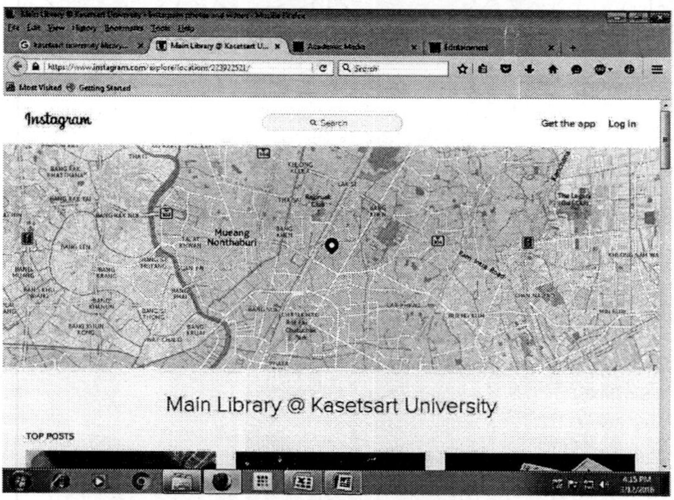

Screenshot 27. Kasetsart University library on Instagram

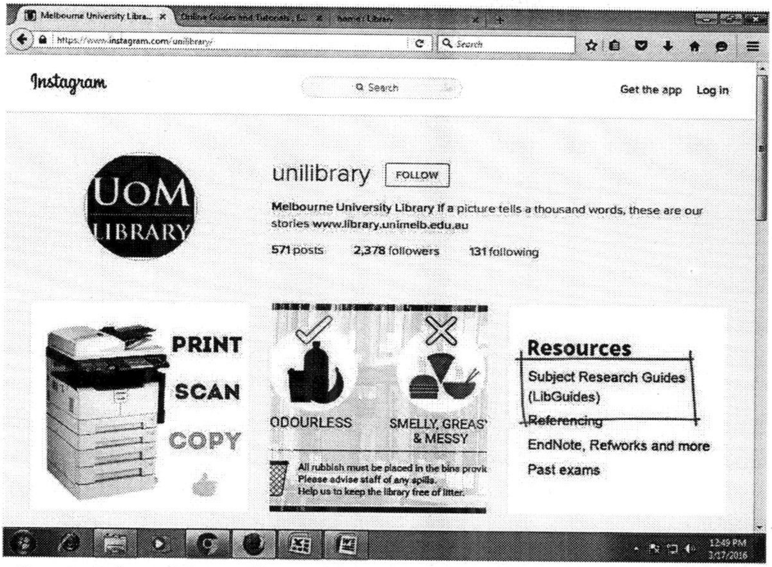

Screenshot 28. Melbourne University library on Instagram

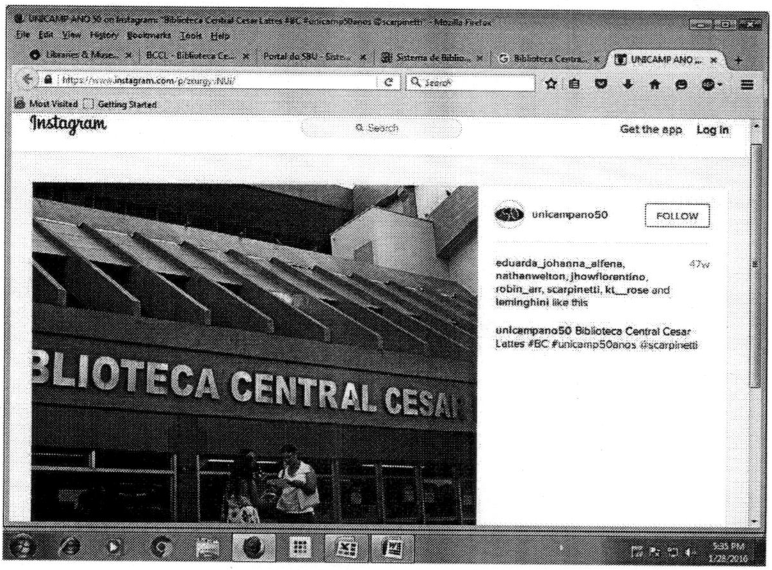

Screenshot 29. Central Library of Universidade Estadual de Campinas on Instagram

Delicious : It is widely used social bookmarking tool on the web. A university library uses this tool to identify, classify and share useful sites. Libraries can make their online resources accessible to patrons using this delicious platform.

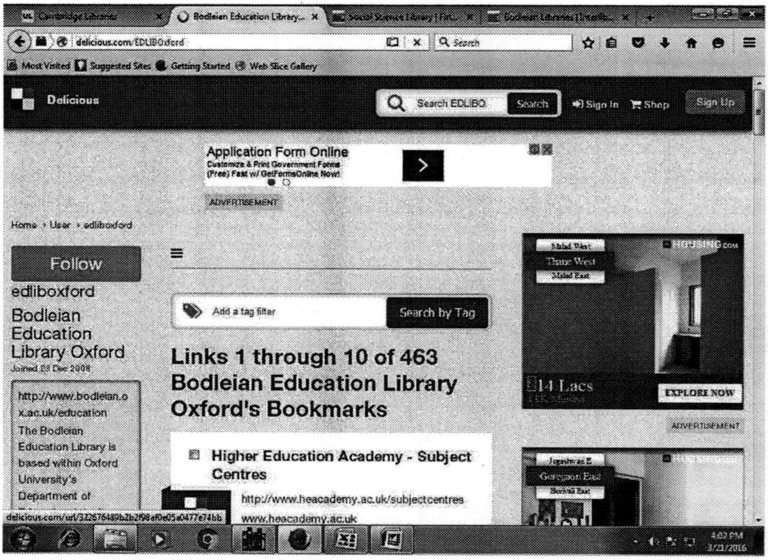

Screenshot 30. Delicious account of the Oxford University library

Google+ : Google+ offers some interesting functionality for sharing and connecting with users and a broader community like Facebook and Twitter. Many university libraries in the world are very active and actively engaging their patrons. Libraries post interesting articles on books and technology, events and refer back to the library (Jackson, A)[4].

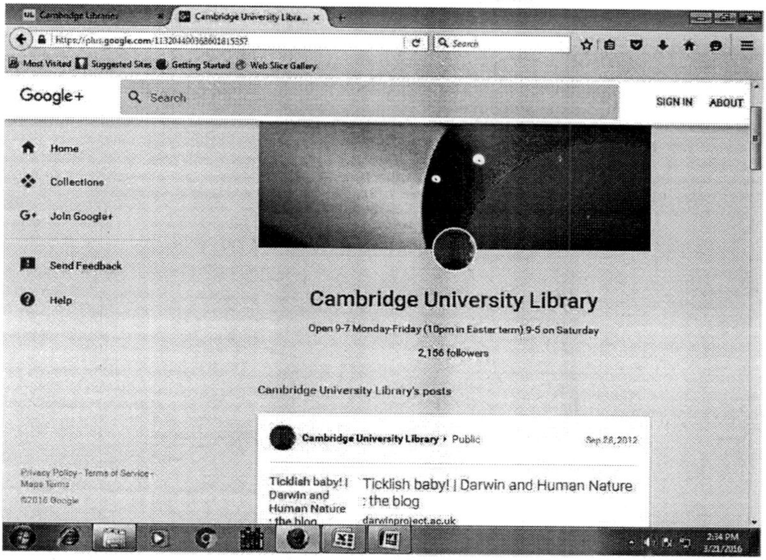

Screenshot 31. Google+ account of Cambridge University library

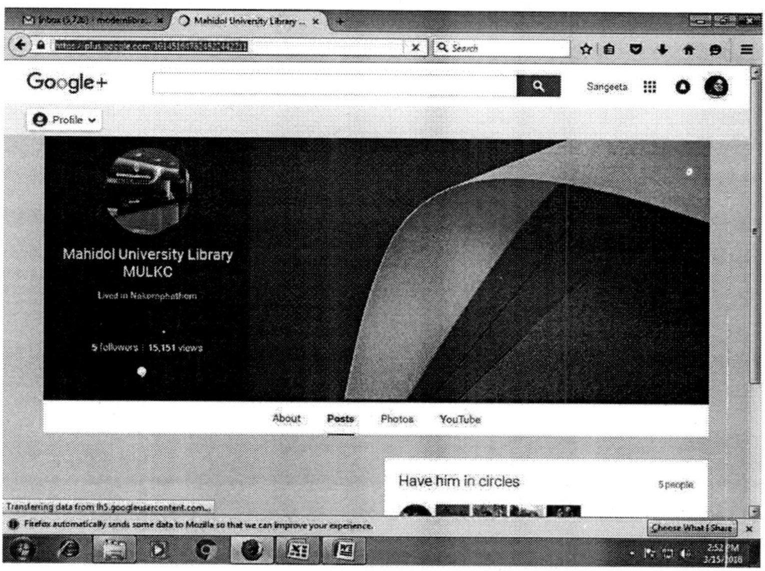

Screenshot 32. Google+ account of the Mahidol University library

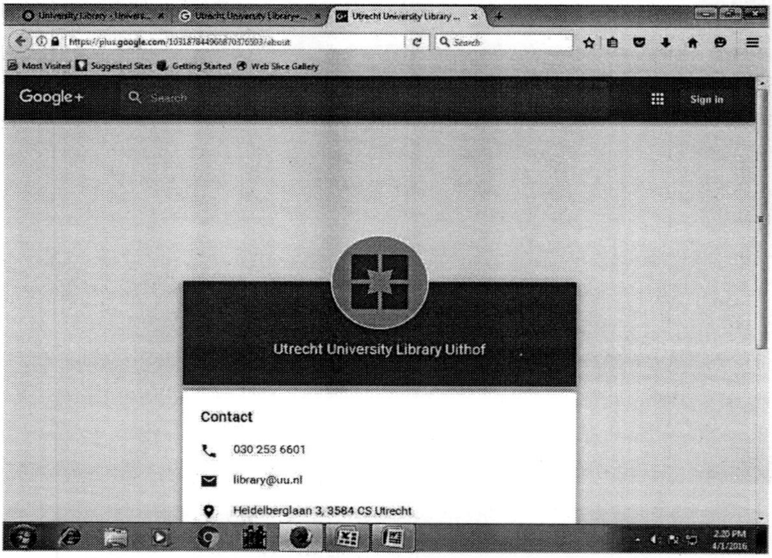

Screenshot 33. Google+ account of the Utretch University library

Foursquare : Foursquare is a mobile application for local search and places discovery within the city. University libraries or academic institutes are using this application to specify or highlight their location so that people will able to locate this place. Foursquare locates university libraries with a Google map of library location.

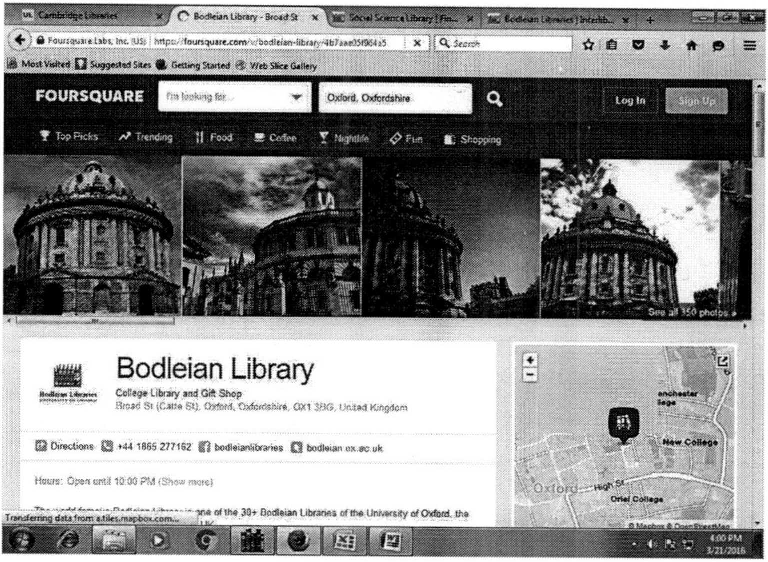

Screenshot 34. Foursquare account of University of Oxford library

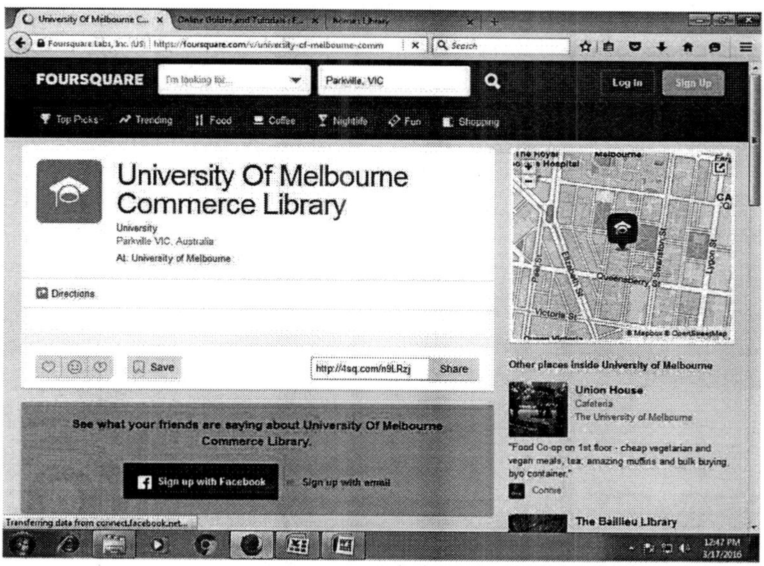

Screenshot 35. Foursquare account of the University of Melbourne library

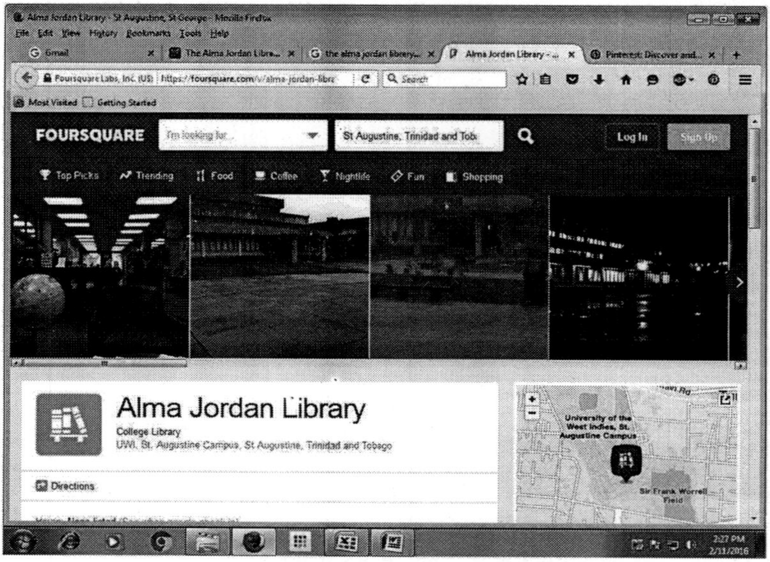

Screenshot 36. Foursquare account of the Alma Jordan Library of University of West Indies

WhatsApp : WhatsApp is most popular, widely used messaging application for mobiles. Few libraries started providing mobile services through whatsapp too. The whatsapp contact number is given on the contact page of the library. Readers can reach them by messaging on this whatsapp. The Tej Aviv University and Hebrew University of Jerusalem provides this service.

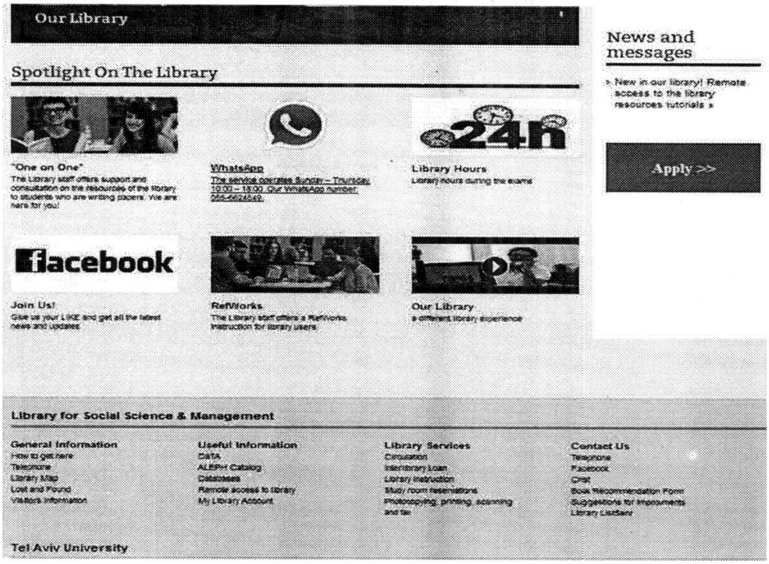

Screenshot 37. Use of Whatsapp at Tel Aviv University library

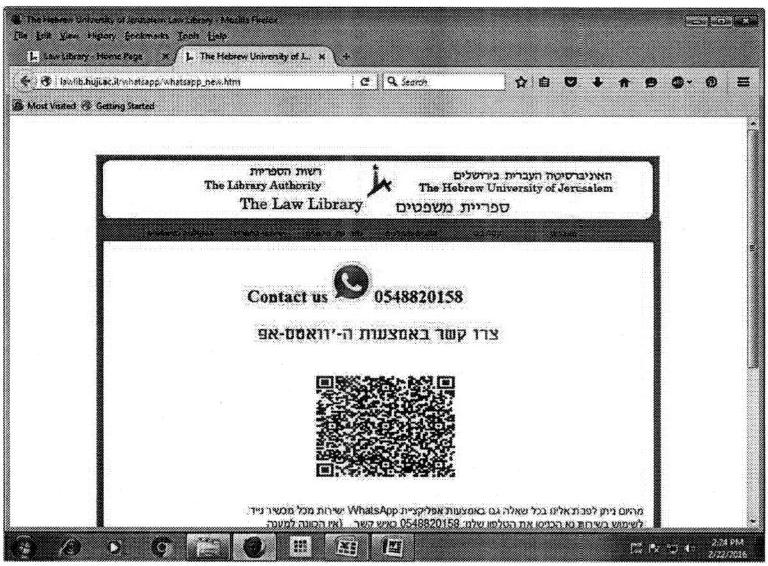

Screenshot 38. Use of Whatsapp at the Hebrew University of Jerusalem

REFERENCES

1. Awang, N. (2012). Towards library 2.0: The adoption of web 2.0 Applications inacademic library websites in Malaysia. International Conference on Libraries: Transformation to Humanized Libraries. Kota Bharu.
2. Dhande, S. (2014). Web 2.0 applications in library. New Delhi: EssEss Publications.
3. Hatua, S. R. Web based library and information services. DRTC Seminar. Institutional repository. (n.d.). Retrieved from https://en.wikipedia.org/wiki/Institutional_repository
4. Jackson, A. (n.d.). How are libraries making use of Google+? Retrieved from http://anjackson.net/zombse/062013%20Libraries%20&%20Information%20Science/static/questions/370.html
5. Loughran, H., & Miller, C. (2012). Libraries and Learning Innovation and the use of Twitter. SCONUL Focus, 56, p. 43.
6. Milstein, S. (2009). Twitter for Libraries (and Librarians). Computers in libraries, 29 (5).
7. Stumbleupon. (n.d.). Retrieved from Wikipedia: https://en.wikipedia.org/wiki/StumbleUpon
8. Stumbleupon. (n.d.). Retrieved from itunes: https://itunes.apple.com/us/app/stumbleupon/id386244833?mt=8
9. Tekulve, N., & Kelly, K. (2013). Worth 1,000 Words: Using Instagram to Engage Library Users. Brick and Click Libraries Symposium Proceedings.
10. Welch, A. (2014). Tumblr: Extending the Reach of Library Websites. Computers inlibraries, 34 (7).

6

Web-based Publishing Platform for Patrons Offered by University Libraries : An Overview

WEB-BASED PUBLISING PLATFORM FOR PATRONS

The fourth cluster is related to library services for the researchers and writers in publishing their work. Time to time readers visits libraries for finding various resources related to their research area. New writers frequently ask information about where to publish, how to write and publish articles and old writers ask about impact factor journals, plagiarism check softwares, referencing and writing styles for articles, patents and citation tools, etc.

This cluster has covered main important web based services universities initiated to support research writers.

Open Access Initiatives : Open Access (OA) is free, immediate, permanent online access to the full text of research articles for anyone, web wide (Roohie, Sehdeep, 2013)[1]. Open access helps to ensure long-term access to scholarly articles. According to 'Budapest Open Access Initiative' (BOAI) the concept of Open Access refers to "World-wide electronic distribution of the peer-reviewed journal literature, completely free and unrestricted access to it by all scientists, scholars, teachers, students, and other curious minds." Open-access literature is digital, online, free of charge, and free of most copyright and licensing restrictions. Open access contents are not restricted only to peer-reviewed research articles, but they can be in any formats from texts and data to software, audio, video, and multi-media. (Suber, P, 2010)[2].

In the beginning years of the 21st Century, scholarly communities got engaged with the global OA movements for opening up scholarly resources, more particularly research literature, with worldwide researchers' communities without any access fee or subscription cost. (Roohie, Sehdeep, 2013)[1] The first Open Access repository was launched in the year 1991 named arXiv.org which helped researchers in self-archiving their preprints of scientific papers in various science and technology fields (Unesco)[2]. In the similar way slowly all universities started practicing and using the same technology to shift from the traditional way of scholarly communication to a revolutionary way of open access by allowing researchers to upload scientific output in Institutional repository. It is an initiative towards sustainable development of institutional scholarly output. After decades also these IRs guarantees its access.

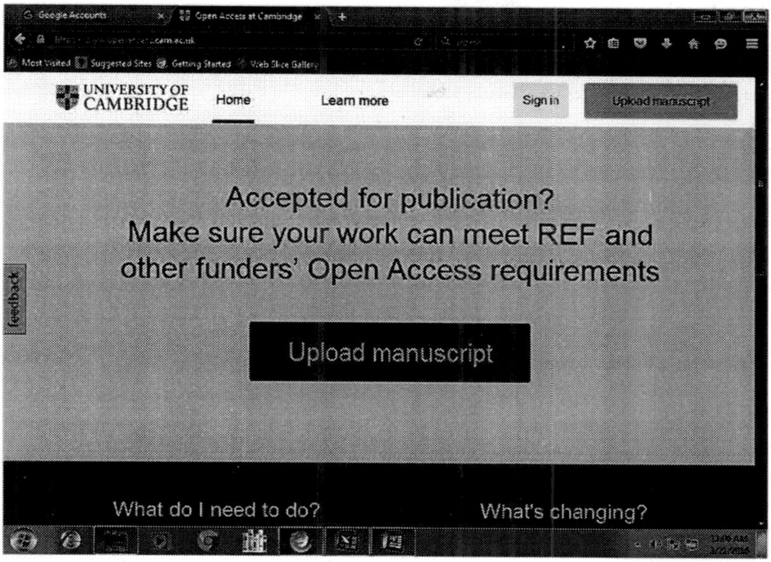

Screenshot 1. OAI at Cambridge University library

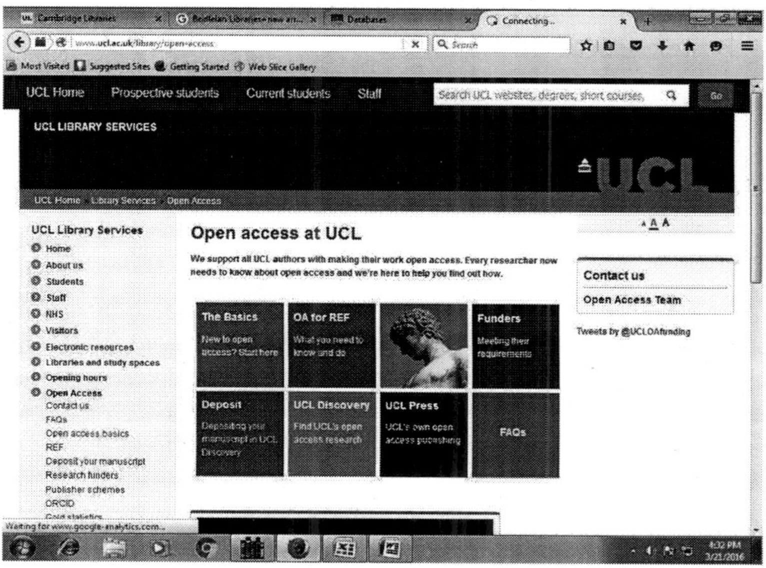

Screenshot 2. OAI at University College of London library

Screenshot 3. OAI at University of Witwatersrand library

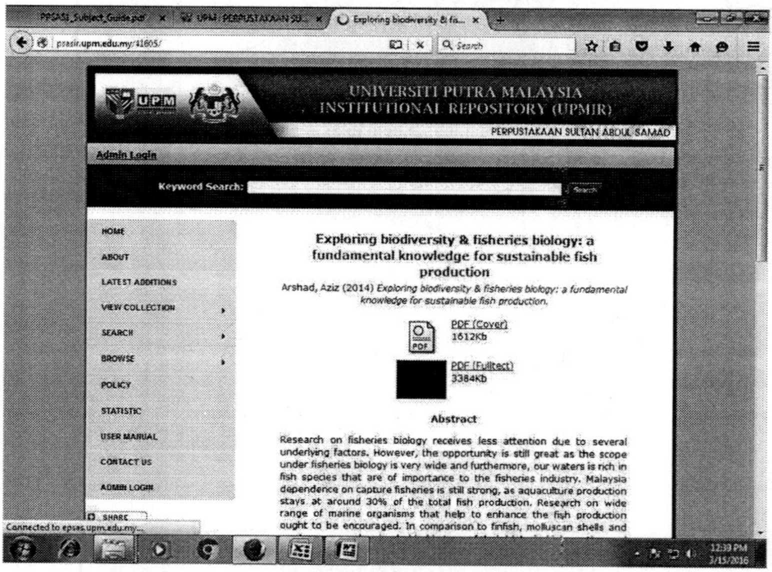

Screenshot 4. OAI at Universiti Putra Malaysia library

Platform for authors and journals : Researchers and patrons are publishing their research work at various level and files patents too. In institutional repository universities tries to add all the resources and even gives facility to upload work individually to enrich the IR. Libraries provide research support to all patrons starting from how to write research papers, how to select impact factor journals, citations, writing style formats, plagiarism, etc. To encourage and create writing skills among the student university libraries are playing major roles. Many libraries offer a platform like online newsletter, book review section, journals, magazines, bulletins, in which they invite articles from the patrons/ researchers/readers.

Below are screen shots of few examples of such platforms offered by sample university libraries.

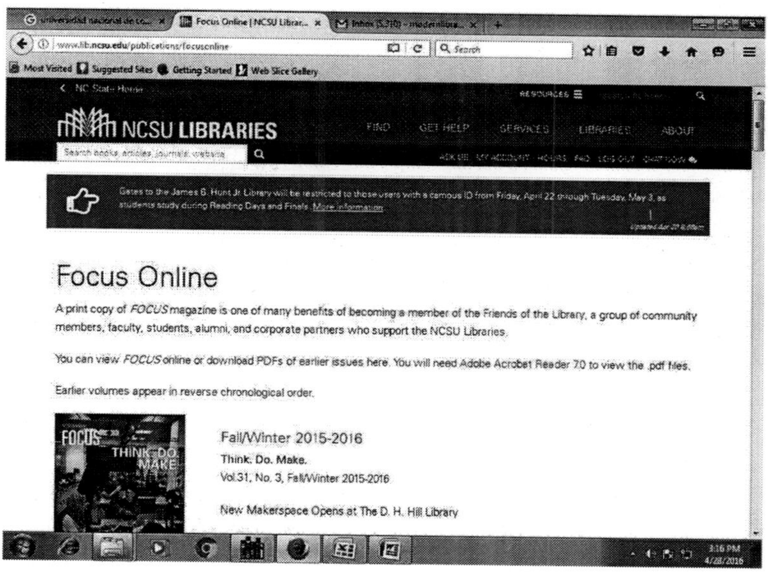

Screenshot 5. NCSU publishes an online magazine Focus for patrons

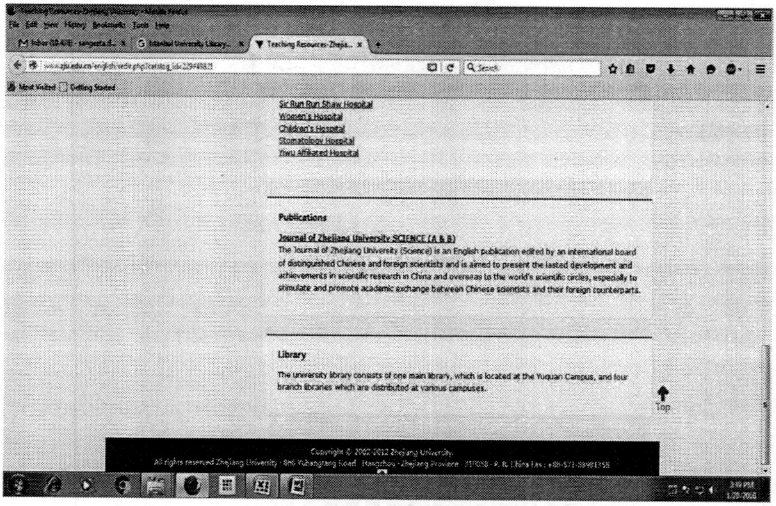

Screenshot 6. Zhejiang University library publishes journal of Science

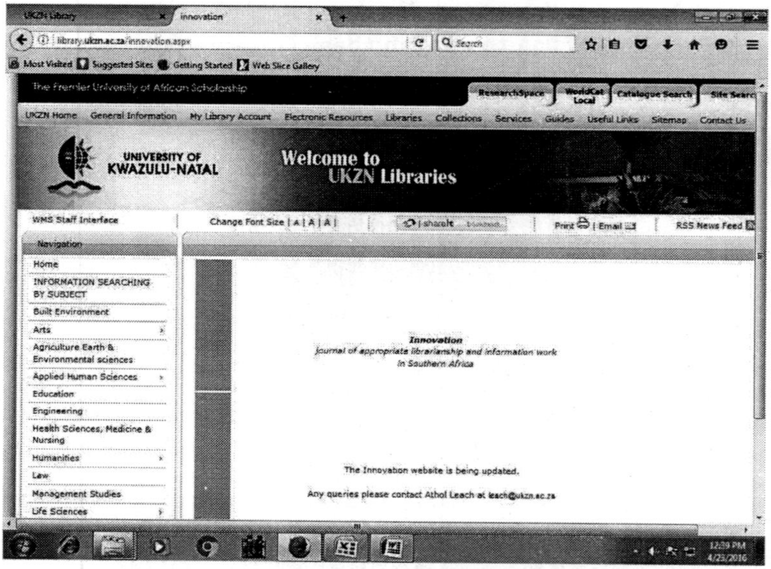

Screenshot 7. University of Kwazulu Natal library publishes journal Innovation

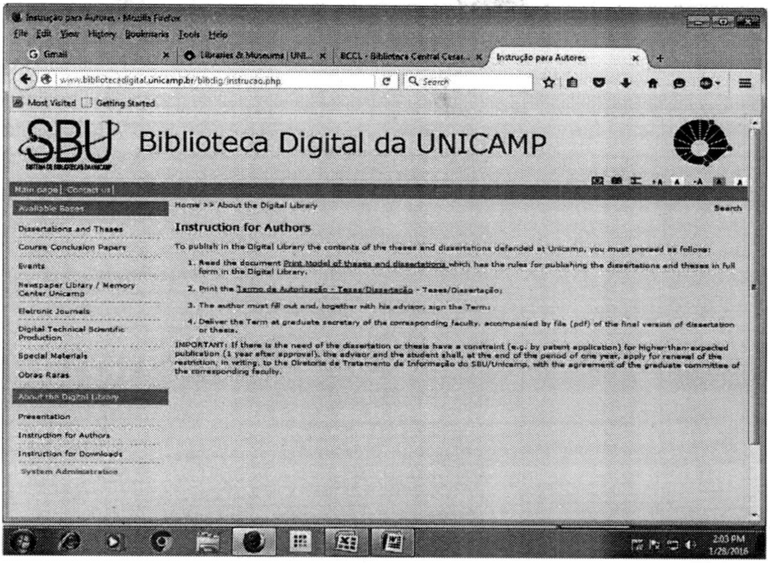

Screenshot 8. Universidade Estadual de Campinas library provides platform to publish thesis and dissertations

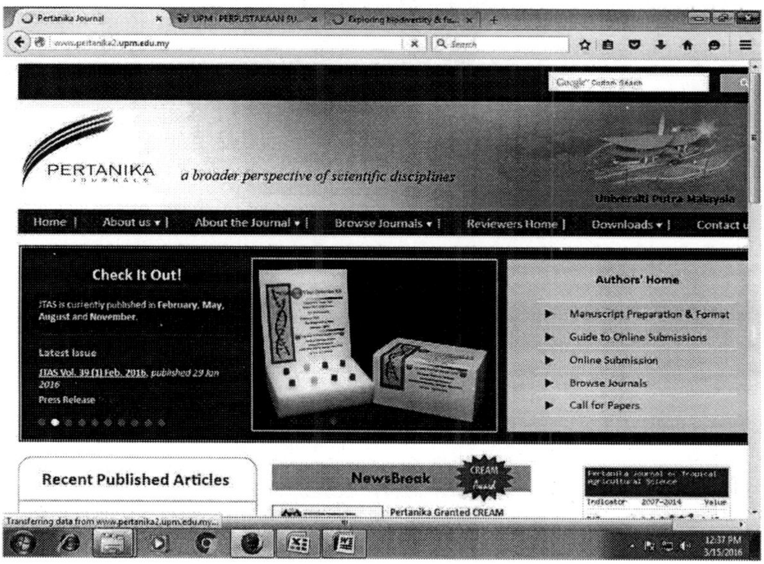

Screenshot 9. University of Putra Malaysia publishes journal Pertanika

University Records management : Many university libraries are managing university records and have a separate digitization unit where they scan all important university documents and preserves as archives. Records are one of the University's most valuable assets. Records support decision-making, demonstrate compliance and document the history of the University (Harvard University). University records are vital University assets requires careful management. Creating and managing records contribute to greater business efficiency, promotes compliance, protects the University from legal risk, and preserves its history. University records include all forms of recorded information, regardless of physical characteristics or a format that are created, received, recorded, or legally filed in the course of University business[11].

University records have historical value and therefore they are transferred to university archives to preserve them for longer time. Their records can be annual reports, event photos, guest speeches, videos of important programs, university projects, test community, maps, projects, lectures, audio, video files, interviews, newsletters, administrative documents, historical documents, datasets, and course notes, learning objects, conference proceedings or other special and rare collection. Management and maintenance of university records are part of Institutional repository. Access to some important documents is restricted.

Below are screen shot of selected Institutional Repositories of university records.

Screenshot 10. Seoul National University collection maintained by the library

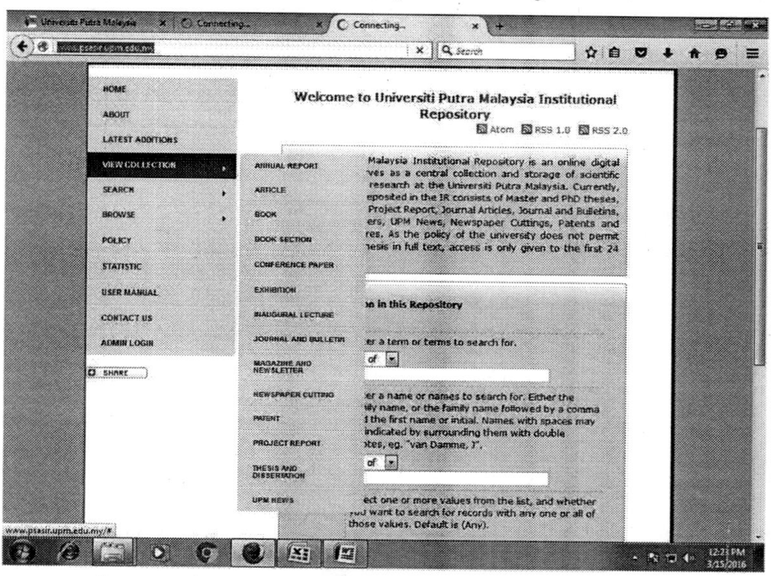

Screenshot 11. IR of Universiti Putra Malaysia

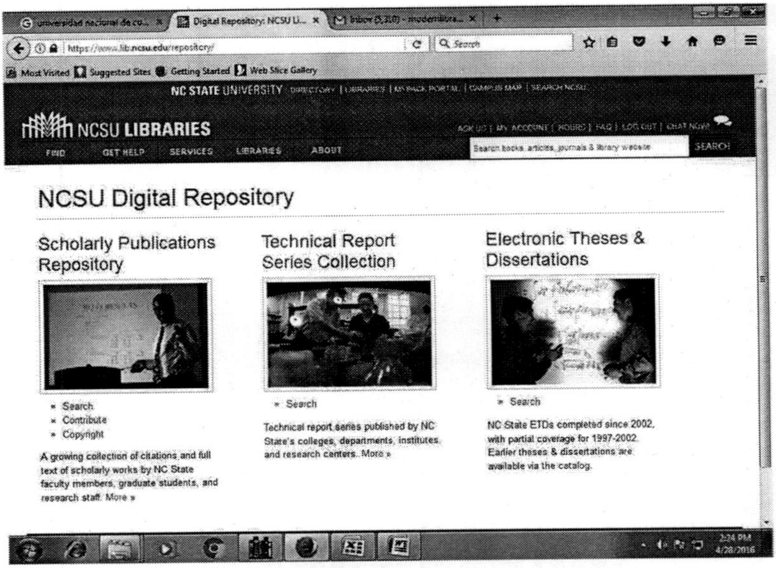

Screenshot 12. NCSU Digital repository managed by the library

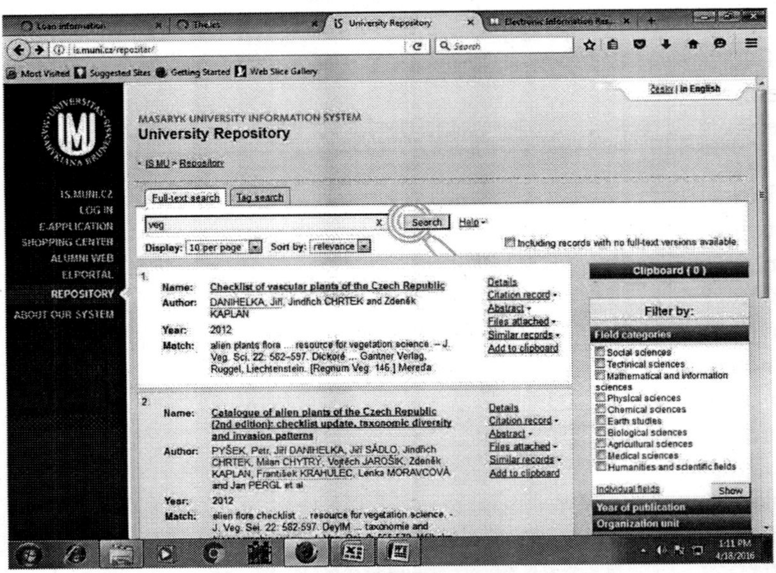

Screenshot 13. Repository of Masaryk University

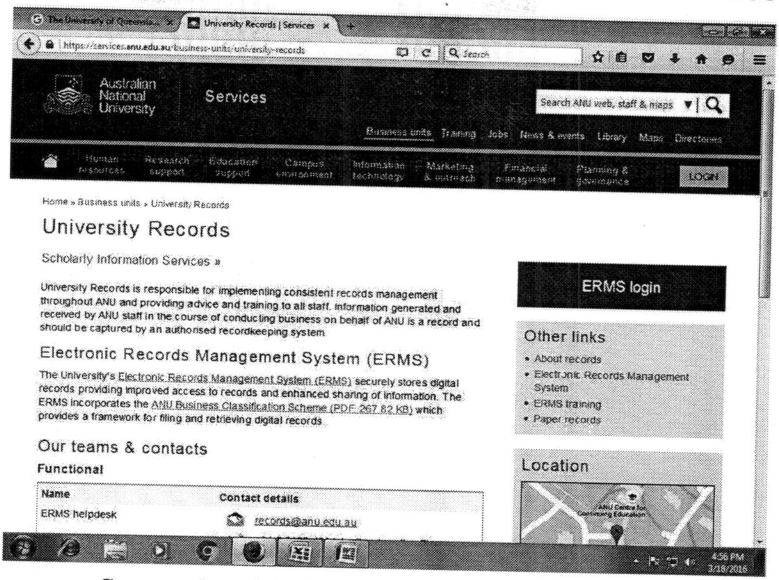

Screenshot 14. Austalian National University electronic records management system

Anti-plagiarism Software Access/ Help : Because of ICT, information explosion, mobile technology, web technologies and open access initiative in academic and research community plagiarism (cutting and pasting a work of unreferenced texts)has become new problem. Many students found plagiarizing in their assessment, projects, publication and even thesis. It is an intentional or unintentional attempt, but it is becoming a serious issue in academic institutions as it is an offense. It can destroy the reputation and profession of students as well as institutes and therefore universities are under pressure to tackle this problem. To solve this problem universities understood that just monitoring, policing the plagiarism is not enough, but to educate students and teacher to use technology, e.g. softwares like Turnitin, iThenticate software to avoid plagiarism and also teach them academic referencing norms e.g. EndNote reference manager software. Researchers and students get benefited if all this important information and software made available online. Many top university libraries are providing all this information related to plagiarism to their patrons on the website. They provide video tutorials, text instructions, demonstrations, guides to educate patron.

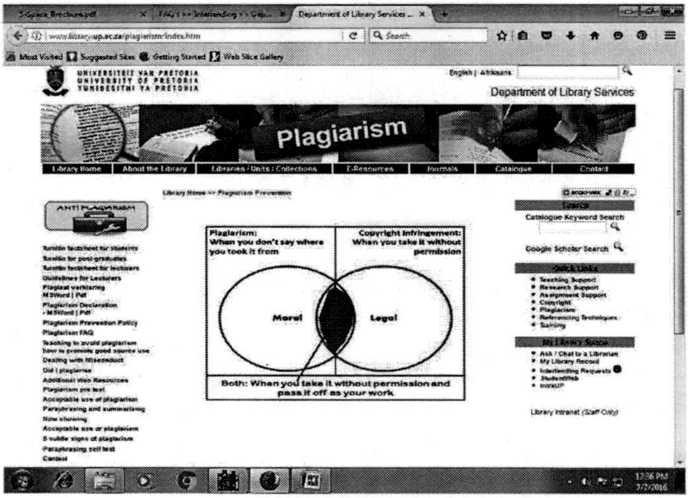

Screenshot 15. Plagiarism prevention help at University of Pretoria library

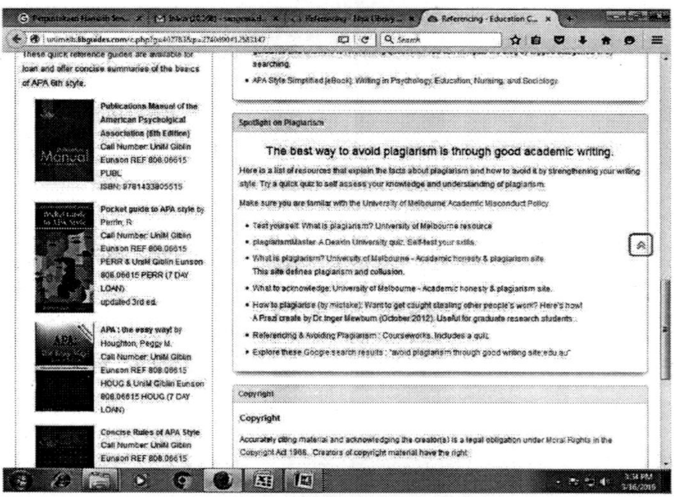

Screenshot 16. Plagiarism prevention help at University of Melbourne

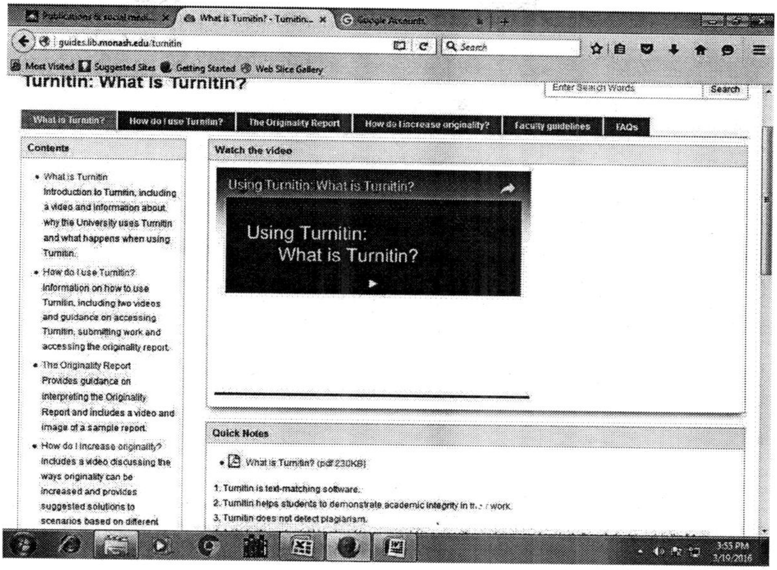

Screenshot 17. Access to Turnitin at Monash University library

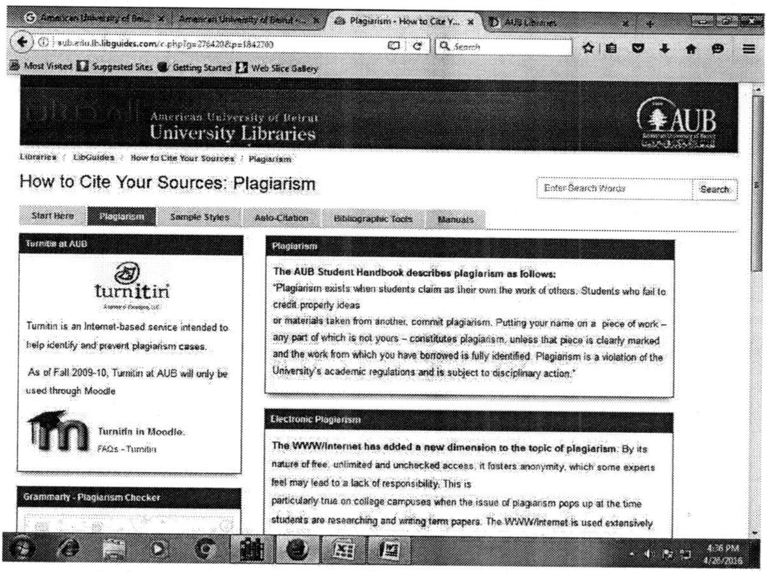

Screenshot 18. Access to Turnitin and help at American University of Beirut

Citation Tools/Help : Patrons doing research always need the help of the library when they cite any work in their publications. Different journals need papers in different formats of citations and referencing style. To avoid plagiarism author needs to give due credit to the original author by citing his work. To promote the research environment, giving information related to writing quality papers in proper format and without plagiarism, university libraries are taking more efforts to train users by proving them information about citation tools.

Following are few examples of the top universities offering citations related service.

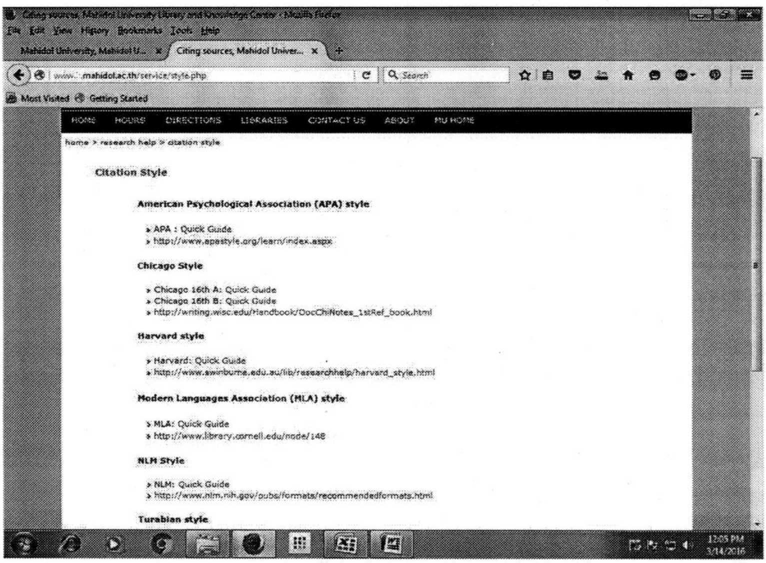

Screenshot 19. Citation help at the Mahidol University library

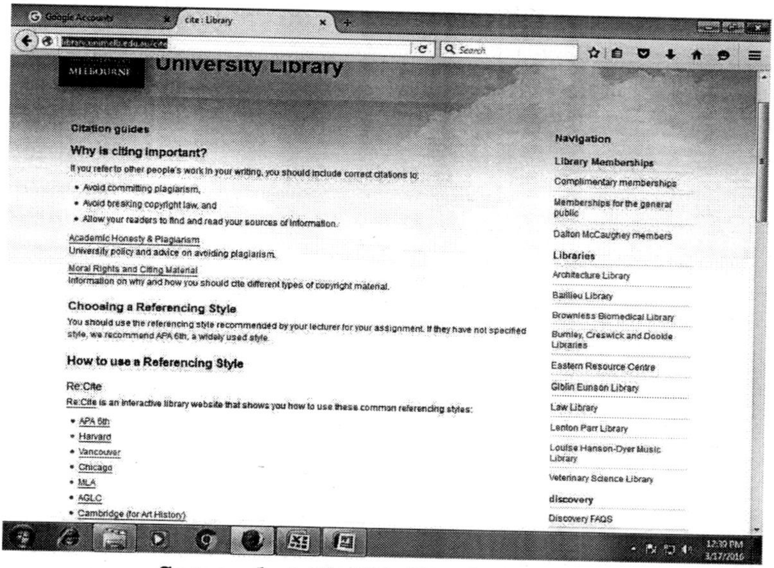

Screenshot 20. Citation help at the Melbourne University library

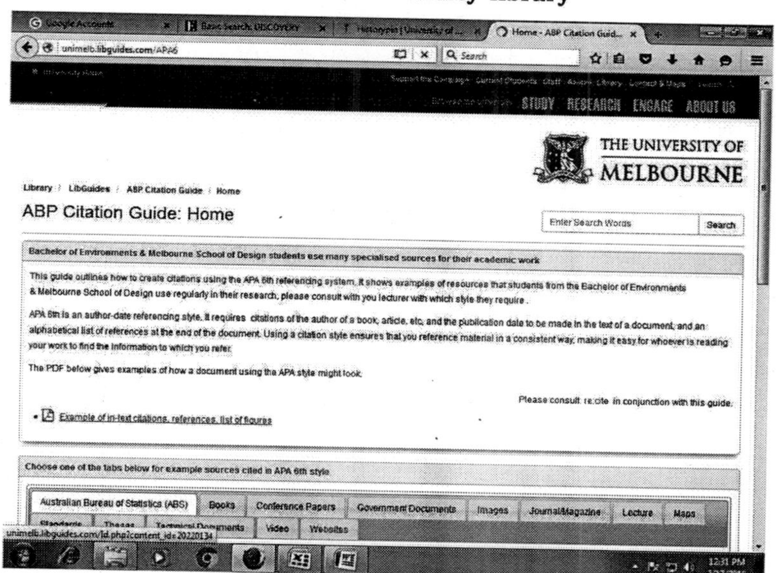

Screenshot 21. Citations guide at the University of Melbourne

Coursework : Libraries play an important role in all coursed conducted by the university. Universities are conducting many online courses and providing reading material online. Libraries started working with the teachers and tutors to provide course related reading material. Few university libraries providing coursework help including reading materials and tools are Taiwan University Library provides a course search facility through Taiwan University library information processing system (TULIPS). Another example is of Shanghai Jiao Tong University providing course support to students.

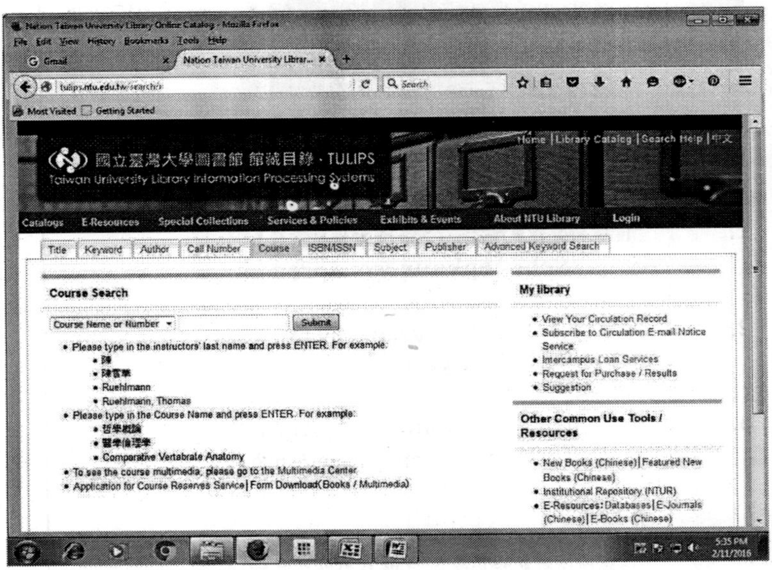

Screenshot 22. Course work/ reserve service at Taiwan University library

Screenshot 23. Course support at Shanghai Jiao Tong University library

REFERENCES

1. Roohie, S. (2013). Open access in India. Retrieved from https://sehdeepkaur.wordpress.com/category/open-access-2/
2. Suber, Peter (2004). A Very Brief Introduction to Open Access. Retrieved from https://legacy.earlham.edu/~peters/fos/brief.htm
3. UNESCO. (n.d.). Introduction to open access. Retrieved from http://unesdoc.unesco.org/images/0023/002319/231920E.

7

Web-based Best Practices Offered by University Libraries: An Overview

INTRODUCTION

In this chapter authors have listed the best practices few top university libraries are following while providing web based services apart from the services mentioned in first three clusters. Best practice requires active participation, willingness, creativity and problem solving attitude from all library stakeholders. On the basis of feedback for overall performance improvement university libraries takes continuous efforts. A best practice may be innovative and be a philosophy, policy, strategy, program, process or practice that solves a problem or create new opportunities and positively impact the whole organization (NAAC, 2006).

Online Exhibitions : University libraries conduct exhibition of books and other reading materials, museum, archives in their libraries frequently. Notifications circulated among the students about time and place of exhibitions. Few top university libraries like the Australian National University, the University of West Indies, the Jagiellonian University Library, the Alma Jorden Library, the AUB University libraries organize and display online exhibitions of their archives, Bibliographies, special collection and life and work of eminent personality[2]. Many exhibitions are named by renowned eminent personalities and founders of those universities.

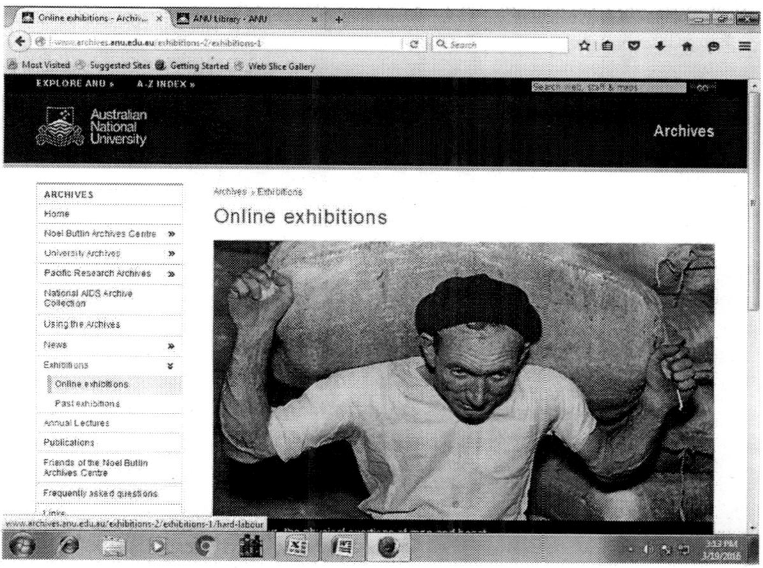

Screenshot 1. Online exhibitions at the Australian National University library

Screenshot 2. Online exhibitions at the University of the West Indies library

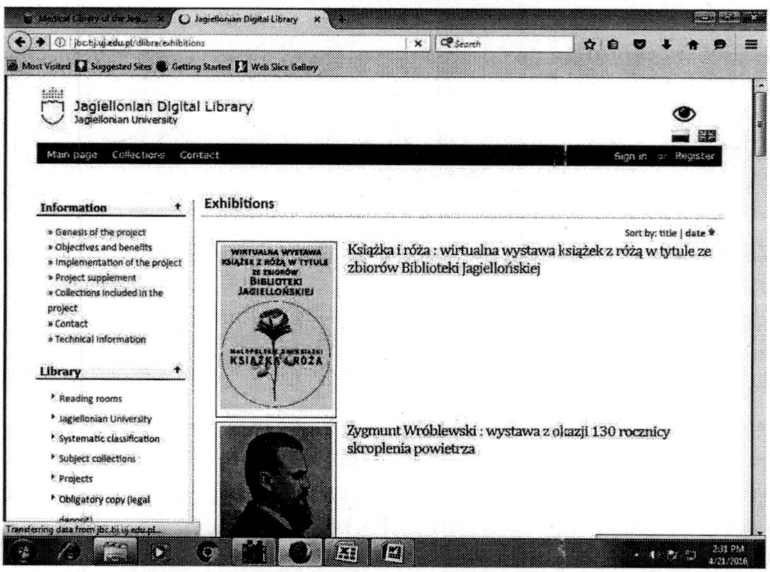

Screenshot 3. Online exhibitions at Jagielionian University library

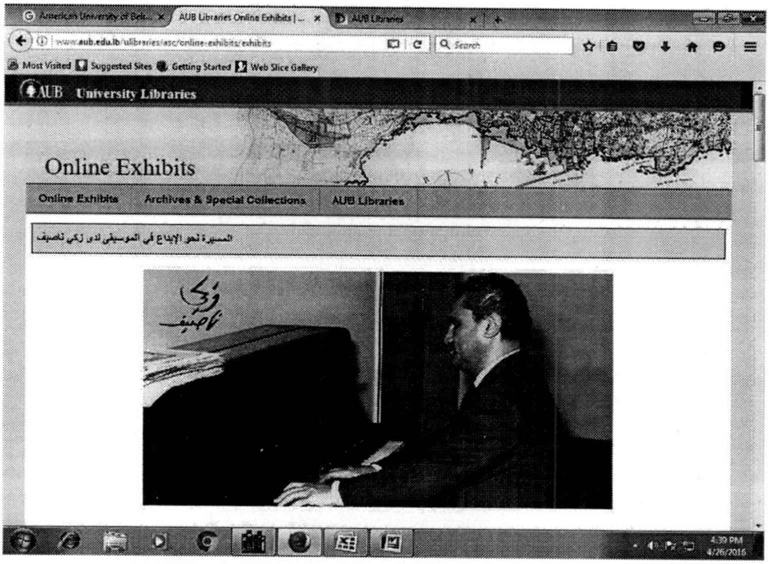

Screenshot 4. Online exhibitions at American University of Beirut library

Virtual Library Tour : University libraries are always open to university stakeholders, but restricted to public. The virtual tour is nothing but self guided tour with an interactive pathway and library map that highlights importance of that location/section or services. It can be a beautifully shoot video of the library sections with its brief information and an overview, self guided audio form or mobile application form in which, when you approach with your smart phones to library building or section these tour guide provides important information about Harvard programs you will be able to hear the information about that section or point or map or floor plans or maps in pdf file. These online tours gives features of each location to find your way and library policies and specialized collection in the library and takes you to its appearance from inside, different sections, facilities and history of that library to public and non members. Harvard University Library gives self guided tours in audio form, map pdf form and mobile tour as university campuses and library has a rich history.

While Cambridge, Peking, Columbia and Mahidol University libraries provide virtual tour in video form.

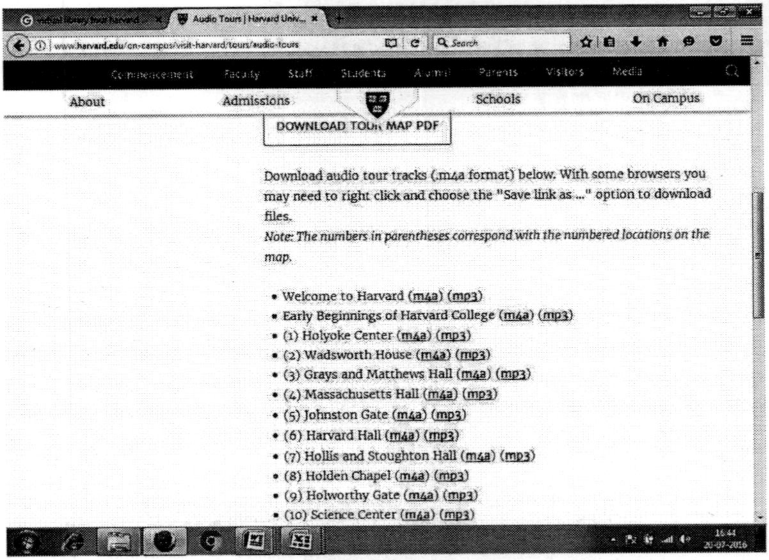

Screenshot 5. Virtual (Audio-visual) tour of Harvard University library

Screenshot 6. Virtual tour of Columbian university library

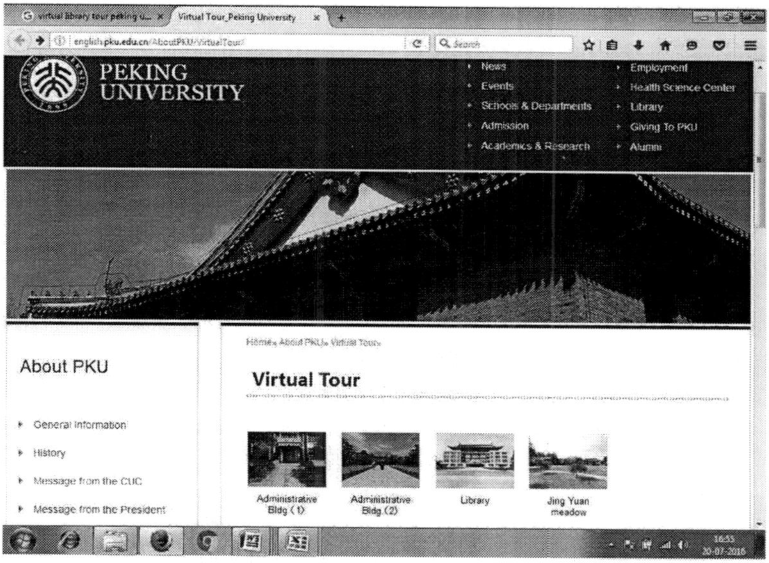

Screenshot 7. Virtual tour of Peking University library

Screenshot 8. Virtual tour of Peking University library

Screenshot 9. Virtual tour of Mahidol University library

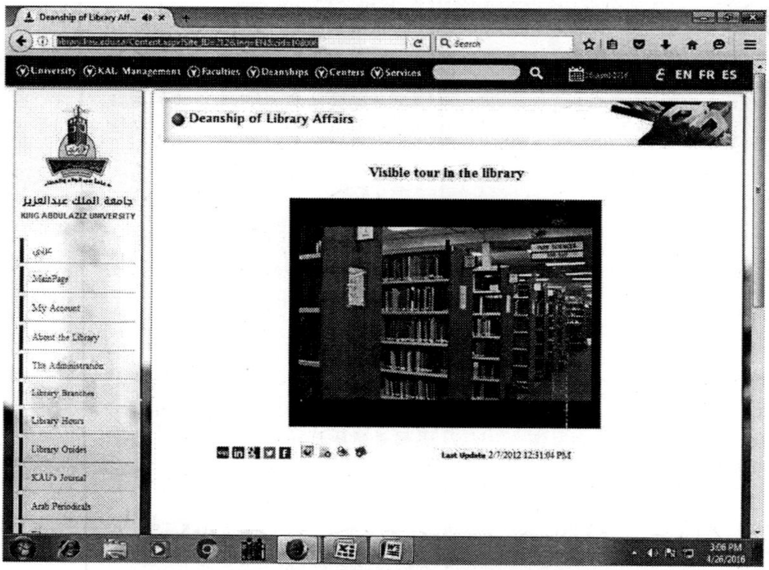

Screenshot 10. Virtual library tour of King Abdul Aziz University library

Wikis : Since 2001 Wikis facilitate collaborative authoring. In library,wikis are used for various purposes like collaboration among libraries, library staff and patrons, sharing information, collecting software documentation, supporting conferences, facilitating librarians to faculty collaboration, creating digital repositories, managing web contents, creating intranets, providing reference desk, creating a knowledge base, subject guides and collecting readers reviews. At large level wikis were used to support collaboration among library staff intra-organizational and extra-organizationally (Bejune, M, 2007)[4]Many university libraries created their wikis for giving overview of library and its services.Below are few examples of top university librarywikis.

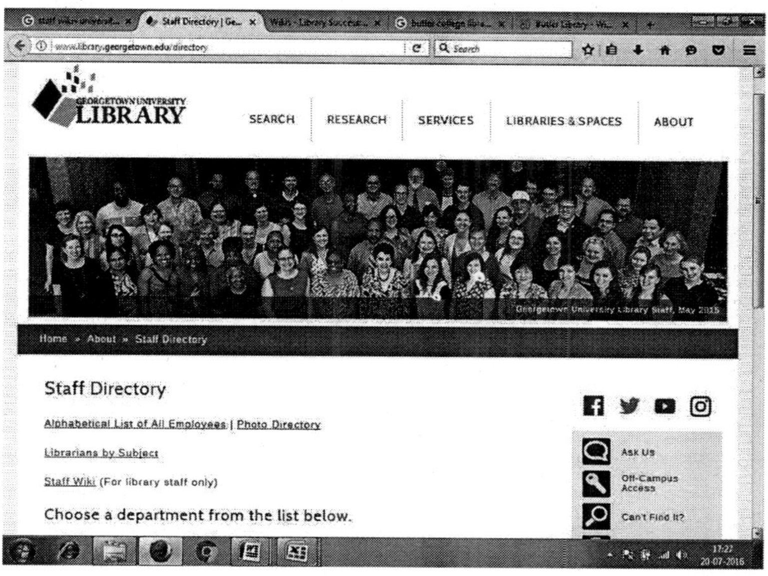

Screenshot 11. Staff wiki of Georgetown University library

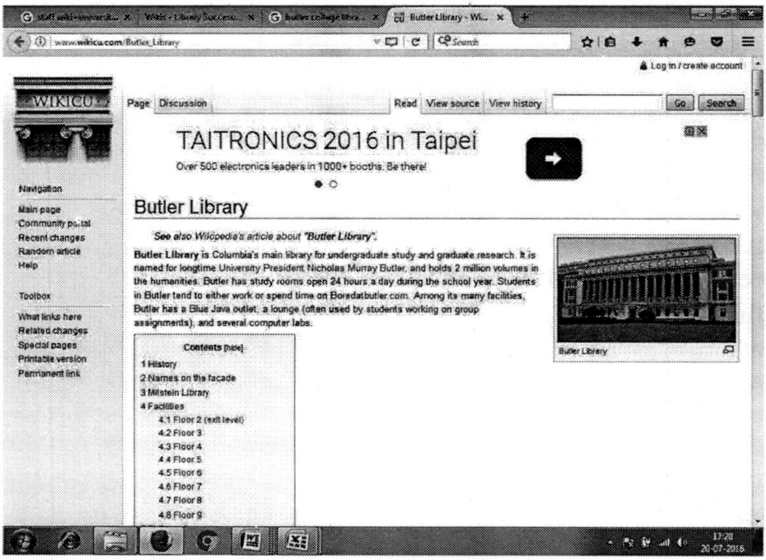

Screenshot 12. Wiki page of Columbia University library

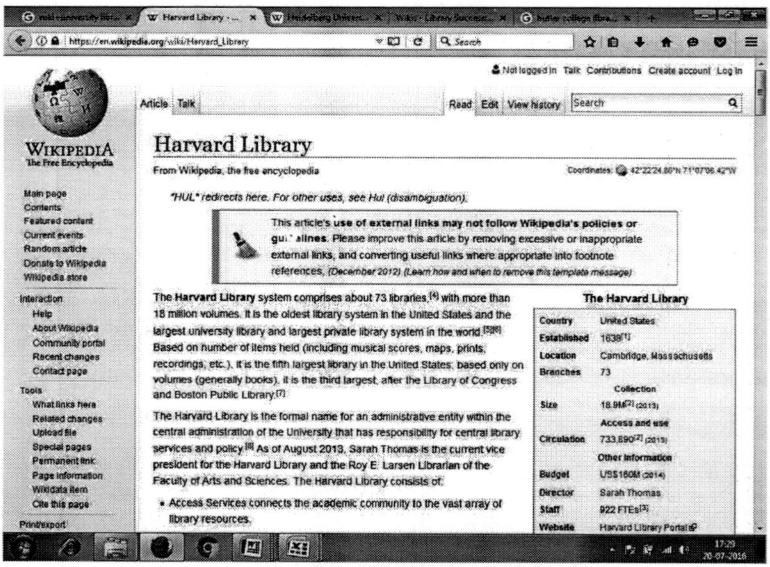

Screenshot 13. Wiki page of Harvard University library

Interactive Games, Puzzles and Movie/Short Films : University libraries making the patron education more interesting by introducing interactive online quiz, games and puzzles and movie/short film. University Sains Malaysia is inviting their patrons to participate in Web of Science discovery quiz. University of Pretoria created an interesting interactive kind of online quiz and in which multiple choice based answers are given through which they get feedback also how patrons understand the library and use of the library. The University of Melbourne conducts a library orientation quiz every year so that patrons will know library more. Winners get prize. There are many free software available which can be used to create such puzzles, games and conduct quiz like Jigsaw Puzzle, Eclipse Crossword, iSpring, online quiz creater, Qzzr, Quizstar, ProProfs Quiz maker, etc.

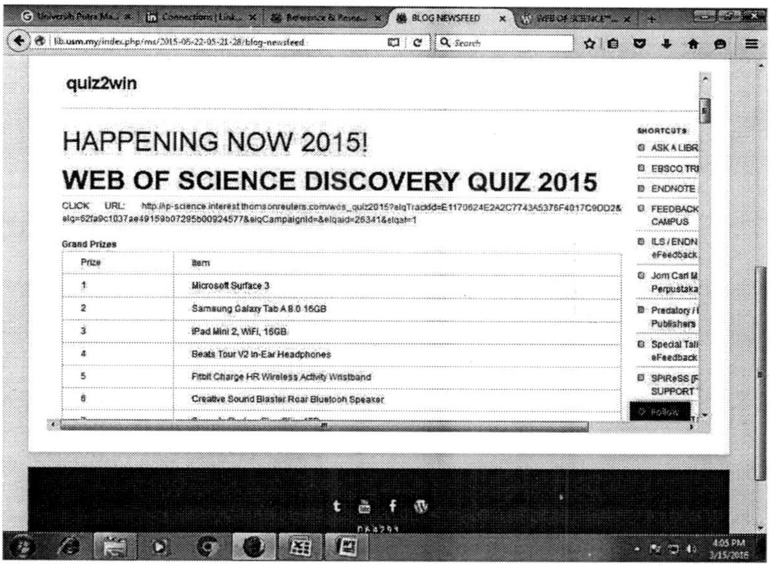

Screenshot 14. Online quiz competition at University Sains Malaysia library

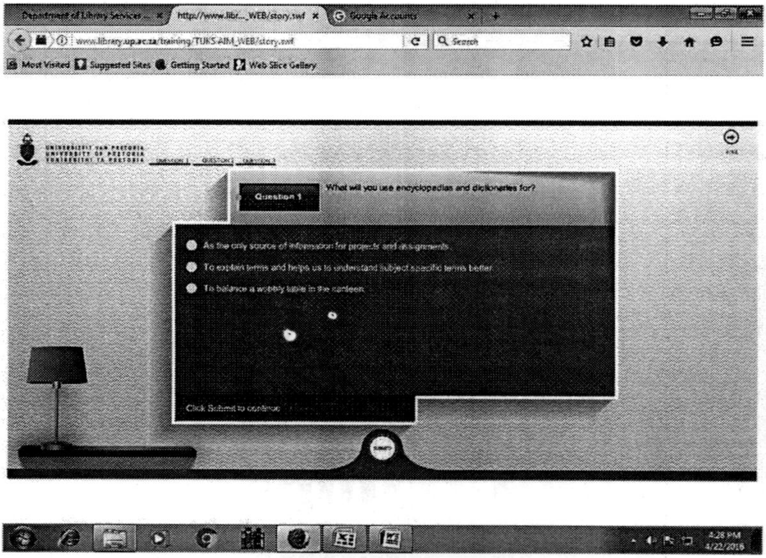

Screenshot 15. Interactive quiz competition at University of Pretoria

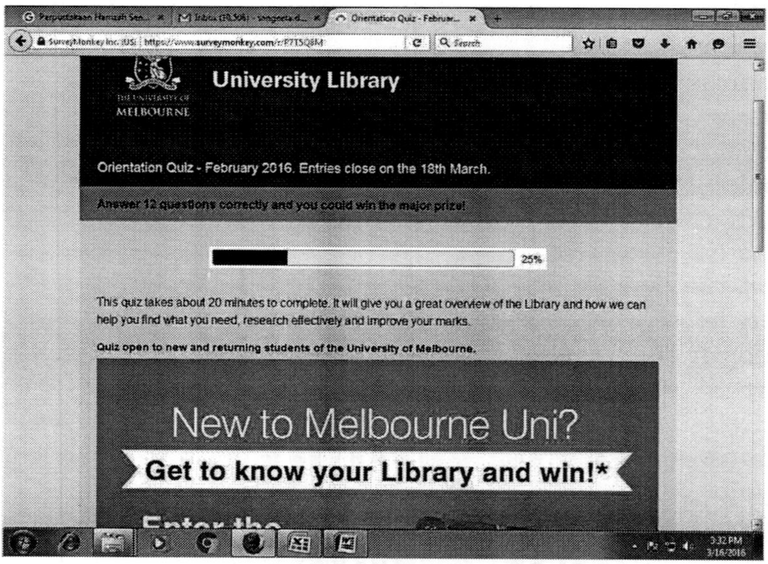

Screenshot 16. Orientation quiz at Melbourne University library

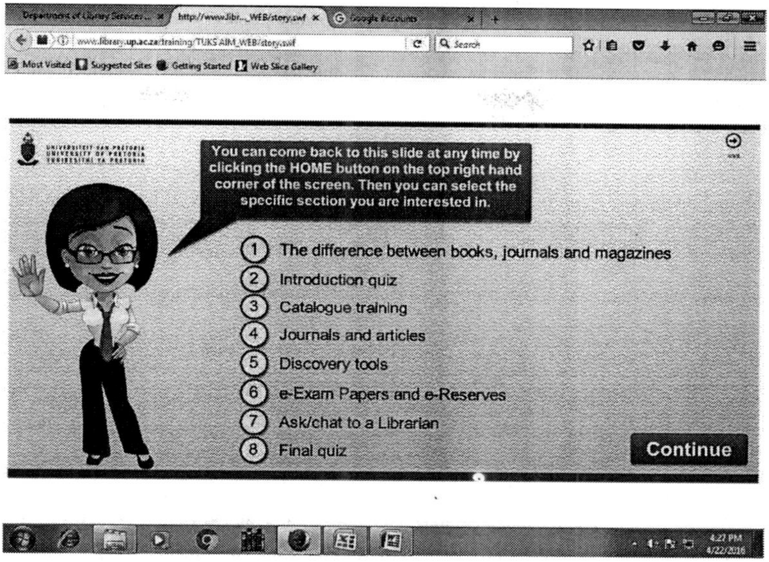

Screenshot 17. Online quiz at University of Pretoria library

OTHER BEST PRACTICES

Blackboard/Moodle/Open Courseware : Blackboardis virtual classroom software. It is paid software many universities are using to conduct virtual classes in developed countries. The American University in Cairo took initiative to educate their patrons and engage them with reading material and instructional material and interact with them. Blackboard provides high quality audio and video sharing facility. Because it is paid software so very few libraries use this software to educate and conduct information literacy classes for patrons. Moodle is a free virtual classroom software and easy to use. Hebrew university of Jerusalem library uses Moodle software to educate their patrons and conduct sessions. Similarly Kyoto university library is using Open Courseware which is a free platform to publish course material.

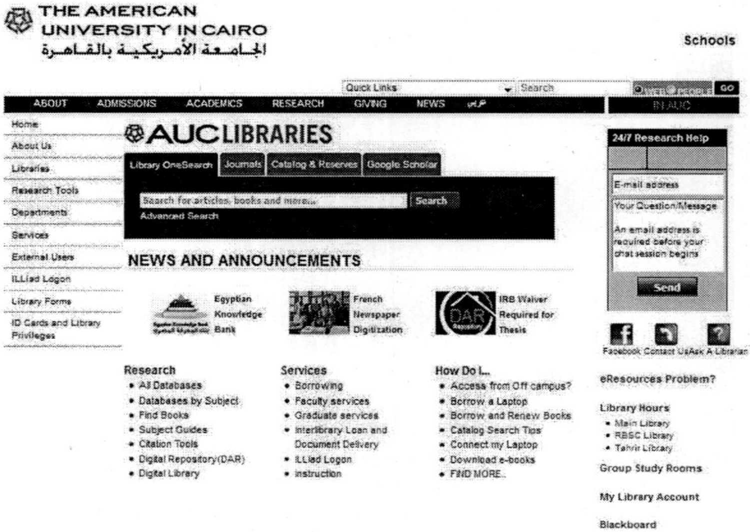

Screenshot 18. Blackboard at the American University in Cairo library

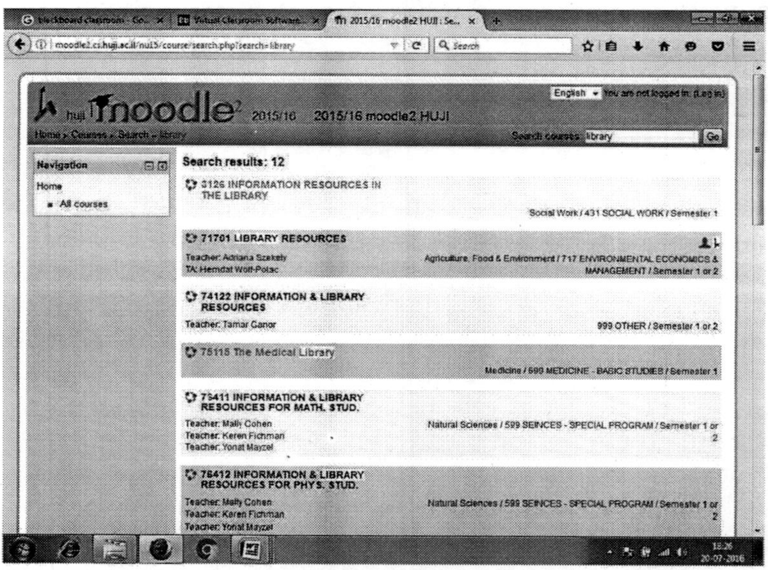

Screenshot 19. Use of Moodle courses at Hebrew university of Jerusalem library

Screenshot 20. Use of Open Courseware at Kyoto University library

1. Access or Borrow Rankings : Kyoto University practices to display Borrowed Ranking of reading material as well as Access Rankings on their website. This university also updates new reviews written by their patrons of books on their website.

Screenshot 21. Kyoto University display of Boorowed Rankings

Screenshot 22. Access rankings and new reviews at Kyoto University library

Screenshot 23. New collection reviews at Kyoto University library

The Tsinghua University library practices to display latest books review on their website to inculcate reading habits among the students, to involve and attract readers in library activities.

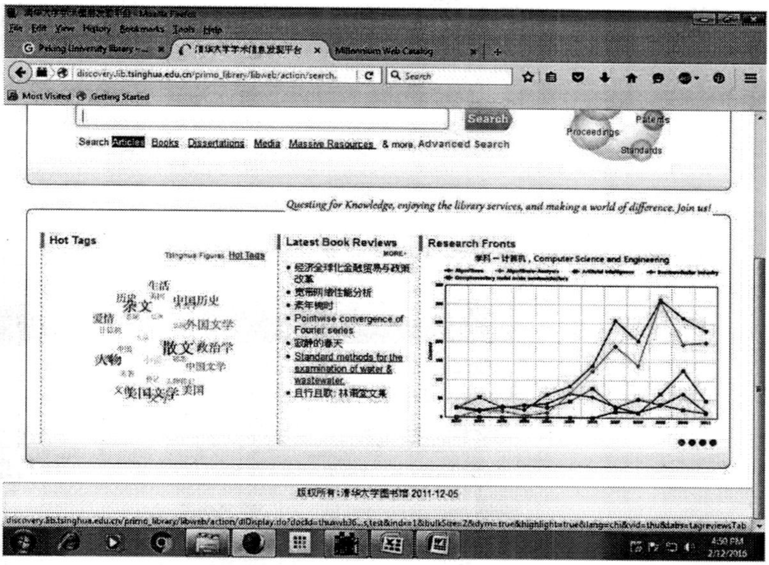

Screenshot 24. Latest book reviews at Ksinghua University library

2. The American University of Beirut library has taken innovative steps to provide tools for physicians, nurses, public health users and patients along with subject guides and research support[1]. Its Saab Medical library conducts PubMed quiz in collaboration with PubMed for their patrons to create interest and increase use of PubMed.

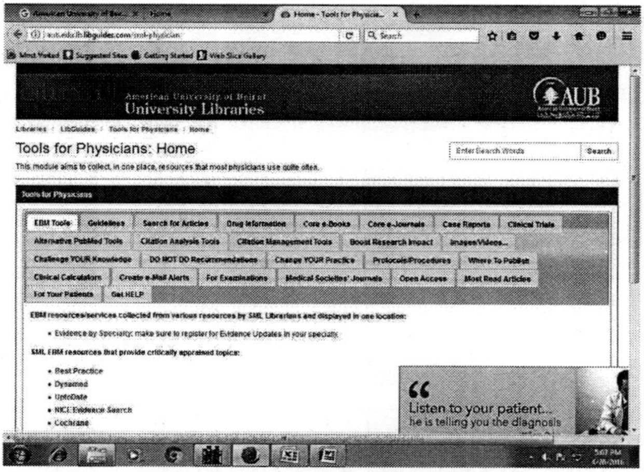

Screenshot 25. Special tools for specific patrons at the American University of Beirut

3. The Australian National University library archives departments organize lecture of prominent researcher and all lecture archives made available on the library website for reference purpose in the vodcast format and lecture flyers in pdf format

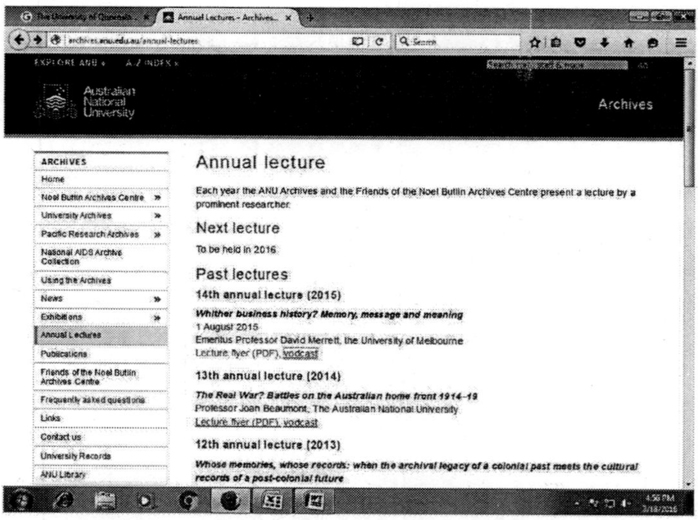

Screenshot 26. Archieve of Annuallectures organized by Australia National University library

4. The University of Queensland provides online training in research and I.T. skills to support UQ's teaching, learning and research. University library uses "Lynda.com" software and skills training websites and is free for UQ students and staff. Alibrary created 101 online tutorials about locating and using your Library in different modules. Patrons can select the tutorial modules as per their requirement.

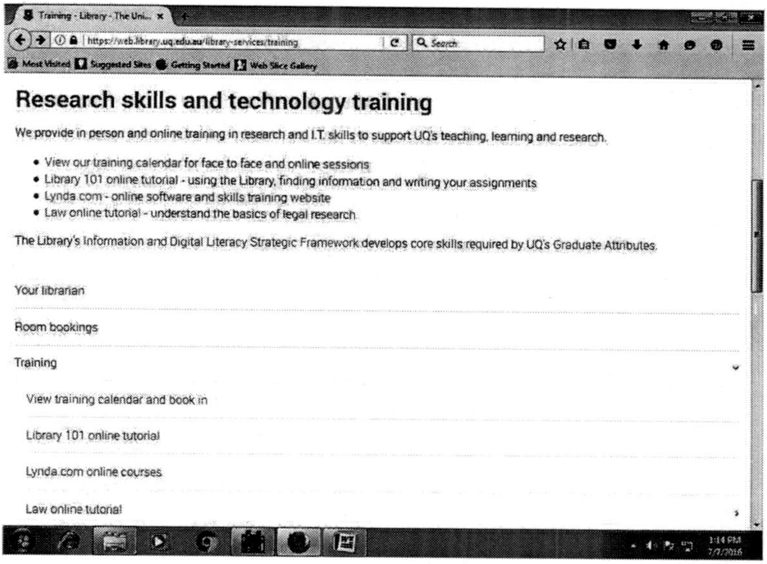

Screenshot 27. Skills training at Queensland University library

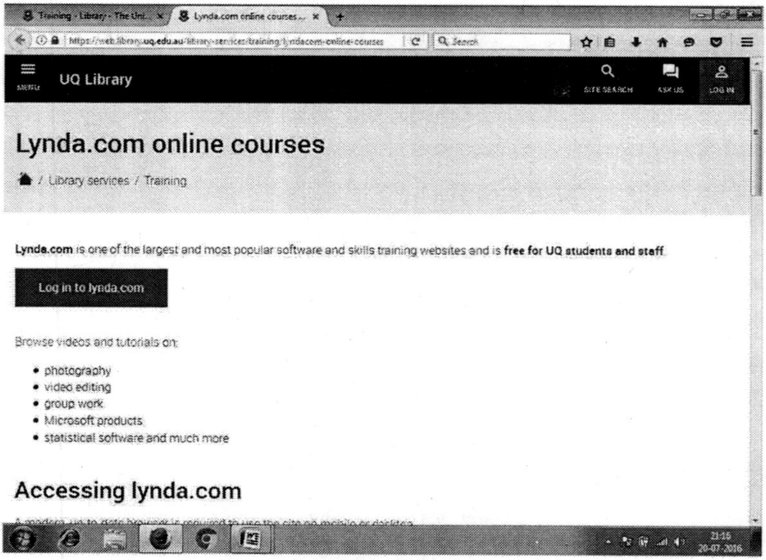

Screenshot 28. Lynda.com online courses at the University of Queensland library

5. A Kesetsart University's Green library created webpage for all books cover pages. It helps readers to select the books. Also, this library organizes an annual event for every year and invites all pass out students. The KU library maintains statistical records of services offered and made available to all on their website. To promote reading library form Reading Promotion Network.

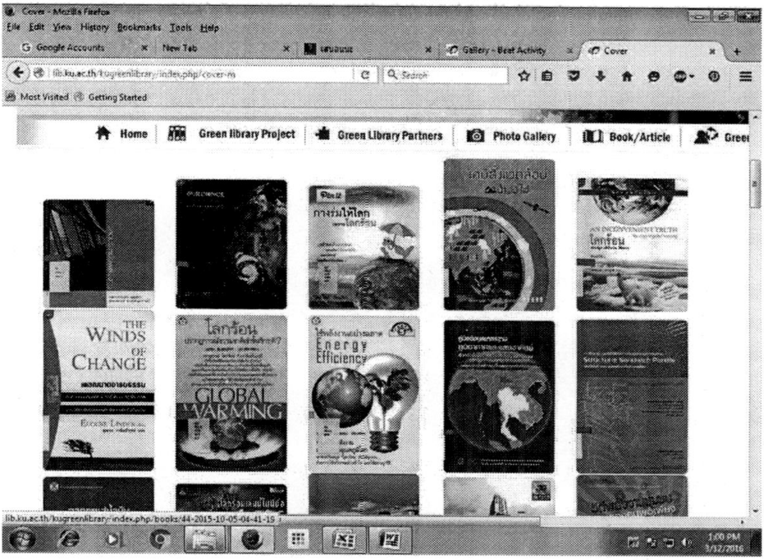

Screenshot 29. Green library project at Kesetsart University library

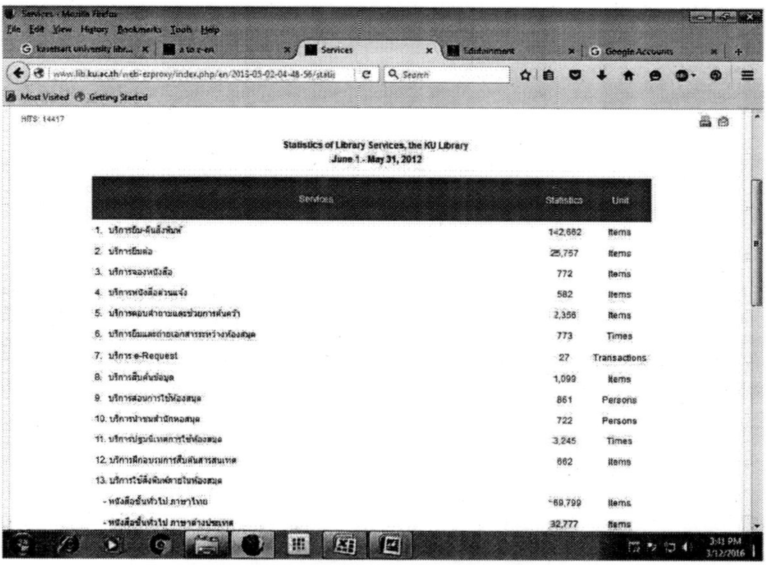

Statistics of Library Services, the KU Library
June 1 - May 31, 2012

Services	Statistics	Unit
1. บริการยืม-คืนสิ่งพิมพ์	142,662	Items
2. บริการยืมต่อ	25,757	Items
3. บริการจองหนังสือ	772	Items
4. บริการหนังสือด่วนแจ้ง	582	Items
5. บริการตอบคำถามและช่วยการค้นคว้า	2,356	Items
6. บริการยืมและถ่ายเอกสารระหว่างห้องสมุด	773	Times
7. บริการ e-Request	27	Transactions
8. บริการสืบค้นข้อมูล	1,099	Items
9. บริการสอนการใช้ห้องสมุด	861	Persons
10. บริการนำชมสำนักหอสมุด	722	Persons
11. บริการปฐมนิเทศการใช้ห้องสมุด	3,245	Times
12. บริการฝึกอบรมการสืบค้นสารสนเทศ	662	Items
13. บริการใช้สิ่งพิมพ์ภายในห้องสมุด		
- หนังสือชั้นทั่วไป ภาษาไทย	69,799	Items
- หนังสือชั้นทั่วไป ภาษาต่างประเทศ	32,777	Items

Screenshot 30. Display of statistics of library services at Kesetsart Univerity

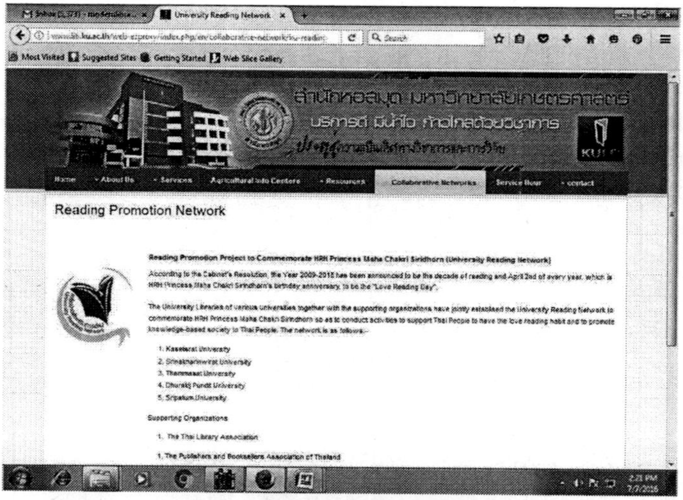

Screenshot 31.Reading promotion network by Kesetsart University Green Library

6. The King Abdul Aziz University has separate libraries for women and men. This university conducts reading marathon competition and shows no. of visitors to the library website.

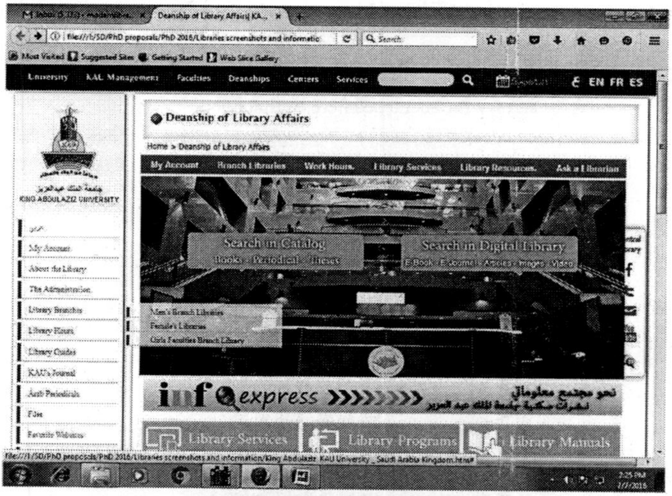

Screenshot 32. Genderwise King Abdul Aziz University libraries

7. Amazon Associate Program : Amazon is providing links to libraries. That link libraryprovideon their website. If readers or library buys books and all other kinds of products using the link allotted to university 5% amount of thetotal purchase is added tothe library accountwith a few terms and conditions. Tel Aviv University and many other Israel universities participating in the Amazon Associates Program and earning financial benefits.

Screenshot 33. Amazon Associate Program at Tej Aviv University library

Screenshot 34. Tel Aviv University libraries associate program with Amazon

8. Plurk : Unlike all other free social network services like Facebook, Twitter, Foursquare, Stumbleupon, etc. mentioned above NTU Library uses Plurk freesocial networking and micro-blogging service that allows libraries to send updates through short messages or links[4].

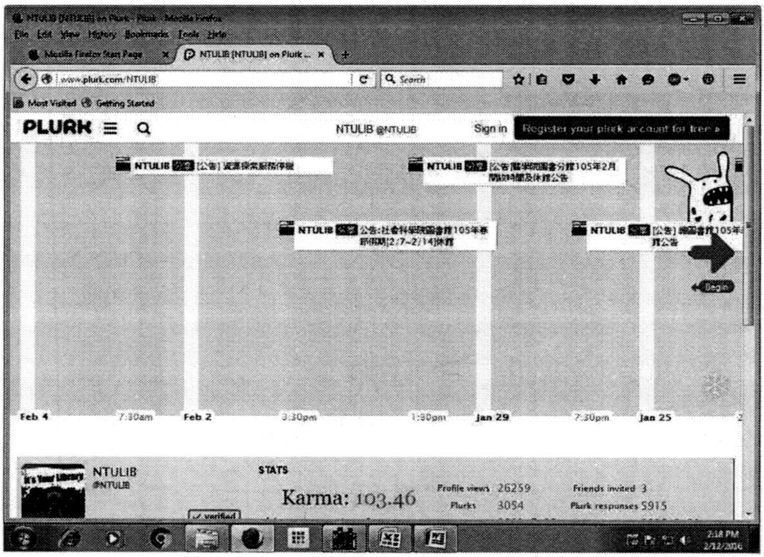

Screenshot 35. Plurk patron communication platform by NTU library

9. Writing and Referencing : Similar to Citations and plagiarism related help university libraries also playing an important role in providing writing and referencing related help and services. Patrons can avail this facility and refer the guides, instructions, tutorials is providedby libraries while writing their projects, theses, academic papers, patents, standards, trademarks.

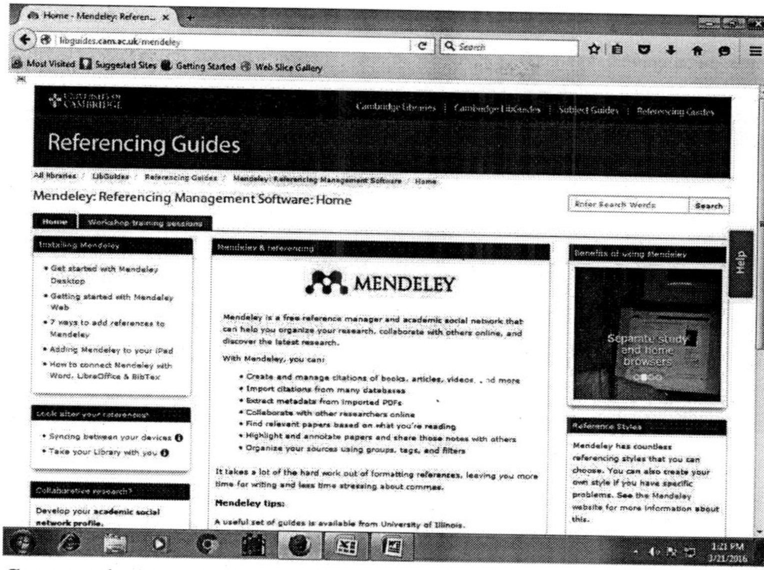

Screenshot 36. Referencing guides by Cambridge University

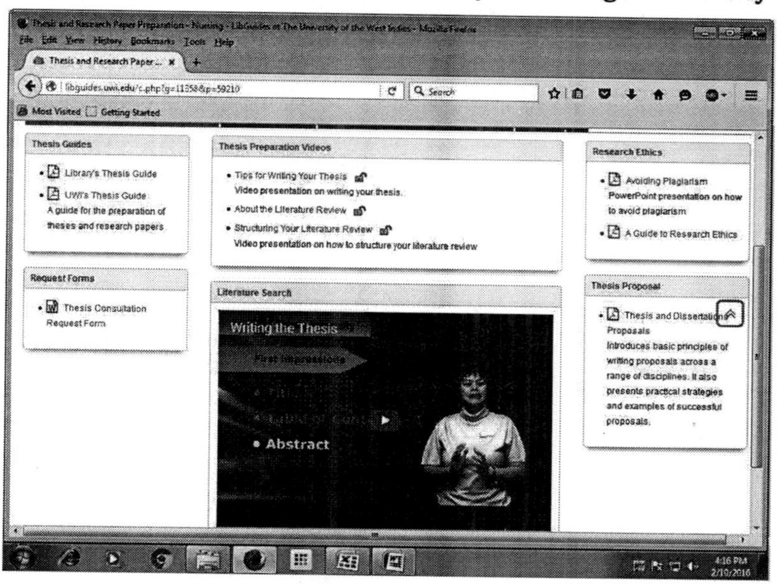

Screenshot 37. Referencing guides by University of West Indies

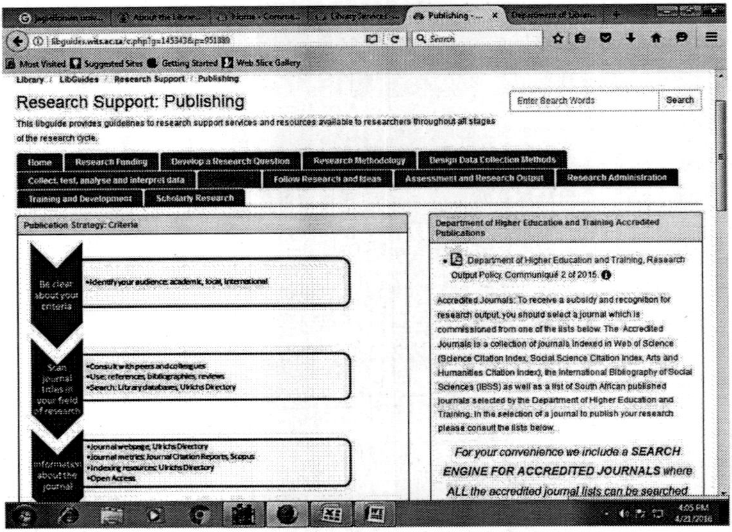

Screenshot 38. Referencing guides by University of Witwatersrand

10. E-Brochure : Every library prepares two, three, four or multiple fold brochures for their patrons and visitors for publicity and also marketing purpose. It contains all information about library along with a few photos. Many top university libraries give these brochures to all visitors. It is mirror of that library. Along with print university libraries uploads these brochures in pdf form on their website. The brochure gives a quick view of the library and its services. Those readers who do not have much time to read all the library webpages library brochure helps them to understand the library. As it is easy to upload brochures university prepares brochure for separate sections, departments, services too.

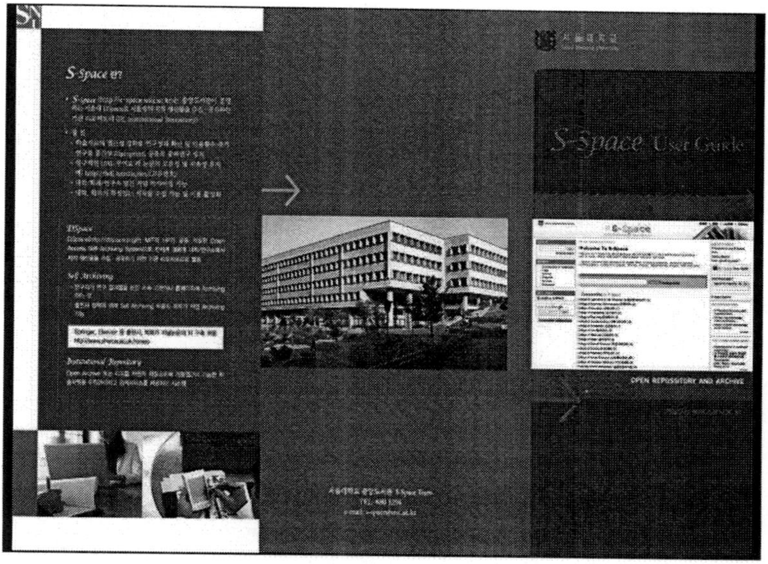

Screenshot 39. e-brochure of Seoul National University library

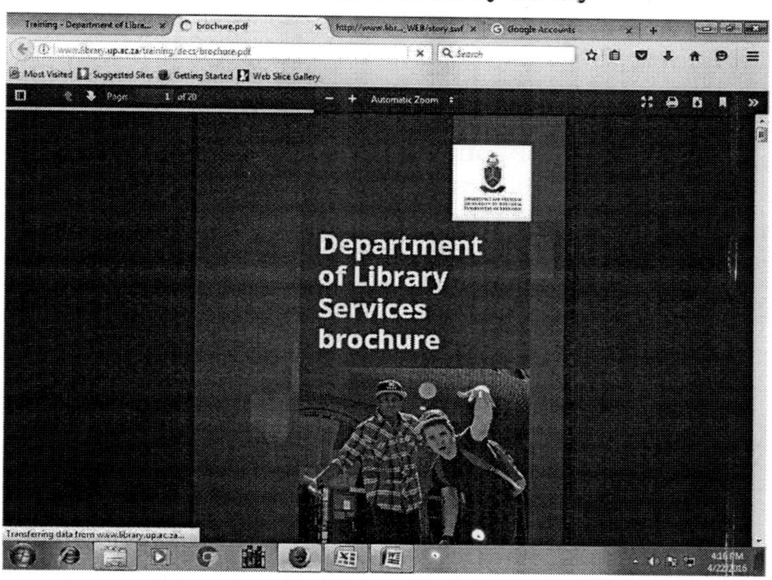

Screenshot 40. e-brochure of library services of the University of Pretroria

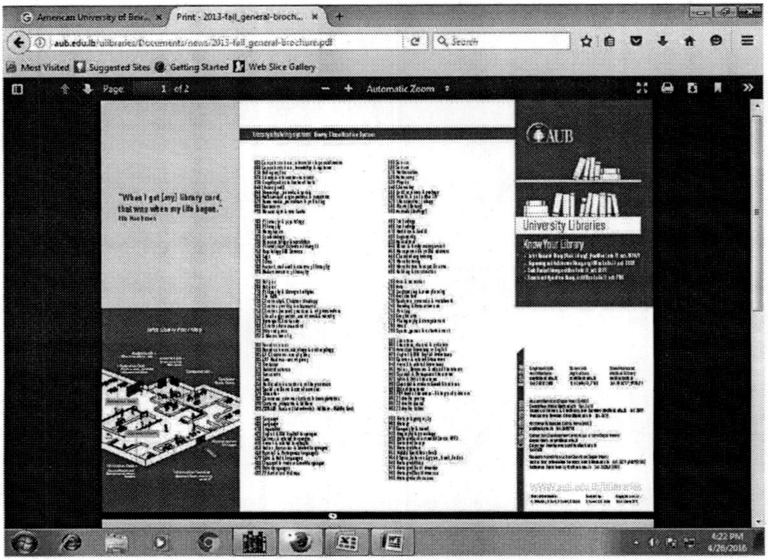

Screenshot 41. e-brochure of the American University of Beirut

The overview of all the web-based library best practices wasdiscussed here in detail using screenshots of those services offered by different libraries in different ways. While reading this chapter, the readers will understand how the specific service is offered by university libraries in the globe and how these services are user centric and beneficial in the future to attract users, reach patrons and make maximum use of library resources.

REFERENCES

1. NAAC. (2006). Best practices in library and information services. Retrieved from www.naac.gov.in/docs/Best%2520Practices%2520in%2520%2520Library%2520and%2520Information%2520Services%2520A%2
2. Stumbleupon. (n.d.). Retrieved from Wikipedia: https://en.wikipedia.org/wiki/StumbleUpon
3. Stumbleupon. (n.d.). Retrieved from itunes: https://itunes.apple.com/us/app/stumbleupon/id386244833?mt=8
4. Wikipedia. (n.d.). Plurk. Retrieved from https://en.wikipedia.org/wiki/Plurk

8

Suggestions and Revolutionary Changes on the Basis of Statistical Analysis of Web-based Services and Best Practices at World and India Level

INTRODUCTION

This is last and very important chapter, which gives the overview of web-based services and best practices offered by top world university libraries and give suggestions to other academic libraries for improvement and revolutionary change of web-based services and best practices in university libraries.

WEB-BASED SERVICES OFFERED BY UNIVERSITY LIBRARIES

If we compare all 59 web-based services count offered in four clusters by 'world' and 'Indian' university libraries were analyzed by applying T-test. It is observed that sample 70 world university libraries mean score ofweb-based services was 33.629 (±10.9705) and that for 39 Indian university libraries, the mean score were 8.103 (±8.1201). The mean difference between the mean score of all web-based services offered by 'Indian' and 'world' university libraries was 25.5260. This mean difference was statistically significant at 0.05 significant levels (t-12.710, df =107). This indicates that world university libraries offer four times better web-based services for patrons than Indian university libraries. Among all web-based services percentage score of offering text instruction on websites service by both 'world' and 'India' was 81.7%, and for access to web OPAC and database services was 78%.

WEB-BASED BIBLIOGRAPHICAL SERVICES

It is observed that, among web-based bibliographical services score of offeringaccess to the database and web OPAC score in both 'world' and 'India'university libraries was high i.e. 78% and access to dataset score was very low i.e.7.3%. The overall score of web-based 'federated search/e-discovery tools service', 'access to archives/ digital collection/IR service', 'Off campus access service' and ILL service is above 60%, whereas 'access to visual databaseservice', 'new arrival service', 'e-document delivery service' and 'book recommendation service' is below 35%. In all bibliographical services, except Dataset service world universities scored much higher than Indian universities.

Below Graph 1 is self-explanatory to show the score of each bibliographical service area wise.

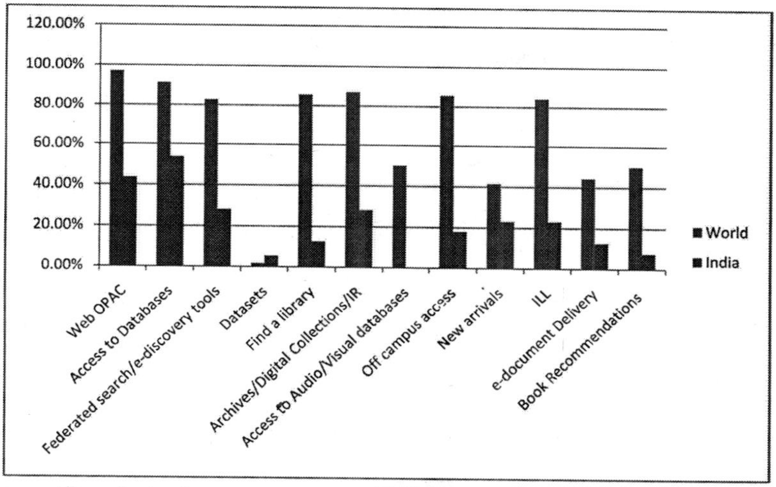

Graph 1. Average score of bibliographical services of 'world' and 'Indian' university libraries

The Chi-Square test indicated that the p value for Datasets and New Arrival services is not significant to significance level 0.05. Remaining all services shows a strong relation between the 'world' and 'Indian' university libraries.

From the top fiveworld university libraries Harvard University, Stanford University and Cornell University are offering allbibliographical services and ranked first. From India,Jawaharlal Nehru University, New Delhi, ranked first in offering 10 out of 12 bibliographical services and TISS ranked second in offering 3/4th bibliographical services in India. Still 13 universities out of 39 do not offer a single bibliographical service. In Indian universities, libraries are good enough in providing access to databases, Web OPAC, federated search/e-discovery tools to search information, university archives, displaying new arrivals, inter library loan facility, but still need to improve in providing web-based bibliographical services mentioned in this study like preparing and providing access to datasets, find a library service, providing access to visual databases, providing e-document delivery service and online book recommendation services.

Annexure 1 shows which universities bibliographical services count was high and low from different continents and regions.

WEB-BASED PATRON EDUCATION TOOLS/ SERVICES

It is observed that, the use of text instruction to educate and train patrons in both 'world' and 'India' university libraries is high i.e. 81.7% and conducting online or live sessions for patron's service scored very low i.e. 4.6%. So not only in India but university libraries from different parts of the world can adopt this method of delivering instructions or educating patrons.

At world university level, is observed that for educating patrons score of 'tips for access and use', 'ask us', 'help/user guides' and 'text instruction' was above 90% and 'News service', 'library calendar' and 'PPTs/PDFs' for updating and educating patrons score is above 80%. More than 50% world university libraries are educating patrons using 'upcoming events', 'service directory', 'research/subject guides', 'you tube', 'FAQs', 'feedback', 'photc gallery', 'research tutorials', 'maps directions', 'RSS feeds' and 'video tutorials' services and tools. Range of 35-50% world university libraries were providing and using 'mobile application', 'weblog', 'newsletter', 'prezi/ slideshare', instant chat/messaging' tools/service. 21.4% universities use WordPress platform, 15.7% prepares audio tutorials and gives online or live video library and 7.1% universities conduct live or online sessions for educating patrons.

On the contrary, Indian university libraries score of these services was below 62%. The score of Indian university libraries for educating and orienting patrons by publishing text instructions on library website was 61.50% and all other services score was below 50%. The score of photo gallery was 46.2%, service directory was

41%, library calendar was 35.9%, PPTs/PDFs was 33.3%, ask us is 28.2%, help/user guides was 17.9%, news and feedback service is 15.4%, research/subject guides and FAQs is 12.8% and score of upcoming events, YouTube, research tutorials, video tutorials, weblog, instant chat/ messaging service was 7.7%. No Indian library is using RSS feeds, newsletter, Prezi/Slideshare, WordPress, audio tutorials, live/online video library or live/online sessions for patron education.

Below Graph 2 is self-explanatory to show the score of each patron education tool/service area wise.

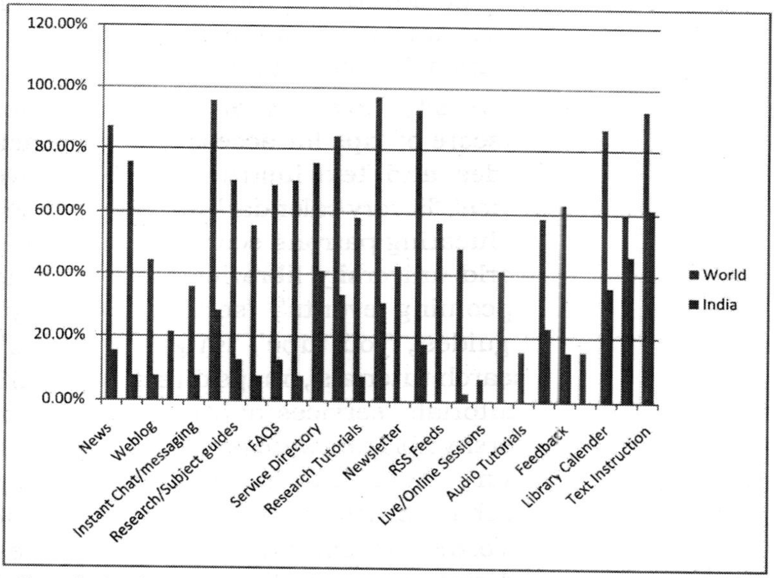

Graph 2. Average score of patron education tools/ services of 'world' and 'Indian' university libraries

T-Test results were showing that there were 70 world university libraries offering total web-based patron education services mean of 16.229 (±5.7513) and that for 39 Indian university libraries, the mean score was 4.231 (±4.1133). The 'world' university libraries are offering better, i.e. four time patron education services than Indian university libraries.

From the 'world' university libraries Stanford University offers maximum patron education tools and services, i.e. 26 services out of 27 services. In India, Jawaharlal Nehru University scored high by offering 19 patron education services. Indian universities are good in providing text instructions, photo gallery service, providing library calendar/timings, service directory, use of PPTs/PDFs, providing tips for access and use of library, ask us service, providing user guides and updating library news. Indian libraries have scope to improve their patron education services like updating them about upcoming events in the library, using blogs, WordPress, providing instant chat or messaging service, providing research or subject guides, preparing video tutorials, preparing FAQs for solving common queries, using video tutorials and publishing on YouTube platform, preparing research tutorials to support and promote research, publishing library newsletters, RSS feeds, use of mobile application, live/online presentations, use of interactive Prezi tools for presentation, preparing audio tutorials for patron education.

Chi Square test indicate p=.088 and p=.164 live/ online sessions and photo gallery tools/services respectively which were not significant at .05 significance level. All other results were significant at .05 significance level.

Annexure 2 shows which universities are offering maximum patron education services using different web tools and technologies along with the universities which are not good enough in providing web-based patron education.

WEB-BASED PATRON COMMUNICATION SERVICES/TOOLS

From T-Test for comparing the means of the world and Indian university libraries given is in the score data format shows that world university libraries are offering a total web-based patron communication services mean of 5.957 (±2.8460) and that Indian university libraries, the mean score was 0.821 (±1.2747) given in Table 25. The mean difference between the mean score of web-based patron communication services offered by 'Indian' and 'world' university libraries was 5.1366. This mean difference was statistically significant at 0.05 significant levels (t-10.674, df =107). This indicates that world university libraries are offering total patron communication services much better (five times) than Indian university libraries.

From Chi-Square analysis and percentage analysis of data collected for 109 university libraries it is observed that from 14 web-based patron communication services and tools Email communication scored high i.e. 71.6% university libraries use email for communication and vice versa only 2.8% libraries use Stumbleupon platform for patron communication. Chi-Square test indicated that Stumbleupon, Delicious and Whatsapp communication tools and services are not significant at .05 significant levelsof 'world' and 'Indian' university libraries.

The score of world university libraries and Indian university libraries using these patron education tools showed major difference. If we see email then 90% world university libraries use this media while only 38.5% Indian universities using this media for patron communication which is overall higher in both cases. Facebook tool was used by 84.3% world university libraries and 12.8% university libraries. Twitter was used by 77.1% world university libraries and 10.3% Indian university libraries. A Linkedin platform for networking used by 65.7% world university libraries and 7.7% Indian university libraries. 50% world university libraries were using the Flickr platform while only 5.1% Indian university libraries were using the Flickr platform. Instagram and Pinterest tools 47.1% world university libraries and 2.6% Indian university libraries were using. Google+ platform is used by 37.1% world university libraries and 2.6% Indian university libraries. World university libraries were using Foursquare 34.3%, Tumblr 25.7%, iTunes 22.9%, Delicious 5.7%, Stumbleupon 4.3% and Whatsapp 4.3% on the contrary not a single Indian university library was using this platform for patron communication.

Below Graph 3 shows the score of each patron communication tool/service area wise.

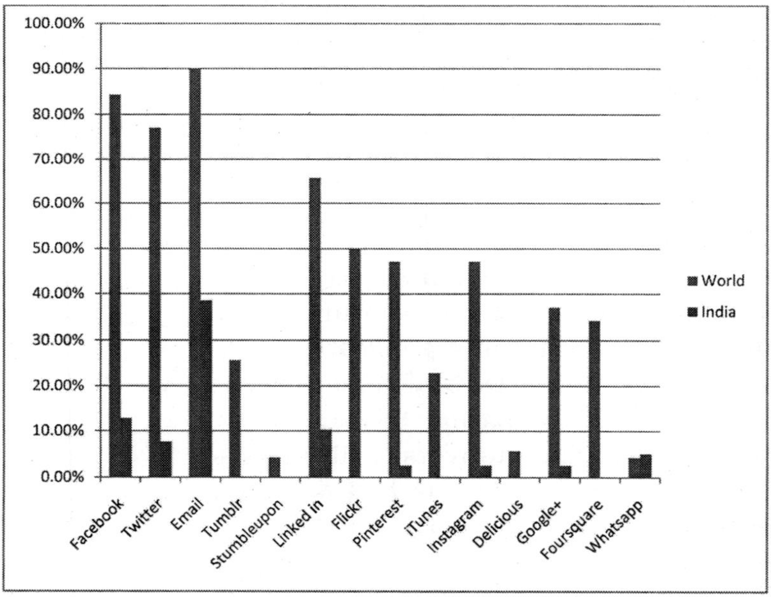

Graph 3. Average score of patron communication service of 'world' and 'Indian' university libraries

From world sample Harvard University and Oxford University offer about 12 patron communication tools whereas UniversitéDjillaliLiabes, Mansoura University from North Africa and University of Tehran from Middle East uses only one patron communication tool whereas Behna University and Alexandria University from North Africa does not use as a single web-based communication tools to communicate with patrons. Jawaharlal Nehru University from India offers only 6 web-based communication tools for patron communication. About 21 universities in India out of 39 are not using any web-based communication platform. Indian universities need to adopt new ways of communication for reaching to patron like Tumblr, Stumbleupon, Flickr, Pinterest, iTunes, Instagram, Delicious, Google+, Foursquare, Whatsapp along with Facebook, Twitter, Email, Linkedin etc.

Annexure 3 shows that which universities uses more web-based communication tools for patron education and which are used very less tools from different regions of the world.

WEB-BASED PUBLISHING PLATFORM FOR PATRONS

The total percentage scores of the web-based publishing platform for patrons by universities in India and the world are 57.8% at higher side and 9.2% at lower side. The maximum score is for undertaking open access initiatives for university publications and archives and the minimum score is for Course work.

T-Test for comparing the means of these services by world and Indian university libraries showed world university libraries were having total web-based publishing platform for patrons mean of 3.357 (±1.5883) and that for Indian university libraries, the mean score was 0.487 (±0.9140). The mean difference between the mean score of web-based publishing platform for patrons offered by 'Indian' and 'world' university libraries was 2.8700. This mean difference was statistically significant at 0.05 significance levels (t-10.356, df =107). This indicates that world university libraries are offering total publishing platform and services for patrons about three times better than Indian university libraries.

From the percentage score (cross tables) and Chi-Square test tables it has been observed that score of world university libraries taken open access initiatives was 81.4% and of Indian university libraries 15.4%, Publishing platform provided by 62.9% world university libraries and 2.6% Indian university libraries, 84.3% world and 7.7% Indian university libraries keeps and manages university records, 40% world and 17.9% Indian university libraries provides anti-plagiarism software or help, 52.9% world and 5.1% Indian university libraries were proving citation tools or help, 14.3% world university libraries were helping or providing course work for patrons while no Indian university yet started online coursework.

Below Graph 4 is self-explanatory to show the score of each patron publishing platform or help to patrons' area wise.

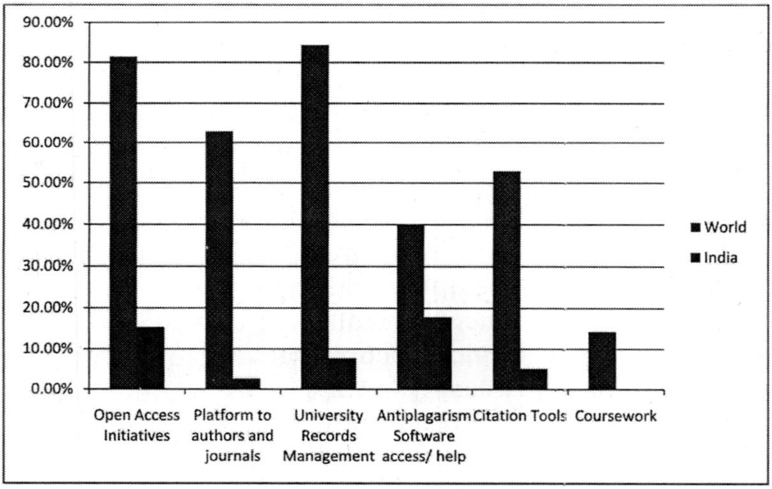

Graph 4. Average score of patron publishing platform and help service of 'world' and 'Indian' university libraries

Out of six services or initiatives by university libraries all over the world to support publishing and research activity among patrons Harvard University from USA, University of Melbourne from Oceania and Universidad Nacional de Colombia from Civet are much ahead than other universities from the world who have not yet taken any initiatives in this direction like Peking University, Lomonosov Moscow State University, Universidade Federal do Rio de Janeiro, Cairo University and Universidad de Puerto Rico (UPR).

From India, University of Hyderabad, Maharishi Dayanand University, Rohtak and BanasthaliVidyapith, Banasthali are using about half of the services to help and provide a platform for patrons to publish their research. Out of 39 Indian universities about 28 Indian universities are yet to initiate these kinds of activities. As there are no distance learning or flipped or online classes are going on in these university coursework or course related material providing services is not yet initiated in these universities.

Annexure 4 shows which universities are much ahead in providing these services and which universities are yet to work hard along with their service score.

TOTAL WEB-BASED LIBRARY SERVICES

Below Graph shows an overall average of web-based services offered by all world and Indian university libraries were 41.53%. Average of total score of different web-based services offered by all sample worlds and Indian university libraries were for bibliographical services was 50.90%, patron education services score was 44.21%, patron communication tools score was 29.44% and publishing platform and help for patron score was 38.85%.

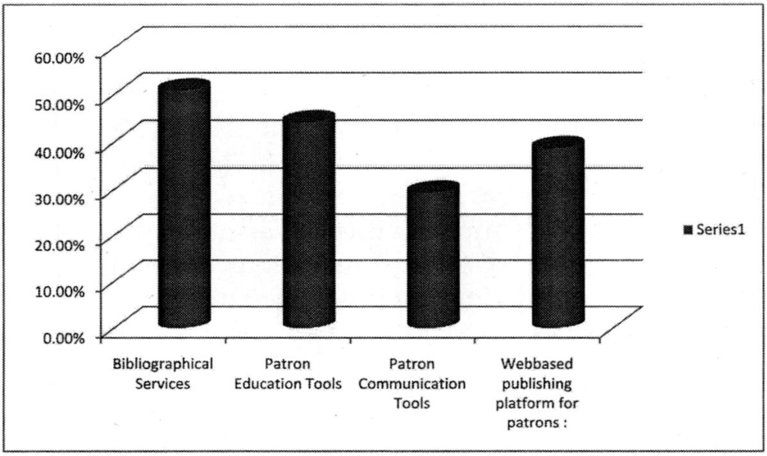

Graph 5. Average score of bibliographical services of sample university libraries

Comparison of average score of web-based bibliographical services for World University libraries was 66.81% and for Indian university libraries 21.39%, patron education services/tools for world university libraries was 60.10% and for Indian university libraries 15.67%, patron communication services for world university libraries was 42.54% and for Indian university libraries 5.87% and last cluster of publishing platform for patrons service for world university libraries was 55.97% and for Indian university libraries was 8.12%. It clearly shows that Indian university libraries are poor in providing web-based services to their patrons.

When we consider all web-based services offered by all 109 top world and Indian universities, it has been observed that top five world universities, according to webometric ranking of universities, i.e.Harvard University, Stanford University, Cornell University, University of Michigan and University of California Berkeley(Avg. 51) are also topper in offering web-based services too. European universities ranked second position (Avg.44.2) and South East Asian universities ranked third position

(Avg.40.6) in offering web-based library services. North African universities took the last position in offering web-based library services. In India, Jawaharlal Nehru university took first position (36) and Tata Institute of Social Science took second position (30) and Maharishi Dayanand University, Rohtak took third position(20) in offering web-based library services.

Annexure 5 shows the universities from different region of world offering maximum and minimum score of web-based services.

WEB-BASED BEST PRACTICES

Authors shortlisted four best practices offered by sample university libraries and found that 24.8 % university libraries were having their wiki pages and 18.3% libraries were conducted online exhibitions of their collection at a large level, 9.2% libraries were created virtual library tour and only 3.7% libraries were practicing interactive games, quiz, puzzles, movies or short film type activities for their patrons to create interest in this subject or libraries.

The T-test applied to compare all best practices by world and Indian university libraries score showed that world university libraries are offering a total web-based practices mean of 0.843 (±0.9111) and that for Indian university libraries, the mean score was 0.051(±0.2235). The mean difference between the mean score of web-based best practices conducted by 'Indian' and 'world' university libraries was 0.7916. This mean difference was not statistically significant at 0.05 significance levels (t-5.327, df =107). This indicated that world university libraries are conducting a total web-based best practices better than Indian university libraries.

The percentage score of world university libraries for best practices 'online exhibition' was 28.6% and for Interactive games, puzzles, movie/short films was 3.7% whereas no Indian university libraries were providing these best practices. Virtual tour practiced by 12.9% world and 2.6% Indian university libraries, wikis were created by 37.1% world and 2.6% Indian university libraries.

Below Graph 6 is self-explanatory to show the score of best practices offered by area wise libraries.

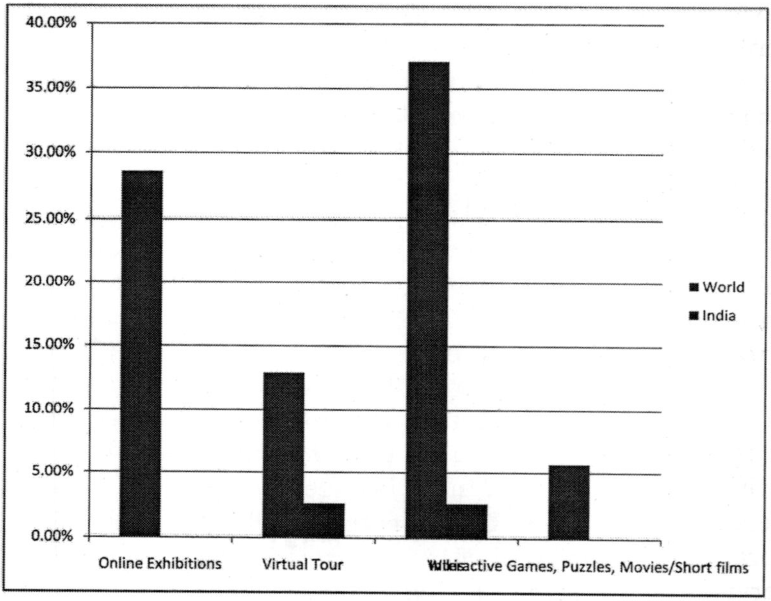

Graph 6. Average score of best practices of 'world' and 'Indian' university libraries

Annexure 6 shows that which universities are conducting best practices in their libraries at large scale and which libraries are yet to take such initiatives.

SINGLE WEB PAGE UNIVERSITY LIBRARIES

In this research it was found that from India 12universities hadsingle web pages through which they reach and interact with patrons. They offered hardly 18 web-based services through that webpage. As compared to other world university websites and web-based services offered those by these libraries needed to improve their library website designing to their contents.

CORRELATION OF UNIVERSITY AND LIBRARY RANKINGS

On the basis of total score of web-based services offered investigatorranked the university libraries and calculated Pearson and Spearman Correlations between world/India rankings of universities with their library rankings depending on web-based services offered and found that world university ranking and library rankings was statistically significant at 0.05 significance level while Indian university library rankings and Indian university rankings according to NAAC (CGPA) score was statistically not significant at .05 significance level. In all accreditation systems and ranking of university libraries plays major role in research, infrastructure and facilities criteria. It is observed that world university rankings and university library rankings show correlation between them and therefore we can say that while ranking universities at world level library web-based services were taken into consideration and libraries play major role in getting university higher rank. In Indian scenario we found there were no correlation between university rankings and library rankings though NAAC has covered different library services and facilities under criteria IV. Now many discussions going on, why Indian universities are not reflecting in top world university ranking? So it is suggested that if Indian university libraries will offer more various web-based services including research and patron education, communication tools Indian universities will also get higher rankings than present rankings in the world ranking system. Many world university ranking systems see the presence of university on the web and Google scholar for their research output and libraries plays major role in initiating open access publishing institutional repository and publications.

SUGGESTIONSON WEB-BASED SERVICES AND BEST PRACTICES

Through this study investigator studied 70 university libraries spread all over the world evenly and 39 university libraries from India. From the data analysis, findings and observations there is scope for Indian libraries to improve their web-based services and best practices. Both worlds and Indian university libraries average score for bibliographical services is better compared to all other web-based services. After bibliographical services the score of patron education services was good. Patron communication services are average in both cases and poorly in offering publishing platform and help. As discussed in findings and observations Indian universities are four times backward in providing different web-based bibliographical services and patron education services and eight times backward in using web 2.0 tools and other web-based communication tools to communicate with patrons. In case of bibliographical services Indian libraries should give details of library automation, digital library and e-discovery softwares they are used in their libraries on their website. It is possible that libraries are providing all the bibliographical services within campus or using login passwords but they failed to mention the details or path on their library websites. Similarly, it has been found that many librarians have their social network accounts and actively communicates with patron using various web 2.0 platforms, but they failed to create an account with their university library names. So there is suggestion for Indian university library professionals to run the account with their university or library names.

In this study many examples of web-based services and practices offered by top world universities are mentioned. Many patron education tools are free of cost and with some initiatives and efforts Indian libraries can also offer these services. Libraries all over the world are offering various web based services to the users. Since last one decade, researchers are seeing a huge difference between world and Indian university library web-based services, but still Indian universities are lagging behind in offering web based services because of various reasons like lack of trained staff to manage these kinds of services, websites are outsourced and lack of knowledge of technologies and tools used behind such services.

Though because of web and new library technologies it has become very easy to reach patrons and provide them resources at their finger tip where ever they are, but due to not sufficient trained staff such as web librarians, subject librariansto take care of web-based services Indian libraries are lagging behind. In developed country libraries there are teams of special librarians are working on library web-based services, website updating and to offer need based services to the patrons. They are ahead of time in using ICT and web communication technologies. Many Indian library staff is interested to offer new services, but still students in India are interested in personalised training and education than offering them online using different web platforms and tools.

Libraries in developed countries are using most of these technologies and are visible on their websites. But in developing and underdeveloped countries, many library professionals are not aware and trained about using these technologies. Library professionals are not aware about what technologies they use behind these services. Here are few new educational technologies and tools investigator suggesting which all libraries can use and implement which are not covered in this study.

Educational Technologies

The educational technologies now a day used all over the world in periodic table form which covers social networks, online learning technologies, multimedia technologies, coding technologies, classroom technologies, hardware and educational conferences. (*http://*

www.schrockguide.net/uploads/3/9/2/2/392267/ edtech_periodic-table.pdf)

Social Networks : Twitter, Facebook, Edmodo, Slideshare, Google+, Edublogs, Wikispaces, Linkedin, Scoop.it, Pinterest, Grockit, Skype, Diigo, Quora, Ning, Openstudy and Instagram

Online Learning technologies : Khan academy, Animoto, Socrative, Knewton, Kerpoof, StudySync, Udacity, Udemy, Corsera, edX and Skills Genius.

Multimedia technologies : Prezi, Wordle, Quizlet, YouTube, TED-Ed, eduCanon, Evernote, Planboard and Bitstrips

Coding technologies : code.org, Hour of Code, Scratch, Kodable, W3Schools, Code Avengers, Raspberry pi and Minecraft

Classroom Technologies : Doceri, Google Apps, Groupboard, Schoology, ePals, OneNote, edShelf, Book Creator, Canva, Pikochart, iBeacons, WordPress, Popplet, Jing, Stumbleupon, Slack, Camtasia, Videonot.es, LiveBinders, Dropbox, Office 365, QR Codes, Remind, Class messenger, ClassDojo, Kidblog, Showme, iKeepSafe, Mastery Connect, Explain Everything, Skitch, iMovie, Pinkmonkey, Doodle, Storify, Osmo, iRubric and Rubistar

Hardware Technologies : Apple iPad, Chromobook, MacBook, Android, iOS, IWBs and Apple TV.

Education Conference : ISTE,Edcamp, WISE Summit, SXSWedu, ASUGSV, iNACOL, Integrated, FETC, Excel in Ed, Learning and Brain, DML, EdTech Europe, Miami Device, Educon, EdTech Teacher, ASCD, GESF, BETT, Education Innovation Summit, CUE Conf, New Schools, ST4T, Global Educational Conferences, AIEA, EdNET, Learn Launch, OEB and PBL World.

Flipped Classroom for Information Literacy Programs or Patron Education

Wikispaces Classroom : Wikispaces is an open classroom management platform where teachers and students can communicate and collaborate.It is a social writing platform for education totally free of cost for teachers and students. It provides an easy online platform to create a classroom workspace where you and your students can communicate and work in teams. One can use these wikispaces classroom using any modern browser, tablet and phones too. Millions of teachers and students are using this platform for creative and innovative learning. It gives tools for teachers to quickly and easily create assignments, share resources, make announcements, and foster discussion and community.

Academic libraries can usewikispaces classroom for giving library orientation and information literacy programs to all patrons and even to visitors. Basic aim to create flipped classroom is to reach each and every student and with this each student can learn and work wherever and whenever they can? One can embed video tutorials of video of introduction to library in wikispaces. Various new educational tools can be use to create this wikispacesclassroom interactive and innovative. To create this flipped classroom following technologies and tools are used.

Thinglink : Is a leading provider of an interactive images and video interaction tool in classroom which can help students develop 21st century skills and enrich their enthusiasm for learning. It works on all modern web browsers as well as iPad, iPhone and Android.One can use tagging platform to layer images and videos with web links, photos, texts, videos, polls, Google products and other great content. Libraries too can use this tool to make their presentations more interactive.

Padlet : Padlet is a digital canvas to create beautiful projects and easiest way to share and collaborate in the world. It is an empty page works like a sheet of paper where you can post or uploadwhatever you like whether it is images or snap or selfie or videos or documents or text altogether with anyone from anywhere via device like PC, ipad, phone, etc. It is widely used for teaching, brainstorming, note taking, website publishing, bookmarking, blogging or selling good. One can make it more beautiful by choosing custom wall papers and themes given. It is very flexible so it is called as inspiration board. Libraries can use this tool to collect feedback from the patrons in interactive way.

Screencast-O-Matic : is a tool to create and share screen recordings. This tool is used by many educators, businesses for fast recording app to create a video file, share on YouTube, or even uploading to a custom branded site. In its free feature it allows users to record up to 15 minutes on-screen activity for short tutorials, visual presentations, and communicates while you demonstrate and publish on YouTube directly or save as MP4 video file. It supports screen plus webcam recording also. Using this tool libraries can give information literacy training or can demonstrate how to access online electronic resources, OPAC, databases etc.

Rubistar : is a tool to help the teacher who wants to use rubrics, but does not have the time to create quality rubrics.Rubrics have become popular with teachers as a means of communicating expectations for an assignment, providing focused feedback on works in progress, and grading final products. Rubrics help students to develop understanding and skill and also make dependable judgments about their own work quality. It helps students as well as teachers to clarify the standards for a quality performance and to guide ongoing feedback about work in prcgress. Libraries and teachers can use this tool for assessing or evaluating the students' assignments too or how much they understand from the lectures.

Jeopardy Labs Game : Jeopardy is danger or risk. Jeopardy is America's favorite game. Jeopardy Labs allows us to build our own jeopardy template without PowerPoint. The games we make can be played online from anywhere in the world. One can create Jeopardy Game of own choice and theme without login also. It is very easy to create the game just by adding title and categories one needs to add answer and create question for points given to specific category questions.

Videonot.es : It is open source tool for taking notes while watching video for future reference. All the notes taken are automatically synchronized with the video and one can just click on a line for the video to jump to the relevant part. We can save or integrate these video notes on google drive and can access them from anywhere. Once we add videonotes we can share or give permission to specific group of students or colleagues to view and whenever we want we can make it private.

Libraries can create video notes for the tutorial videos and made them available to the students on the web. To make online learning more interesting libraries can added questions in notes and asked students to answer after watching the video. If students fails to answer they can click on the question and it takes them to the particular strip of video where the answer is there.

edShelf : is a socially-curated discovery engine of websites, mobile apps, desktop programs, and electronic products for teaching and learning. Anyone can create an account free of cost. For creating a shelf you need to add Title, Description, privacy (Public or Private) and then you can search for tools or websites or programs related to your topic chosen and add the sources in your tray. You can filter the sources by price, platform, subject, age, category and sort by popularity, date added and last update.

Libraries can create edShelfs for specific groups of patrons as per their interest by conducting academic audit and make these shelfs available to patrons.

Flubaroo : Is a free open access tool to create multiple choice based or fill-in-blank type assignments quickly. Teachers need to create an assignment, then create an answer key for the same then assign and then review the grades. Flubaroo not only used for grading but it can Computes average assignment score, average score per question, flags low-scoring questions, shows a grade distribution graph, gives the option to email each student their grade, and an answer key and let teacher send individualized feedback to each and every student.

Audacity and Vocaroo : Audacity is a free open source digital audio editor and recording computer software application, available for all operating systems while Vocaroo is a quick and easy way to share voice messages over the interwebs. Audacity is used for post processing of all types of audio including podcasts. We can add effects such as normalization, trimming, fading in and out, srub, cut, copy and paste within limited levels of undo, mix the tracks, noise and vocal reduction and isolation, precise adjustments to the audio speed and pitch and import or export WAV, MP3, AIFF, AC3, AAC, AMR file formats.

Video Ant : It is another web-based video annotation tool for mobile and desktop devices used to add annotations, or comments, to web-hosted videos. VideoAnt-annotated videos are called as "Ants". To create video ants one need to create a user account and save collections of Ants. Authenticated users can manage their Ant Farm. You can export annotations in various formats. You can embed your ants on website, wikispaces, LMS or any HTML page.

Voicethread : Voicethead is one of the most diverse communities in the world and that is by design. It is more human way to connect. One can participate in this using voice, video or text in comment box using any computer, device, internet connection or mobile. We can integrate it it in our LMS, ERP, website or HTML pages like Video ant.

Ted-Ed : is an education initiative which aims to amplify the voices and ideas of teachers and students around the world. Any scholar can create worth sharing lesson, new topics and spread their great ideas on this platform to learners. It is growing library of lessons. It is good platform for collaborative research. The lessons or educational videos uploaded on the TED platform easily create customized questions and discussions around the video. We can distribute lesson publicly or privately and track its impact on community, students, individuals we shared. Till date 185,903 lessons are created and 10, 183, 478 questions are answered. (28/06/2016, 2.55pm) ed.ted.com

Google Groups : Library professionals can create Google groups for teaching staff and group of students depending on their interests and update them with new information in their interest fields.

Survey Monkey : Libraries can use survey monkey tool to collect online feedback from patrons. It enables to get analyzed report automatically.

Annexure 1. Higher and lower bibliographical service count of university libraries region wise

Region	*Universities offering maximum bibliographical services*	*Universities offering minimum bibliographical services*
Africa	University of Pretoria (10/12)	University of the Western Cape (6/12)
Arab_world	American University of Beirut (9/12)	University of Jordon(2/12)
Asia/Pacifico	National Taiwan University & Kyoto University(11/12)	University of Tokyo (5/12)
Brics	Tsinghua University and Shanghai Jiao Tong University (10/12)	Universidade de São Paulo (5/12)
Caribbean	University of the West Indies at St Augustine (10/12)	Universidad de la Habana (5/12)
Central Eastern Europe	Jagiellonian University (8/12)	Lomonosov Moscow State University (3/12)
Civets	University of Cape Town and Universidad Nacional de Colombia (11/12)	Cairo University (7/12)
Europe	University College London (11/12)	Utrecht University (7/12)
Latin America	UniversidadeEstadual de Campinas (8/12)	Universidade Federal do Rio de Janeiro (4/12)
Middle East	Tel Aviv University (10/12)	Univeristy of Tehran (1/12)
North Africa	American University in Cairo (7/12)	Alexandria University (4/12)
Oceania	Australian National University (10/12)	University of New South Wales (6/12)
South East Asia	Mahidol University (11/12)	Universiti Putra Malaysia (7/12)
World	Harvard University (12/12)	University of Michigan (11/12)
India	Jawaharlal Nehru University, New Delhi (10/12)	13 universities does not offer a single bibliographical service

Annexure 2. Higher and lower patron education services count of university libraries region wise

Region	*Universities offering maximum Patron Education services*	*Universities offering minimum Patron Education services*
Africa	University of Pretoria (24/27)	University of Nairobi (16/27)
Arab_world	American University of Beirut (20/27)	University of Baghdad (8/27)
Asia/Pacifico	National Taiwan University (21/27)	University of Tokyo (11/27)
Brics	Shanghai Jiao Tong University (20/27)	Peking University (6/27)
Caribbean	Universidad de Puerto Rico (UPR) And University of the West Indies (19/27)	Universidad de la Habana (8/27)
Central Eastern Europe	Charles University in Prague / Univerzita Karlova v Praze (16/27)	Lomonosov Moscow State University (6/27)
Civets	University of Cape Town (23/27)	Cairo University (8/27)
Europe	University College London (24/27)	Utrecht University / Universiteit Utrecht (15/27)
Latin America	Universidad de Chile (18/27)	Universidade Federal do Rio de Janeiro (4/27)
Middle East	Hebrew University of Jerusalem (18/27)	University of Tehran (7/27)
North Africa	American University in Cairo (18/27)	Alexandria University (3/27)
Oceania	University of Melbourne (23/27)	University of New South Wales (15/27)
South East Asia	National University of Singapore (24/27)	Kasetsart University (15/27)
World	Stanford University (26/27)	University of California Berkeley (23/27)
India	Jawaharlal Nehru University, New Delhi (19/27)	KLE Academy of Higher Education and Research and Kannada University (0/27)

Annexure 3. Higher and lower patron communication count of university libraries region wise

Region	*Universities offering maximum Patron Communication services*	*Universities offering minimum Patron Communication services*
Africa	University of Nairobi (8/14)	University of the Western Cape (4/14)
Arab_world	American University of Beirut (9/14)	University of Baghdad (4/14)
Asia/Pacifico	National Taiwan University (9/14)	University of Tokyo (3/14)
Brics	Tsinghua University China (5/14)	Peking University (3/14)
Caribbean	University of the West Indies at St Augustine (7/14)	Universidad de Puerto Rico (UPR) (4/14)
Central Eastern Europe	University of Ljubljana (8/14)	Masaryk University in Brno (3/14)
Civets	University of Cape Town (9/14)	Istanbul University (4/14)
Europe	University of Oxford (12/14)	University of Helsinki (9/14)
Latin America	Universidad de Chile (7/14)	Universidade Federal do Rio de Janeiro (2/14)
Middle East	King Saud University (10/14)	University of Tehran (1/14)
North Africa	American University in Cairo (5/14)	Alexandria University (0/14)
Oceania	Monash University (10/14)	Australian National University (4/14)
South East Asia	National University of Singapore (9/14)	Universiti Putra Malaysia (6/14)
World	Harvard University (12/14)	University of California Berkeley (7/14)
India	Jawaharlal Nehru University, New Delhi (6/14)	21 universities in India (0/14)

Annexure 4. Higher and lower patron publising service count of university libraries region wise

Region	*Universities offering maximum publishing platform for patrons*	*Universities offering minimum publishing platforms for patrons*
Africa	University of Nairobi (5/6)	University of the Western Cape (4/6)
Arab_world	American University of Beirut (5/6)	University of Jordan (1/6)
Asia/Pacifico	Seoul National University (5/6)	University of Tokyo (2/6)
Brics	Shanghai Jiao Tong University (5/6)	Peking University (0/6)
Caribbean	University of the West Indies at St Augustine (3/6)	Universidad de Puerto Rico (UPR) (0/6)
Central Eastern Europe	Jagiellonian University / UniwersytetJagielloński (4/6)	Lomonosov Moscow State University (0/6)
Civets	Universidad Nacional de Colombia (6/6)	Cairo University (0/6)
Europe	University College London (5/6)	University of Helsinki (4/6)
Latin America	Universidade Federal do Rio Grande do Sul UFRGS (3/6)	Universidade Federal do Rio de Janeiro (0/6)
Middle East	Hebrew University of Jerusalem (4/6)	Univeristy of Tehran (2/6)
North Africa	American University in Cairo (5/6)	Alexandria University (2/6)
Oceania	University of Melbourne (6/6)	University of New South Wales (1/6)
South East Asia	National University of Singapore (4/6)	Kasetsart University (3/6)
World	Harvard University (6/6)	University of California Berkeley (3/6)
India	University of Hyderabad, Maharishi Dayanand University and Banasthali Vidyapith, Banasthali (3/6)	28 universities from India (0/6)

Annexure 5. Higher and lower web-based service total count of university libraries region wise

Region	*Universities offering maximum web-based services*	*Universities offering minimum we-based services*
Africa	University of Pretoria (45/59)	University of the Western Cape (31/59)
Arab_world	American University of Beirut (43/59)	University of Baghdad (19/59)
Asia/Pacifico	National Taiwan University (45/59)	University of Tokyo (21/59)
Brics	Shanghai Jiao Tong University (38/59)	Peking University (19/59)
Caribbean	University of the West Indies at St Augustine (35/59)	Universidad de la Habana (19/59)
Central Eastern Europe	University of Ljubljana (32/59)	Lomonosov Moscow State University (15/59)
Civets	University of Cape Town (46/59)	Cairo University (23/59)
Europe	University College London (49/59)	Utrecht University / Universiteit Utrecht (36/59)
Latin America	Universidad de Chile (34/59)	Universidade Federal do Rio de Janeiro (10/59)
Middle East	Hebrew University of Jerusalem (38/59)	University of Tehran (11/59)
North Africa	American University in Cairo (35/59)	Alexandria University (9/59)
Oceania	University of Melbourne (46/59)	University of New South Wales (27/59)
South East Asia	National University of Singapore (47/59)	Kasetsart University (35/59)
World	Harvard University (55/59)	University of California Berkeley (46/59)
India	Jawaharlal Nehru University, New Delhi (36/59)	Kannada University and KLE Academy of Higher Education and Research (0/59)

Annexure 6. shows that which universities are conducting best practices in their libraries at large scale and which libraries are yet to take such initiatives.

Region	*Universities offering maximum web-based practices*	*Universities offering minimum web-based practices*
Africa	University of Pretoria (2/4)	University of the Witwatersrand (0/4)
Arab_world	American University of Beirut (1/4)	University of Baghdad (0/4)
Asia/Pacifico	University of Hong Kong (1/4)	Seoul National University (0/4)
Brics	Peking University (2/4)	Universidade de São Paulo USP (0/4)
Caribbean	University of the West Indies at St Augustine (2/4)	Universidad de la Habana (0/4)
Central Eastern Europe	Jagiellonian University (2/4)	Lomonosov Moscow State University (0/4)
Civets	Universidad Nacional de Colombia (2/4)	Cairo University (0/4)
Europe	University of Oxford (2/4)	Utrecht University (2/4)
Latin America	Universidade Federal do Rio Grande do Sul UFRGS (1/4)	Universidad Nacional Autónoma de México (0/4)
Middle East	Hebrew University of Jerusalem (1/4)	University of Tehran (0/4)
North Africa	American University in Cairo (1/4)	Alexandria University (0/4)
Oceania	Monash University (2/4)	University of New South Wales (0/4)
South East Asia	Universiti Sains Malaysia (2/4)	Universiti Putra Malaysia (0/4)
World	Harvard University (3/4)	University of California Berkeley (2/4)
India	Mysore University and Tata Institute of Social Sciences, Deonar, Mumbai (1/4)	37 universities offers 0 services

Other Reading List

1. Abram, S. Web 2.0, Library 2.0, and Librarian 2.0: Preparing for the 2.0 World. SirsiDynix OneSource 2. Available at IAML UK & IRL. Best practices for libraries. Accessed at *http://www.iaml.info/iaml-uk-irl/accessibility/best.html*
2. Augment the UK library net with the best. Available at http://www.reddit.com/r/Policy2011/comments/l114j/augment_the_uk_library_network_with_the_best/
3. Ariaden (2004). Reaching Out to Your Community: Policies and practice for public library service. Accessed at http://www.ariadne.ac.uk/issue38/talis-rpt/
4. Battleson, B. Booth, A., &Weintrop, J. (2001). Usability testing of an academic library web site: a case study. *The Journal of Academic Librarianship, 27*(3), 188-198.
5. British Library Digital Preservation Strategy. Available at http://www.bl.uk/aboutus/stratpol prog/ccare/introduction/digital/digpresstrat.pdf
6. Debra Engela & Sarah Robbinsb. Improving Reference Services through a Library Website: Strategies for Collaborative Change. The Reference Librarian. Volume 40, Issue 83-84, 2004. pp 157-173. Accessed on http://www.tandfonline.com/doi/

abs/10.1300/J120v40n83_13[6/21/2012 4:53:37 PM]

7. Emily Symonds, (2011) "A practical application of Survey Monkey as a remote usability-testing tool", Library Hi Tech, 29(3), 436 – 445

8. Faisal, S. Library-20-and-beyond. Accessed at http://www.slideshare.net/slfaisal/library-20-and-beyond-42206751

9. Guha, T. K., & Saraf, V. (2005). OPAC usability: assessment through verbal protocol. *The Electronic Library, 23*(4), 463-473.

10. Holmberg, Kim ; Huvila, Isto; Kronqvist, Maria; Gunilla, Berg&Wulff, Widén (2009) "What is Library 2.0?", Journal of Documentation, 65(4), pp.668 – 681

11. IAML UK & IRL. Best practices for libraries. Available at http://www.iaml.info/iaml-uk-irl/accessibility/best.html

12. Jason Vallery. What is Web 3.0?: A review of the ICWSM Available at http://vallery.net/2007/03/27/what-is-web-30-a-review-of-the-icwsm/

13. Jeffrey Zeldman. Web 3.0. Available at http://www.alistapart.com/articles/web3point0

14. Jharotia, Anil Kumar. Web 1.0, 2.0 & 3.0 in Electronic Era: A New Paradigm for Library and Information Centre. Accessed from https://www.academia.edu/11384468/Web_1.0_2.0_and_3.0_in_Electronic_Era_A_New_Paradigm_for_Library_and_Information_Centre

15. Kaur, Kiran, (2009) "Marketing the academic library on the web", Library Management, 30(6/7), pp.454 – 468

16. Kim Holmberg, IstoHuvila, Maria Kronqvist, Berg Gunilla & WidénWulff, (2009)

17. Lorraine Paterson, Boon Low, (2011) "Student attitudes towards mobile library services for smartphones", Library Hi Tech, Vol. 29 Iss: 3,412 – 423

18. Mallikarjun & Maharana, Balu (2008). A-Lib 2.0: New Avatar Academic Libraries with Web 2.0 Applications. International CALIBER-2008.467-476

19. McNicol, S. (2010). User-centered Library Websites: Usability Evaluation Methods. *New Library World, 111*(1/2), 76-77

20. MLA.Best practices. Available at http://www.mla.gov.uk/what/raising_standards/best_practice

21. Moyo, L. M. (2002). Collections on the Web: some access and navigation issues. *Library Collections, Acquisitions, and Technical Services, 26*(1), 47-59.

22. Nagabhushanam, V. Web based services in University libraries. Available at http://dlis.du.ac.in/RC%20IN%20LIS/pdf/Presentations/V.Nagabhushanam.pdf. Accessed on 7/7/12 at12.02pm

23. Office of Digital Collections and Research University of Maryland, College Park.Best Practice Guidelines for Digital Collections at University of Maryland Libraries. Accessed athttp://www.lib.umd.edu/dcr/publications/best_practice.pdf

24. Paterson, Lorraine& Low, Boon, (2011) "Student attitudes towards mobile library services for smart phones", Library Hi Tech, 29(3),412 – 423

25. Reaching Out to Your Community: Policies and practice for public library service. Accessed at *http://www.ariadne.ac.uk/issue38/talis-rpt/*

26. Sconul. Library services for international students. Available at http://www.sconul.ac.uk/groups/access/papers/international_students.pdf

27. Steve Spalding. How to Define Web 3.0. Available at http://howtosplitanatom.com/news/how-to-define-web-30-2/

28. Stover, M, & Zink, S.D (1996). World Wide Web home page design: patterns and anomalies of higher education library home pages. Reference Service Review. 1996, 24, 7–20.

29. Symonds, Emily, (2011) "A practical application of SurveyMonkey as a remote usability-testing tool", Library Hi Tech, 29(3), 436 – 445

30. Tikam, M. Best practices in academic libraries. Accessed at http://knol.google.com/k/madhuri-tikam/best-practices-in-academic-libraries/35muq6i9t1aro/3#

31. World's Best Universities: Top 400. Available at http://www.usnews.com/education/worlds-best-universities-rankings/top-400-universities-in-the-world Accessed on 7/4/2012 at 2:40:38 PM

32. Xisle graphics (2012) Available at http://www.xislegraphix.com/website-types.html. Accessed on 16/7/2012 at 2.55 PM on

33. *http://www.imakenews.com/sirsi/e_article000505688.cfm?x=b6yRqLJ,b2rpQhRM*

34. *http://www.1st-tech.com/services/advantages.html accessed on 22/6/2016*

35. http://slq.nu/?article=library-1-0-library-2-0-library-3-0

36. http://drtc.isibang.ac.in/ldl/bitstream/handle/1849/506/Use_of.pdf?sequence=1&isAllowed=y

37. http://southernlibrarianship.icaap.org/content/v10n03/mcmanus_b01.html

38. http://course1.winona.edu/vleighton/webind2/webind2.htmhttp://muse.jhu.edu/article/209023

39. http://www.emeraldinsight.com/doi/abs/10.1108/LR-06-2015-0069

40. http://eprints.uni-mysore.ac.in/18300/1/8.pdf
41. http://www.slideshare.net/cdtrini/library-2011-web-tools-peltierdavis
42. *http://dsim.in/blog/2013/10/03/10-people-who-changed-the-internet-forever/*
43. *http://www.emeraldinsight.com/doi/abs/10.1108/LR-06-2015-0069*